LEARNING TO SPEAK

LEARNING TO SPEAK

The Church's Voice in Public Affairs

Keith Clements

T&T CLARK
EDINBURGH

T&T CLARK LTD
59 GEORGE STREET
EDINBURGH EH2 2LQ
SCOTLAND

First published 1995

ISBN 0 567 29266 5

British Library Cataloguing-in-Publication Data
A catalogue record for this book is available from the British Library

Typeset by Trinity Typesetting, Edinburgh
Printed and bound in Great Britain by Hartnolls Ltd, Bodmin

For Margaret

Contents

Preface

This book seeks to discuss a perennially fraught area of Christian witness: the addressing of public issues by the churches.

Books do not always grow from a single seed, and in retrospect I am aware that in this case several concerns and levels in my experience, recent and more distant in time, have been trying to find a voice. Early in my career as a minister, and subsequently as a teacher in a theological college, I became deeply interested in the history of the churches' witness in modern times in contexts of conflict and oppression, and the theological basis of that witness. The First World War, and then the responses of the German churches to Nazism, were the first main foci of that interest. More recently I found myself drawn into engagement with contemporary issues on the international scene, above all the churches' role in South Africa, a country I first visited in 1985 when I had the memorable experience of being present at the public launch of the now famous *Kairos Document.*

Such interests, when they are those of an academic without any official church responsibility, can all too easily encourage the indulgence of criticizing church leaders and official bodies for their failures to take "a more prophetic stand" when the occasion demands. However, since 1990 when I became Co-ordinating Secretary for International Affairs in the Council of Churches for Britain and Ireland, the issue of whether the churches can or should speak out on particular issues has become far more immediate for me. A defining experience came that fateful morning in January 1991 when I was woken by the telephone at two o'clock. It was the news desk of a national newspaper, telling me that Desert Storm had been launched against Iraq — and 'What is the churches' view?' One was now in a rather different position from the theological tutor conducting a seminar on the Just War — was *this* a just war? Almost weekly, I now experience the pressure of the expectation that the churches will have 'something to say' on whatever is hitting the headlines. In good measure I too share that concern, and often feel frustrated, even shamed, that the Christian community and its leadership so often seem tongue-tied or unable to utter more than bland generalities.

At the same time I have long felt a pull from another direction. Thirty years ago as a student at Cambridge, I well recall the stern injunctions of my teacher Alec Vidler against the verbosity of churches and especially their leaders. 'Far too much talking', he once growled in the course of one his agreeably short sermons in King's College Chapel. Vidler, as one who had been deeply concerned with the churches' social witness, especially through the Christian Frontier Council and his long association with J.H. Oldham, was certainly convinced that there was a Christian contribution to social and political affairs, but more through the informed actions of committed laypeople than through the words of clerics and assemblies. His little book on the whole issue of Christian social responsibility, *Christ's Strange Work* (SCM Press 1963) is still to be relished for such pungent, if over-generalizing, comments as:

> Political resolutions by ecclesiastical assemblies or political pronouncements by clerics frequently encourage irresponsibility. They give those who pass them or make them or hear them the illusion that, because something has been said and written down and even published, something has been done, or at least something will be done by somebody, which unfortunately does not follow at all. A witty archbishop once said: 'The clergy have just now a strange mania for signing declarations. I think I could manage to get three-fourths of them to sign a declaration against an eclipse, if I could only persuade them that in some oblique way it expressed some party feeling which they happened to be indulging in at the moment.' (p. 115f.)

Then, too, Dietrich Bonhoeffer, who knew the shame of a church woefully silent in face of evil deeds, warned also of 'speaking the Word of God to excess'. That remark increasingly troubled me as a theological college tutor. Our students were going out to minister in a publicity-hungry, media-dominated and materialistic society with its own canons of what looks good and sounds good and counts as success. Are not the ministry, life and death of Jesus deeply at odds with all this? How could ministry in this age be equipped theologically and spiritually to maintain its integrity under such pressures? That the church must become more media-conscious I have no doubt, and to have been involved in a certain amount of broadcasting has been one of the most satisfying activities I have known. But there is a point where the desire for audibility and visibility witnesses to the spirit of the age rather than to the gospel.

Reflecting on these matters has led me to the conviction that underlying the churches' anxiety about how to address the public sphere is a certain assumption, that the church's role is primarily that of teacher, instructing the world how to behave. It is the dominance of this self-image which is at the root of so much Christian insecurity in the modern west. It drives the church to be over-hasty in speech — we feel we *must* 'have a voice' if we are to be taken seriously. Equally often, it results in a demoralizing sense of failure and irrelevance when what we do say is dismissed or simply ignored by the naughty world.

This book does not argue against the church's proper teaching role, and certainly not against its 'prophetic' calling, a concept to which a whole chapter is devoted. I suggest however that there is another image which, in faithfulness to the biblical tradition, continually needs to be upheld for the sustenance and vitality of the witnessing community. It is so basic that it probably appears too naive to mention: the role of learner, of disciple, which in fact is crucial to that of prophet — 'as one who is taught' (Is. 50.4). To affirm this as a paradigm for the church would, I believe, make the church in its address to the world more disciplined yet more imaginative, more humble yet far more creative. It would involve the church freely and gladly being prepared to *learn* to speak in the course of its mission, and so to be liberated from false pretensions about its status and from unnecessary fears about its effectiveness.

Several important studies of church pronouncements on

social and political questions have recently appeared. Henry Clark's *The Church Under Thatcher* (SPCK 1993) examines statements by the Church of England over the past decade, while Mark Ellingsen in his *The Cutting Edge* (WCC and W. B. Eerdmans 1993) surveys in detail a worldwide range of denominational and ecumenical pronouncements. It will be evident however that my concern has less to do with the content of such statements than with some of the underlying questions in the debate about the rightness of the church 'speaking out' in the public sphere at all. Because of my particular interests and responsibilities, the public issues on which this book focuses tend towards the international level. I hope, however, that the argument will be seen to apply more generally. Furthermore, while it is usually 'leaders' and 'official bodies' who are thought of as speaking in the name of the churches, the issues are such as concern all who are committed to the church's witness in the world, at whatever level. At more than one point I draw attention to instances of local communities playing a crucial role in exemplifying the wider church's witness, and indeed in some cases actually stimulating and catalysing it. Nor do I apologize that this book uses a variety of approaches and disciplines — including church history, biblical studies, systematic theology and social sciences — together with a certain amount of personal experience and observation. If this raises problems for librarians uncertain about which shelf the book belongs on, I hope it will at least not be too far from the section on mission, a subject which, as so many are reminding us these days, must be understood and acted upon holistically.

I gratefully acknowledge the help of a number of friends and colleagues in the ecumenical enterprise, in Britain and elsewhere, with whom I have discussed the general theme or particular sections, and who have offered their wise counsel in encouragement and criticism, in some cases also pointing me towards additional and important sources. Particularly to be mentioned are John de Gruchy, Christopher Duraisingh, Alan Falconer, Duncan Forrester, Gillian Paterson, Elizabeth Salter and Charles Villa-Vicencio. Finally, a special word of appreciation is due to my wife Margaret. Not only has she had to bear yet again with the preoccupations of a nascent book, but at a critical point she was able, with the aid of her university computer department, to redeem the consequences of my own computer-illiteracy and to retrieve a large section of the text which would otherwise have been lost for ever. It is therefore much to be hoped that, in this and in other ways, I too have been learning something.

Keith Clements
Bristol,
Ash Wednesday 1994

1

Required to Speak?

'Will you be issuing a statement?' Bishops and archbishops,
moderators and general secretaries of denominations, directors
of aid agencies and boards of social responsibility, are all
familiar with the question. Yet another famine in Africa, or an
upheaval in eastern Europe, or an explosion of violence in our
own inner cities, or a government announcement of public
spending cuts, prompts the hope (or perhaps the fear) that
'the churches will say something'. The question may in fact be
too late. As likely as not, the machinery of ecclesiastical
pronouncement will already be turning: drafts being faxed
hither and thither for comment and amendment and eventual
signature, church press officers being briefed on the importance
of the issue, and final versions being released to the avid
attention, it is supposed, of the world's waiting media.

That 'the voice of the church should be heard' on this or that
issue is one of the most widespread demands from within
Christian circles, and surprisingly often from outside them
too. Not that all are agreed, of course, on which particular
issues the churches should be most vociferous, whether
pornography or abortion or racism or the arms trade. In this
book I am mostly concerned with the churches' addressing of
public, political issues and especially in the international field
where my own responsibilities within the ecumenical bodies of
Britain and Ireland lie. Nor is there any single pattern of
statements proper to the church. They can assume a variety of
dress, from the personal utterances of church leaders to
resolutions passed at synods or assemblies, from lengthy reports

carefully prepared over months or even years to urgently typed letters in the national secular press. Despite frequent accusations that the churches have been 'silent' on one crisis or another, the evidence is usually that they have been fairly talkative though not necessarily mouthing quite what those who charge them with 'silence' have been wanting them to say.

That the churches are expected to 'speak' on major public issues is perhaps not surprising, given that Christianity is very much a religion of speech. It shares with Judaism and Islam a basic belief in a self-communicating, speaking God and in using a collection of sacred texts or 'scriptures' as a central source for knowledge of the divine self-revelation. But it is distinctive in asserting that the divine speech (or 'Word') ultimately became a human being, speaking human words, and in turn generating a great deal of further speech about him. This word-nature of Christianity is embedded at every level of its tradition. At an unsophisticated level, but all the more striking for that, take for example just three verses of the old English carol (emphasis mine):

This is the truth sent from above,
The truth of God, the God of love,
Therefore don't turn me from your door,
But *hearken* all both rich and poor.

The first thing which I do *relate*
Is that God did man create;
The next thing which to you I'll *tell* —
Woman was made with man to dwell.

And at that season of the year
Our blest Redeemer did appear;
Here he did live, and here did *preach*,
And many thousands he did *teach*.[1]

'Preaching', the proclamation of the good news of what through Jesus Christ God has done and is doing for humankind, and 'teaching', the setting out of how life is to be lived in response

---

[1]No. 68 in *The Oxford Book of Carols*, Oxford University Press, 1928.

to that good news, are not incidental extras to some wordless, mystical 'essence' of Christianity, but have been integral to it from its birth.[2] A visit to almost any church, of any tradition, will show how this is literally embodied in the very architecture of Christianity. It is not only in decidedly Protestant churches that the pulpit is given prominence and that, as the Scottish poet Edwin Muir ironically observed of the Calvinist kirk, 'The Word made flesh is here made word again'.[3] The most ornate devices for elevating preachers 'six feet above contradiction' (or still higher) are to be found in some medieval cathedrals where supposedly the priestly service of the altar took precedence over the ministry of the Word. It is perhaps not just a matter of practicality, but of important symbolism, that the single most expensive piece of equipment in the sanctuary these days will be the voice amplification system.

It is therefore a natural assumption that the voice of the church needs amplifying in society at large as well as in the sanctuary. A 'prophetic' ministry of the church is required, this being equated with 'speaking out' on issues of national and international justice and peace. I certainly share this concern, but am equally concerned that little attention is paid to examining what makes for authentically 'prophetic' utterance as distinct from talking for its own sake, or simply for the sake of being heard. The writer Katherine Mansfield famously decried 'poor, talkative little Christianity'. She may not have sufficiently appreciated that a church which believes in 'good news' has to speak about certain things which have happened and other things that can and ought to happen, '... for we cannot keep from speaking about what we have seen and heard' (Acts 4.20). But the warning must be heeded. Belief in God's word does not justify our wordiness. In fact that belief should remind us that speaking is a deeply serious responsibility, and the Bible itself warns against verbosity. Speaking idly, or even speaking earnestly for its own sake, is irreverence before

[2]The classic short work on the New Testament evidence for this is C. H. Dodd, *The Apostolic Preaching and Its Developments*, Hodder and Stoughton, 1936.

[3]Line from 'The Incarnate One', in *The Penguin Book of Religious Verse*, ed. R. S. Thomas, Penguin, 1963.

God and a disservice to our neighbour: 'Never be rash with your mouth, nor let your heart be quick to utter a word before God, for God is in heaven, and you upon earth, therefore let your words be few' (Eccles. 5.2f.); 'Let everyone be quick to listen, slow to speak, slow to anger, for your anger does not produce God's righteousness' (Jas. 1.19f.); 'When you are praying, do not heap up empty phrases as the Gentiles do, for they think that they will be heard because of their many words' (Mt. 6.7). True, such injunctions are aimed in the first place at individuals, but do they apply any less to the community as a whole when it claims to require 'a voice'?

It is one thing to want a voice and to be heard. It is quite another to know just what is to be said, and when, and how, and to whom, and (still more significantly) to precisely what purpose. Finding time to reflect on these fundamental questions is all the more difficult when, as in public and international affairs, more and more issues crowd on to our agendas demanding our attention and 'our voice'. We talk about being 'prophetic', but were the prophets of old quite so frantic as we often make ourselves with one problem after another on which 'the church must speak'? Is there not indeed a talkativeness here which is symptomatic of some inner nervous disorder? The malaise is best illustrated with a single recent case-study.

A paragraph too far? The World Council of Churches and the Gulf War

In February 1991 the Seventh Assembly of the World Council of Churches (WCC) met in Canberra, Australia. For nearly two weeks, over 850 delegates from more than 300 member churches, from all over the world, met in common worship, Bible study, discussion and debate, under the overall theme 'Come Holy Spirit, renew the whole creation'.[4] It was an especially poignant time to gather under such a motto, for war was raging in the Gulf and tearing apart the creation, both in terms of human lives and the natural environment. Indeed,

---

[4] See *Signs of the Spirit: Official Report of the Seventh Assembly,* ed. M. Kinnamon, WCC Publications, 1991.

beforehand there had been serious questioning in some quarters as to whether the Assembly should be held at all during a conflict of such threatening proportions. As it happened, the Gulf War sounded an obviously dominant note throughout those two weeks.

On the final morning of the Assembly, the Public Issues Committee presented a statement on 'The Gulf War, the Middle East, and the Threat to World Peace'. This had already been presented briefly in a draft form earlier in the Assembly, and several suggestions for revision had been included. By any standards, for a 'statement' it was a lengthy document, running to nearly twelve pages in the published Assembly Report. Admittedly about three-quarters of it comprised a 'Preamble', which dealt with the churches' involvement in efforts to prevent the crisis developing into armed conflict, the wider context of unsolved disputes and problems in the Middle East, the global implications of the war, the role of the United Nations and so forth. The second, shorter section consisted of 'Appeals and Affirmations' addressed to the churches, the United Nations and the leaders and peoples of the nations participant in the war. In fact, the Preamble itself at certain points was strongly hortatory: 'Cease the bombing! Still the missiles! Stop the fighting! Restrain your armies! Negotiate! Trust in the promise of peace!'[5] Taken as a whole, the statement had the merit of being both comprehensive and concrete. It dealt with broader issues, such as the need for an enhanced role for the UN, in some historical depth and without bland abstractions. Equally, it could be quite specific in calling for consistency in the application of particular UN resolutions dealing with the illegal occupations of Palestine, Lebanon and Cyprus.

However, to let loose an assembly of getting on for a thousand people on such a wide-ranging document, and at such a fraught time, was taking a big risk, as was quickly proved when comments on the Preamble were invited from the floor. Certain paragraphs relating to Israel and to relations with Muslims were strongly contested by some speakers. 'There was much debate about the procedure for revising [the Preamble],

<hr />

[5]Ibid., p. 206.

but the assembly finally agreed simply to request the Public Issues Committee to revise that part of the text in the light of the discussion.'[6] The second, shorter section on Appeals and Affirmations was then moved. This debate persisted until well after the lunch-break, a number of amendments being proposed, most of which were resisted by the Public Issues Committee and defeated by the Assembly. Well into the afternoon, attention focused on certain paragraphs in section 41:

> (a) We call urgently and insistently on both Iraq and the coalition forces led by the United States to cease fire immediately and to work for a negotiated solution of the Iraq-Kuwait dispute within the context of the United Nations.

> (c) We appeal to the government of Iraq to signal its intention and offer guarantees that it will comply with Security Council Resolution 660 by withdrawing completely and unconditionally from the territory of Kuwait immediately upon the cessation of hostility.

The Bishop of Bristol, Barry Rogerson, proposed an amendment appealing to the Iraqi government to *signal* its intention to withdraw from Kuwait, and that immediately upon this indication Iraq and the coalition forces should cease fire and withdrawal from Kuwait should begin. This amendment also was lost, but concern had already been expressed by some delegates such as James Rogers of the Church of Scotland that the Assembly was in danger of occupying such high moral ground (of feeling good) as to be detached from the real world (of doing good) and would not be taken seriously.

This however was not the only piece of contention. In the morning an amendment had been accepted, calling for the churches to give up the theological or moral justification for the use of military power, and to become public advocates of a just peace. In proposing this Konrad Raiser of Germany pointed out that the wording derived from the final document

[6]Ibid., p. 203.

of the 1990 Convocation on Justice, Peace and the Integrity of Creation. By the afternoon, however, it appeared that a number of delegates had spent their lunch hour ruminating on the possibly pacifist implications of the statement, and voiced their misgivings. Following some more confused discussion the assembly allowed itself a U-turn by voting to reconsider the amendment — and then defeating it.

Finally, after four hours of debate, the statement on the Gulf War was voted upon and adopted, though by no means unanimously. Was this whole exercise, as some claimed, a brave piece of witnessing by the churches in baring their divergences and passions honestly before the world and its watching media? Or was it a rather pretentious attempt to say too much, resulting in a somewhat muted and ineffectual voice, a case of ecumenical laryngitis? As one who was not actually present at Canberra, but a keenly interested observer from a distance, I permit myself the luxury of judging that the end result was not prophetic speech, but a statement which allowed itself to become dissipated into a set of too many prescriptions. The world's political leaders might or might not follow these prescriptions, all of which were wholly commendable, for example the calling of an International Peace Conference to settle the Palestinian question in accordance with previous UN resolutions. But would their decisions be materially affected by the fact that the Seventh Assembly of the World Council of Churches had given its 'Yea' to them? What this statement lacked was any assertion as to why these prescriptions really mattered, what was ultimately at stake in them, beyond the fact that they were in accord with previous statements of the WCC and other well-meaning bodies. In short, there was little theology, little sense that the claims of the realm and reign of God were impinging on political decision-making, little sense that a future with fearful consequences was even now in the making.

We can be more precise. The two paragraphs from the statement quoted above do not simply call for an end to the war, but (especially paragraph (c)) prescribe the technique to facilitate this. It is not clear why this prescription was thought to be necessary. After all, paragraph 40 (d) called the UN to 'move with all speed' to convene an International Peace Conference on the Palestinian question but did not actually say who should first be approached on this, Yasser Arafat or President Assad of Syria or Israeli Prime Minister Begin. It simply, and quite rightly, urged the UN Secretary General to get moving as quickly as possible on getting the peace process going. But stopping a war is as technical a matter as starting a peace conference, and to insist on *first* a cease-fire by all parties, and to ask for a signal and guarantees (*what* guarantees?) from Iraq that it would comply with the requirement to withdraw from Kuwait 'immediately upon the cessation of hostilities' is to step into the technicalities of diplomacy when one is no position to play that role. There is, frankly, something unreal in the sight of an assembly prescribing in detail how a conflict thousands of miles away is to be brought to an end, and effectively being asked to speak as if it was in the role of mediator when it was in no such position. It was almost inevitable that once the prescriptive road had been followed thus far, an alternative prescription such as that proposed by Bishop Rogerson would be offered and the debate would become entangled still further in technical possibilities — which within days would in any case be overtaken by events and without the slightest regard being paid to them by the warring parties. This was a signal instance of a perennial dilemma in church utterances on contemporary issues: if bland generalities are to be eschewed, how can the other extreme be avoided, of telling governments not just what they ought to do but precisely how they should do it? The statement had gone at least one paragraph too far, and what resulted was not a 'prophetic word' but a rather ungainly piece of didacticism.

But as far as 'speaking' at Canberra was concerned, this was not all. The Gulf War may have been the overshadowing issue but it was not the only one demanding attention, and the statement on the war was but one of eight such documents brought by the Public Issues Committee. The seven others dealt with Indigenous Peoples and Land Rights, South Africa, Internal Conflicts, the Pacific, the Baltic States and Other Regions of Tension in the (then) Soviet Union, and on Sri Lanka and El Salvador. There was simply neither time nor energy left after the Gulf War debate to take on all of these. The statements on Indigenous Peoples and Land Rights, and on South Africa, were adopted — without discussion. The others were referred to the WCC Central Committee. Moreover, delegates had earlier proposed even more subjects to the Public Issues Committee, 'including global warming, antisemitism, the debt crisis, AIDS, Romania and Albania'.[7]

Crusading: necessity or luxury?

To be critical of what happened at Canberra is not to indulge in the fashionable sport of selecting the World Council of Churches and all its works for condemnation. For one thing, the WCC is a body to whose purposes and principles I am myself strongly committed, and in several of whose activities and programmes I am personally involved. The WCC is a creation of the churches, and its central committee and assembly are composed of representatives from nearly all the major Christian traditions except the Roman Catholic Church (and in any case many Roman Catholic individuals are also involved in one capacity or another in the Council's activities). The 'ecumenism' it manifests is therefore in large part not what the Council itself creates, but what its member churches themselves bring to it. It represents and focuses in peculiarly concentrated form many of the strengths, and not a few of the weaknesses, of its member churches. In saying that it is an institution with a high degree of bureaucracy and a heavy commitment to identifying and pushing through its 'programmes', we are saying no more than what is the case with many of its constituent churches. If we are saying that it tries to do too much, and to say too much at any one time, and suffers from delusions of grandeur about the influence that it wields in the world, we are merely recognizing in it the faults of our own institutions. Perhaps that is why some of the criticisms of the WCC can be so virulent, a case of that psychology which transfers the frustration and anger from the beam in our own eye to the speck of sawdust in our neighbour's. The didacticism of the

[7]Ibid., p. 202.

Canberra statements can equally well be matched in the utterances of many of our own denominations; it merely demonstrates that trait in a singularly conspicuous way.

Nor is there in many of our churches any less of a tendency to want to put the whole world right, as crisis after crisis, calamity after calamity, is brought before us and we put on the assumed role of teacher-cum-manager for the whole world. It is often said that this is a peculiar failing of the late twentieth century, where massive and instant media coverage of events right round the globe batters our consciences mercilessly. The satellite, the computer networks and the fax machine may have had some role here, but only to increase what has always been present as the St George syndrome, the crusading mentality desirous of combating every imaginable dragon. That syndrome however is nothing new, and certainly predates even the cable telegraph. In 1823 Sydney Smith, the greatest English wit of his age, appealed from his Yorkshire rectory to his friend Lady Grey, to be spared yet another passage of arms, with weapons real or metaphorical, however just the cause:

> For God's sake, do not drag me into another war! I am worn down, and worn out, with crusading and defending Europe, and protecting mankind; I must think a little of myself. I am sorry for the Spaniards — I am sorry for the Greeks — I deplore the fate of the Jews; the people of the Sandwich Islands are groaning under the most detestable tyranny; Bagdad is oppressed; I do not like the present state of the Delta; Thibet is not comfortable. Am I to fight for all these people? The world is bursting with sin and sorrow. Am I to be champion of the Decalogue, and to be eternally raising fleets and armies to make all men good and happy? We have just done saving Europe, and I am afraid the consequence will be, that we shall cut each other's throats. No war, dear Lady Grey! — no eloquence; but apathy, selfishness, commonsense, arithmetic! ... I allow fighting in such a cause to be a luxury; but the business of a prudent, sensible man, is to guard against luxury.[8]

---

[8]*Letters of Sydney Smith*, Vol. I, ed. Nowell C. Smith, Clarendon Press, 1953, pp. 396f.

Before that passage is dismissed as a typical case of western liberal cynicism, let us be honest and admit that some selectivity of causes to be supported, given our finite energy and time, is always tacitly assumed. Once again the dilemma is all too apparent. If we want to avoid simply saying, in effect, that all sin is evil, how do we escape having to treat in detail each and every wrong on the agenda? Or are we to deal with each and every socio-political sin merely by statement after statement — an exercise which smacks, in Sydney Smith's words, of being a sheer luxury? Or, in the words of King David, a sacrifice which costs us nothing (II Sam. 24.24)? Just how is a whole world 'bursting with sin and sorrow' to be addressed?

To one American theologian, the late Paul Ramsey, this dilemma facing the churches was particularly apparent a quarter of a century ago. Ramsey used the occasion of the 1966 Geneva Conference on Church and Society to write a trenchant critique of the WCC's style of addressing socio-political issues[9], a style exhibited equally in the National Council of Churches (USA) and many mainline denominations — and presumably by extension in the (then) British Council of Churches and British churches generally. In summary, Ramsey's criticism was that in their pronouncements on public issues all such bodies tended to indulge in specifying detailed policies — particular *directives* — at the expense of the properly ethical task of identifying *directions* for public responsibility, which is the proper role for the church as a theological community. Thus Ramsey inveighed against 'the passion for numerous particular pronouncements on policy questions to the consequent neglect of basic decision- and action-oriented principles of ethical and political analysis.'[10] The churches' proper role, argued Ramsey, is 'to penetrate to a deeper and deeper level the meaning of Christian responsibility — leaving to the conscience of individuals and groups of individuals both the task and the freedom to arrive at specific conclusions through untrammelled

---

[9]Paul Ramsey, *Who Speaks for the Church? A critique of the 1966 Geneva Conference on Church and Society*, Abingdon Press, 1967.

[10]Ibid., p. 13.

debate about particular social policies'.[11] Ramsey did not intend to mean by his preferred approach a retreat into abstractions or counsels of perfection which are of no use to the political decision-maker, but rather, a closer definition of the goals of public responsibility which left open the options of 'political prudence' for their actual implementation. In fact, Ramsey argued, it is precisely the urge for specific directives which results in an air of abstraction irrelevant to the real world of politics, since when this desire is injected into a debate it usually results in the kind of statement which admits that on the one hand there is option X, while on the other hand some support possibility Y. '... Balanced pairs of pieces of specific advice are no more than pious and irrelevant generalities issuing from a great distance above the problems facing the nations.'[12] But above all, for Ramsey the chief weakness of the churches' indulgence in issuing particular directives to the politicians, is that the church, or a council of churches, does not as such carry responsibility for government, and therefore has neither the capacity for nor the responsibility of weighing the feasibility and consequences of one policy in relation to other policies, one context against another, in the total arena of the government's responsibility. The church must not 'yield to the dream of becoming a surrogate world political community, each where we are and in our various groupings particularly instructing one another and then telling the governments of the world how to bring about the solutions, the peace that passeth understanding'.[13]

For the moment I leave open a judgment on Ramsey's thesis, except to say that to reach a fair verdict one ought to have known what it is like to be in a position of church leadership or responsibility where one is exposed to the merciless pressures to 'say something' at a time of public alarm and confusion. Suffice it to say for now that his case has to be heard and answered by anyone concerned for Christian public responsibility.

[11]Ibid., p. 15.
[12]Ibid., p. 37.
[13]Ibid., p. 44.

A right to interfere?

There is of course one way out of these nagging questions: ignore the public, socio-political realm altogether; confine Christian moral discussion and teaching to the sphere of purely personal and domestic behaviour; so far as citizenship is concerned, simply obey the laws of the land and keep out of trouble. This debate has got so hackneyed in the past few years that I have no intention of embarking on it again here. My position for what it is worth can be summed up in a few sentences as follows.

There is no non-political Christianity, because there is no non-political life for any of us, Christian or whoever. We may think we are non-political if we refuse to join a political party, or refuse to campaign on some particular issue, or refuse to vote at a general election out of lack of interest, or simply switch off the television when the party political broadcast comes up on the screen. Such behaviour however is of no less political significance than that of the most dedicated party activist. For we all belong to the *polis*, the one society of human commerce and responsibility, and we are all playing some part in it whether we like it or not, whether we are conscious of it or not. We may attempt to influence it by consciously and positively opting for a certain party or certain priority issues, but equally we are affecting it by *allowing* policies and practices to go unchallenged and by acquiescing in what vested interests are up to. In recent years much has been written pejoratively about the 'politicization' of Christianity,[14] by which is usually meant, in the interests of a 'socially relevant' gospel, an alleged sell-out of Christian belief to a secular ideology such as Marxism. But captivity to ideologies can take many forms. One of the most clearly 'politicized' sermons which I have ever heard was in a white church in Johannesburg, where the decidedly evangelical preacher urged his hearers to develop a 'purely individualistic relation' (yes, those were his exact words) to God, a relation in which what other people thought and said had no influence on

---

[14]Most well known here is E. R. Norman, *Christianity and the World Order*, Oxford University Press, 1979 (the 1978 Reith Lectures).

us whatever. A far cry from Marx, but very close indeed to the
no less secularist ideology of bourgois, capitalistic
acquisitiveness. It was a sermon tailor-made to the interests of
the beneficiaries of apartheid, who knew that no critique of
racial and economic exploitation would ever be offered by
such piety.

God is the one who above all others hungers and thirsts for
righteousness on earth (Mt. 5.6), and a church which does not
experience stomach pangs or a parched throat in the world of
the 1990s is no church of God. Enough said on that score. But
nevertheless I am interested in how various thinkers draw the
active connection between the church and the public, political
sphere. Like other questions we are considering here, discussion
of this one already has a lengthy history in Britain and if only
to underline this fact, in the face of continued accusations in
the right-wing press that Christian social and political concern
is a recent invention of trendy church people, it is worth
glancing briefly at one or two threads in this story.

Half a century ago in 1942 Archbishop William Temple
produced his Penguin book *Christianity and Social Order* which
became a wartime best-seller and a classic statement of the
theologically-grounded, Anglican argument for social reform.[15]
Some have attributed the widespread acceptance of the
Beveridge Report on the Welfare State, and even the unexpected
Labour election victory of 1945, in no small measure to the
influence of this little book. 'What Right Has the Church to
Interfere?' is the title of the first chapter and in the opening
paragraph Temple recalls how during the Coal Strike of 1926
a group of bishops tried to bring government, mine-owners
and miners together to resolve the dispute, and Prime Minister
Stanley Baldwin asked a delegation of bishops how they would
like it if he referred the revision of the Athanasian Creed to the
Iron and Steel Federation (irreverent souls might speculate
that that particular formulary would not fare too badly under
such treatment). Temple, the Archbishop who once described
Christianity as the most materialist of all the religions, lost no
time in answering his own question.

---

[15]*Christianity and Social Order*, Penguin, 1942.

In summary his argument is as follows. Part of the divine commission of the church of God is to bring all human activities into that order which God has intended for his creation. As for *how* the church should 'interfere', the main task of the church is to 'inculcate Christian principles and the power of the Christian spirit' in society. This has often been undertaken in the past: the medieval and reformation churches, and the churches since then, have had very definite if diverse views on the Christian ordering of society and and the responsibilities of Christians in society. Before going on to discuss contemporary matters such as housing, employment and education, Temple devotes significant space to 'Christian principles'. He rejects notions of any social 'ideal' or blueprint revealed to Christians which must then be imposed on the disorderly world. Still less does he claim that Christian principles lead inevitably to Christian support for one political party rather than another (in fact for much of his life he was himself a card-carrying member of the Labour Party). In a nutshell his argument is that:

> The method of the Church's impact upon society at large should be twofold. The Church must announce Christian principles and point out where the existing social order at any time is in conflict with them. It must then pass on to Christian citizens, acting in their civic capacity, the task of re-shaping the existing order in closer conformity to the principles. For at this point technical knowledge may be required and judgments of expediency are always required. If a bridge is to be built, the Church may remind the engineer that it is his obligation to build a really safe bridge; but it is not entitled to tell him whether, in fact, his design meets this requirement ... In just the same way the Church may tell the politician what ends the social order should promote; but it must leave to the politician the devising of the precise means to those ends.[16]

One almost envies the serenity of Temple's assumption that clear principles can first be confidently stated, from which

---

[16]Ibid., p. 35.

programmes can then be deduced and particular problems addressed. The logic seems inexorable, and if we find it a little too much so it probably indicates a cultural distancing which fifty years of social change have placed between ourselves and Temple's starting-point. Today, we are less sure that general starting-points can survive the subsequent clashes with the particularities of experience without themselves having to submit to severe revision. We may speak, for instance, of the principle of the sanctity of life but when we try to apply this to the applications of the most recent medical science we may find that the definition of life itself is required to be reviewed by the advances in knowledge.

There is however another problem with Temple's approach. Has Temple in fact fully answered his precise question, on the right of the church to interfere? The answer he gives, as we have seen, is in terms of the relation between Christian belief and the public realm. Christianity has to do with ordering society. But at the risk of sounding like word-quibbling, is this the same as *the church* 'interfering'? Or, to be more exact, should it not be asked 'What right has *this* church to interfere?' That is, is the church as we know it in a fit condition to engage usefully in the public realm?

This somewhat subversive question was in fact also being asked half a century ago. Indeed, at exactly the same time as Temple was writing, another British thinker was wrestling deeply with the challenge of relating Christian belief to social and political realities, and with a significantly different emphasis. J.H. Oldham, Scottish layperson and pioneer in the ecumenical missionary movement, secretary of the epoch-making Edinburgh Missionary Conference of 1910 and study organizer of the 1937 Oxford Conference on Church, Community and State, was a close ally of Temple (though somewhat suspicious of bishops as a species). From the late 1930s until the end of the Second World War he led a group of thinkers, known collectively as the Moot, who met every few months to discuss many aspects of Christianity and the crisis facing western civilization. The Moot included figures as diverse as the sociologist Karl Mannheim, the poet and literary critic T.S. Eliot, the philosopher H.A. Hodges, the educationist Walter Moberly, the eccentric communist farmer John Middleton Murry and the theologian John Baillie. Oldham also founded the *Christian News-Letter* which appeared fortnightly throughout the war reaching a very large readership of all sorts and conditions of people. Closely related to these enterprises was another of Oldham's brainchildren, the Christian Frontier Council, which sought to engage with the issues lay-people were meeting in their secular responsbilities in society. Much of Oldham's thought, and that of other Moot members, found its way into the *Christian News-Letter* and into such books as Oldham's widely-read *Real Life is Meeting*[17]. That title, borrowed from the Jewish philosopher Martin Buber, itself signals a different nuance to Temple's approach. Oldham is no less concerned to relate Christianity to society, and to find a common purpose which can be given by the church to society. But, he says:

> We want an understanding of Christianity that has been reached, and could only have been reached, by those who have felt the full pressure of the forces that dominate modern society. We are facing a crisis in the life of mankind in which man's very existence as a person is at stake. In this life and death struggle it is essential to know the crucial points at which the Christian understanding of life is in accord or in conflict with the purposes and directions of contemporary society. It is through contact with actual life that truth acquires a dynamic quality, and the power that can save us will come from a new apprehension of the meaning of the Christian revelation for the actual situation of men today.[18]

Not here, then, truth in rounded general principles which descend upon particular issues. Rather, truth learnt as cuts and bruises from bumping against the jagged concrete edges of those matters. Oldham's call is for the church itself to enter into a new learning experience about the nature of contemporary society and what is happening to people in it, as

---

[17]*Real Life is Meeting*, Christian News-Letter Books No. 14, London: Sheldon Press, 1942.
[18]Ibid., pp. 1f.

the prior condition for any effective addressing of the issues. Moreover it is *a new understanding of Christianity itself* that has to be sought by the church as it engages with the world. There are no grand unquestioned assumptions from which to begin. These are basic insights to which we shall have recourse again and again in this book.

The difference between Oldham and Temple is significant. More to the point, so is the difference between Oldham and much of our church life today. The movements which Oldham and his co-workers like Kathleen Bliss and Alec Vidler pioneered, and which catalytic figures like Mark Gibbs and Ralph Morton[19] fostered well into the 1960s and 1970s, of emphasizing the central role in the church's mission of the whole body of Christians, the vast majority of whom are 'lay-people', in their secular vocations and responsibilities in the world, now seem sadly passé. Even in Germany, where after the Second World War the 'lay academies' played such a vital role in nurturing new concepts of Christian social responsibility, the vision is proving hard to sustain. One hot summer evening recently, over a glass of wine on his patio the director of one such academy mused to me that with the churches in numerical decline as far as their committed membership is concerned, there is a subtle but almost irresistible pressure for 'lay leadership' increasingly to be seen as *church-leadership*, and 'lay-training' as training of lay-people for 'clerical' roles of preaching, pastoral care and so forth. No-one can deny the importance of such work in the churches, but to clericalize the lay members at the expense of their primary vocation in the everyday world is a sure sign of retreat, of calling in the frontier troops to man the home defences, of maintenance rather than of mission. Conversely, if not paradoxically, there is now an equal pressure for the church's responsibility of addressing secular issues to be loaded on to its clerical leaders.

---

[19]Alec Vidler's *Christ's Strange Work*, SCM Press, 1963, incorporates material from twenty years earlier but still has trenchant relevance for today. The two books on laity education by Mark Gibbs and Ralph Morton, *God's Frozen People* (Collins, 1964) and *God's Lively People* (Collins, 1971), were among the most creative British writing on mission in the post-war period.

Compulsive talkers

The call for the church to be 'prophetic' rings out again and again in our time. Whatever else, being prophetic in the Old Testament sense certainly meant experiencing a compulsion to speak: '... within me there is something like a burning fire shut up in my bones; I am weary with holding it in and I cannot' (Jer. 20.9). But the compulsion of serving as vehicle of the divine revelation is not to be equated with each and every urge to 'say something'. The wish to make our voice heard can come from a variety of motives, not always healthy. There are the people, as we all know, who simply have to 'offer a comment' on every item of business on the agenda even if all that is worth saying has already been said, and who would depart from the meeting feeling unwanted, useless and unrecognized if they had remained silent throughout. They have to justify themselves by their speech. We all know, too, the embarrassing awkwardness of silence, whether in a personal conversation or in a public meeting when the speaker has sat down, and we just ache for someone, anyone, to break that silence by saying *something, anything.* Speaking can serve a host of felt needs, from filling in the gaps in the mind with verbiage as a substitute for thought, to sheer self-advertisement.

It may not be very different on the corporate level. We are more anxious that the 'voice of the church' should be heard than that we ask the very simple yet searching questions that surround the one basic enquiry, 'Why speak at all?' What pyschology lies behind the insistence that on each and every matter in the newspapers the church should 'have something to say'? Is it truly a desire that the world should be changed by our utterance, or is it simply the wish that the church should be noticed among all the other bodies and interests with 'something to say'? When we wish the church to speak, are we really concerned for the world, or more concerned that *our* (!) concern should be noticed and preferably admired by the world? Are we really doing any more than standing in the market place and saying 'We're here, too'? When people want 'the church to speak out' are they wanting that voice simply to be added to an already resounding chorus of public protest? If so, what is the precise point of adding just one more voice? Moreover, when people want 'the church to speak out' and reveal that by this they mean that church leaders — bishops and councils and the like — should 'give a lead', what are they in fact saying about themselves? That their own voice does not really count? Or, more subtly, that they are not really sure that what they want said is the right word but sense that it would at least sound well over the ecclesiastical loud-hailer system? What insecurities are at work here? Most crucially of all, the question we hardly ever dare ask openly: What assumptions are being made about the effectiveness of such speech? What evidence is there that church statements actually *change* anything in the world, whether in shaping public opinion or influencing governmental decisions?

These questions are not meant to be rhetorical, nor simply ways of debunking the whole idea of the church speaking on public and international affairs. That the church is called to speak in this sphere I am not in the slightest doubt, or I would not be in my present job. But precisely because this calling to speak is so important, it is vital that such questions are asked for the sake of clarification and direction on what should be said by the church, and how, and when, and to whom. If they are not asked resolutely then the 'voice of the church' is going to degenerate into sheer chatter, shrill or bland, talk for the sake of talk. To some this may not matter. After all, it will be said, better talk than complete silence, for at least sometimes the mark will be hit. That is surely a counsel of despair, redolent of the old joke about giving a monkey a typewriter and with infinite time it will eventually produce the complete works of Shakespeare. Or, nearer home, like the description I once heard of a preacher whose verbosity was more apparent than his theological insight: 'Anyone who goes on as long as that is bound to come up with some of the truth sooner or later.' The fact is that endless talk produces the same effect as silence, as dozing congregations will testify. An endlessly statement-producing church is equally likely to experience the same law of diminishing returns. Society can hardly be blamed for not be able to tell whether the church has something to say or just wants to say — something.

The temptation is now to rush towards trying to answer the questions posed above. To try to deal with them as they stand, however, would be to succumb to the very same ailment of which the current verbosity is a symptom. Even Paul Ramsey's critique of the earlier (and by implication much of the current) style of ecumenical and denominational pronouncements falls victim here. On all sides much of the argument about what the church should say about current affairs, and how it should say it, betrays a mighty assumption about the significance of speech in abstraction from other elements in the life and work of the Christian community. Ramsey himself regards the speaking — and by implication the teaching — role of the church as a dimension which can be considered as an entity in itself without regard to all else that the church is and does. This is to risk getting matters quite out of perspective. The body, as the Apostle Paul tells his Corinthian readers, does not consist of one member but of many (I Cor. 12.14–26). If it were all eye, there would be no hearing; if all ear, no smelling, and so on. We may take it that Paul could equally have pointed out that the body is not all mouth, but perhaps significantly he omits to mention the mouth at all. Maybe he thought the Corinthians were mouth-conscious enough already. To be more positive, the 'voice of the church' needs to be considered within the totality of the Christian mission which both includes, yet is more than, speaking (cf. I Cor. 13.1ff.). One begins to see a welcome recognition of the need to view church utterances on ethical and public issues within the wider context of the life of the church, and its wider social context, in the recent study by Mark Ellingsen, *The Cutting Edge*[20]. Commenting on what at first appears to be a remarkable degree of consensus among the churches, even on an international level, on issues such as apartheid and racism, economic development and unemployment, ecology, armaments, family life, and even abortion and genetic engineering, he asks pertinently:

> Is it possible that certain values and patterns of theological thought associated with the West are of perduring and central value to the Christian faith, which accounts for the

[20]Mark Ellingsen, *The Cutting Edge. How Churches Speak on Social Issues*, WCC Publications and W. B. Eerdmans, 1993.

consensus of the church statements regarding these
'Western' values? Or is it rather the case that the church
statements reflect Western values because the social-
statements format is essentially a Western innovation
which inevitably forces the Western ethical agenda on
those who employ it?[21]

The latter question in particular, Ellingsen argues, demands
consideration as the churches begin to tackle more seriously
'the issue of finding better mediums by which to do ethics'. The
extent to which the whole statement-producing mentality may
be reflecting certain cultural pressures of the age as much as
any 'prophetic' impulse, is a question we shall take up in
Chapter 3 of this book.

The power and extent of the assumption that the body of
Christ is primarily mouth, can be judged from the ways in
which not only traditional and 'authoritarian' theologies
manifest themselves in aggressive confrontation of their
audiences (often literally so), but also, on occasion, the heavily
didactic styles of some versions of the more recent theologies
of liberation. It is paradoxical when theologies which proclaim
the end of the hierarchical church and the authoritarian,
patriarchal God still feel bound to announce themselves as
from the podium rather than the round-table. This is not to
criticize theologies of political liberation or feminism as such
for it is in them that so much of contemporary life and promise
for Christianity is at work. It is simply to recognize how much
liberation still awaits Christianity from what the Japanese
theologian Kosuke Koyama calls its 'teacher complex'[22].

That is really the theme of the rest of this book. I believe that
behind much contemporary Christianity lies a didacticism
which must be questioned: the assumption that the church is
primarily here (and qualified) to teach the world how to live.
The church, I would assert, is certainly intended to be the
means whereby God reveals to the world how it should live. But

[21]Ibid., pp. 136f.
[22]Kosuke Koyama, in 'What Makes a Missionary? Toward Crucified Mind not
Crusading Mind', in *Mission Trends*, Eerdmans, 1979, pp. 117-132.

that the church itself can teach this to the world as an authoritative guide is a false assumption, an illusory short-cut, from which many of the church's contemporary problems stem. The church has as much to learn as any other community, and it is precisely in its willingness to learn, and in the manner of its learning, that its vital and distinctive witness is to be made.

What we need to do, therefore, is to probe yet more deeply into some of the assumptions that are being made about the importance of 'speaking', and to enquire into what may be some of the social and cultural pressures of our time which are conditioning us to make these assumptions. We need then to ask what other roles and images of the church may be available to us from the biblical and theological resources of the Christian tradition, which can enable us to identify a more authentic role and means of 'speaking', and a deeper understanding of what being 'prophetic' entails. From these we can build up, utilizing the genuinely creative experiences of the worldwide Christian community of the present-day, a new set of priorities and options for the church to engage in 'public speaking'.

First, however, we do well to recognize that one of the most powerful conditioning influences upon the Christian community is that of historic example — or what it considers to be historic example. We therefore turn next to consider how powerfully recent Christian history can reinforce the 'urge to speak' — and equally how this urge can distort that very same history by which it believes itself to be inspired.

2

Two Case-Studies: Barmen and Kairos

Arguments for the desirability and possibility of certain actions usually appeal to historical precedents. The desire for the church to 'speak out' is no exception, and in the story of modern Christianity there are a number of instances which appear to demonstrate that the church can and should speak out concretely in the political realm. These days, two cases in particular are typically cited: from Germany, the Barmen Declaration of 1934; and from South Africa, the *Kairos Document* of 1985. Separated in time by over half a century, and in space by two continents, these statements have indeed become widely regarded as outstanding examples of Christian pronouncement in the face of politicized evil. In an age when there has been more than enough illustration of evasion, compromise and moral cowardice, they at least witness to occasions when the trumpet did not 'give an uncertain sound.'

Indeed, as already hinted, they seem to reinforce powerfully the imperative for the church to speak decisively in the public realm. But given what was said in the previous chapter about the over-anxiety for the church to speak, these two instances deserve a little more examination than is often afforded them. Too often they are simply appealed to in a short-hand and unqualified way as supportive examples of the church speaking politically, and thereby a good deal of their actual significance is missed. It is the purpose of this chapter to ask just what in fact may be learned from Barmen and *Kairos* about 'the church's voice' in the political arena. In so doing we may uncover a good deal more of the questions which need to be addressed if the church is to speak responsibly.

Let us then look in turn at each of these statements with an eye to what they actually reveal about 'the voice of the church' in a critical political context.

Barmen 1934[1]

The Theological Declaration, or Confession, of Barmen was that statement approved by a Free Synod of the German Evangelical (i.e. Protestant) Church meeting at Barmen-Wuppertal in the Ruhr, 29-31 May 1934, and comprising representatives of those sections most determined to resist the 'nazification' of the church in the Third Reich. The declaration immediately caused at least as much a stir in church circles abroad as it provoked within Germany itself, and it was widely seen as the charter of the Protestant Christian resistance to Hitler's totalitarian regime, being the basic theological manifesto of the Confessing Church. A major German church historian acclaims it as 'without doubt the most important event' of the struggle between the church and the Nazi state,[2] and still today it inspires the whole Christian world with an example of how to say 'No!' to Caesar when occasion demands. In face of the rampant nationalistic cry that the divine was to be found in the exciting resurgence of race, state and Führer, the Christian counter-claim was stated with a power all the more striking for its simplicity, as in the first 'thesis' of the statement:

'I am the way and the truth and the life: no man cometh unto the Father but by me' (John 14.6).

'Verily, verily, I say unto you, He that entereth not by the door into the sheepfold but climbeth up some other way, the same is a thief and a robber: ... I am the door: by me if any man enter in, he shall be saved' (John 10.1, 9).

---

[1] For the German Church Struggle this chapter draws heavily upon Klaus Scholder, *The Churches in the Third Reich*, Vol. I, SCM Press, 1987, and Vol. II, SCM Press, 1988, and *Requiem for Hitler*, SCM, 1989. See also J.S. Conway, *The Nazi Persecution of the Churches*, Weidenfeld and Nicholson, 1968, and E. Bethge, *Dietrich Bonhoeffer. Theologian, Christian, Contemporary*, Collins, 1970.

[2] Scholder, *The Churches*, Vol. II, p.147

Jesus Christ, as he is testified to us in Holy Scripture, is the one Word of God which we are to hear, which we are to trust and obey in life and in death.

We repudiate the false teaching that the Church can and must recognise yet other happenings and powers, personalities and truths as divine revelation alongside this one Word of God, as a source of her preaching.[3]

To set this declaration in context, it must be pointed out that when Adolf Hitler acceded to the Chancellorship of Germany on 30 January 1933, except in those political parties of the centre and left explicitly opposed to National Socialism the event was greeted with widespread acclaim throughout Germany, and in the churches no less than in other circles. We who are only able to look back on that period through the perspectives of the Second World War and the horrors of Auschwitz find it hard to empathize with those who hailed Hitler's ascendancy as the dawn of a new era, but it has to be said that in the eyes of many, that tumultuous week was of deep moral and spiritual significance. It meant a new breakthrough to *united* leadership after the gradual disintegration into chaos of the Weimar democracy. Not all were ardent supporters of Hitler himself, and many had been disturbed by Hitler's anti-semitic rhetoric and the brutality of the storm-troopers. But firebrands are often tamed by the responsibilities of actual power, and many assumed that Hitler would be more 'realistic' once in office, more accommodating to those with whom he would have to co-operate (the Nazi party never had an absolute majority in the Reichstag) and would rein in his more extreme followers. Moreover, Hitler was soon making reassuring noises to the churches, affirming that 'positive Christianity' (that is, co-operating with the new political order), in both Protestant and Catholic forms, would be at home in his Reich, and was also given to lacing his oratory with vague, pious-sounding invocations of the deity. The fact is that many decent Christians, including some highly sophisticated theologians, believed that

---

[3]English version of the Barmen Declaration followed in this chapter is that in E.H. Robertson, *Christians Against Hitler*, SCM Press, 1962, pp. 48-52.

nothing less than an epoch-making revolution was taking place in the life of the German people, and that the job of the churches was to co-operate with its best aspects and to baptize it with Christian impulses. One senior and much respected British church figure, recalling an international Student Christian Movement conference at that time, tells me that in many respects the participants most impressive for their moral earnestness were those from Germany in Nazi uniform. Indeed for this particular period it is estimated that the majority of Protestant theological students were members of the National Socialist Party.

Of course in the event Hitler proved not to be so tameable. Within weeks all alternative political parties and the trades unions were eliminated, draconian and dictatorial powers were assumed and justified by the necessity to ensure 'the safety of the Reich', the mechanisms of the police state appeared overnight, concentration camps were set up and the persecution of the Jews began with organized boycotts of Jewish businesses and the expulsion from civil office of all 'non-Aryans'. The public acquiesced in a great deal of this because it seemed to be sheer, if unfortunate, necessity. The awful alternative of a *bolshevik* take-over had been powerfully conjured up by Hitler, and that nightmare alone was enough to convince many middle-class, Christian people that Hitler represented the nation's salvation in this hour of crisis.

Within Protestant circles, real trouble began when the Nazi revolution started to make claims upon the life, teachings and structure of the church itself. The Nazi watchword in the early days of the revolution was *Gleichshaltung*, co-ordination or conformation of all German activities and institutions with the goals, ethos and methods of the new Reich. Quite what Hitler's own plans and policies for the churches were in pre-1939 Germany is a matter of some debate. Probably, he simply desired that they keep themselves out of all political matters and remained quiet, leaving him to run the state as he pleased, and inculcating a loyal subservience to himself among all their adherents. There were a number of Nazi propagandists such as Alfred Rosenberg who attacked Christianity on a theoretical level and believed that the Nazi confection of blood, race and soil could itself become a new religion for the German people in place of Christianity. But the greatest enthusiasts for the *Gleichshaltung* of Protestantism with the new Nazi order were to be found within the churches themselves, and especially in the so-called German Christian movement. This movement, led by a young pastor, Joachim Hossenfelder, not only believed (as did many other godfearing Germans) that the sudden emergence of 'the new Germany' out of the defeatism and disunity following the débâcle of 1918 was nothing less than a manifestation of the divine will, a kind of theophany in contemporary German experience; they also believed that the categories of 'people' (*Volk*), 'race' and 'nation' were in themselves of supreme significance in the divine dispensation, They were 'orders of creation', that is, decreed by the Creator as indissoluble realities for human life and to be preserved in their perfection. Thus, to believe in God the Creator meant first to bind oneself to the *Volk* in and for which one had been created. The prime calling for Germany was to become truly German in every respect — in its political ordering and in its 'racial purity'. Only by freeing itself politically, culturally and biologically from all 'foreign' elements could Germany become its true self. Christians were to welcome and co-operate with this task as a God-given duty, and at the same time realize the opportunity now presented to them to missionize the *Volk* and ensure that the gospel was brought to the people in a truly 'Germanic' form.

In the months following Hitler's accession the German Christians grew strongly in number, and in the summer of 1933 achieved major successes in a number of church elections in the various *Land* (district) Protestant churches, capturing synods and official posts. Among their chief successes were the Church of the Old Prussian Union (the largest Protestant church), and the eventual election of Ludwig Müller, a hitherto unknown former naval chaplain who had already been appointed by Hitler as his special adviser on Protestant affairs, as 'Reich Bishop'. But opposition was also growing. The 'Young Reformation' movement struggled valiantly to resist the complete take-over of theological faculties, universities and parishes by the German Christians. Moreover, increasing alarm was felt when it emerged just what comprised the 'Germanic' gospel which the more extreme German Christians considered appropriate for the unique national context: a bible without the Old Testament (because of its Jewishness), and a Christ without his cross (on account of the need to stress heroism rather than suffering). It also became clear just what was being demanded of the church in the name of *Gleichshaltung*: the removal from office of all 'non-Aryan' (i.e. of Jewish descent) pastors, and the introduction of 'Germanic' forms of leadership in accordance with the *Führer*-principle. Those pastors already resisting such moves were experiencing intimidation and in some cases arrest, and in response a 'Pastors' Emergency League' emerged, in which Martin Niemöller of Berlin-Dahlem became increasingly prominent.

There was however yet another element of opposition. As anyone who encounters German Protestantism very soon becomes aware, almost on a par with the sacred scriptures is the historic *confession* which defines the fundamental beliefs and form of church order for that particular branch of the church of the Reformation. Most famous perhaps is the Lutheran Augsburg Confession of 1530, but the Reformed and 'United' churches were (indeed are) equally jealous of their particular enshrinements of belief, with which their particular identity was bound up. As the clamour and confusion within Protestant circles wore on towards the end of 1933, a number of pastors and theologians felt increasingly that the fight with the German Christians, if it was to be nothing more than a church-political power struggle, was not worth waging. What was at issue was nothing less than the confession of the true faith. Did the German Christians still confess the faith as it came to light in the Reformation and based on the Scriptures? If not, then even if they 'won control' of the church they would not in fact be the Evangelical Church of Germany but, in both theological and legal terms, something quite different.

It was this issue which finally brought together on 29 May 1934, at Barmen in the Ruhr, 83 pastors and 55 lay-people (though only one woman among them) as the Free Confessing Synod. Two tense days later, after much debate, it unanimously and with acclamation approved the now famous Theological Declaration. Its single greatest inspiration was Karl Barth. His severely Reformed theology of revelation, admitting only the Word of God in Jesus Christ as the source of revelation for the Christian church, and stressing the majesty and sovereignty of the one and triune God over all that is human and earthly, had only a few years previously sounded shocking and crude to sophisticated modern ears. Now, it seemed, a prophet's time had come.

The Barmen Declaration is short and succinct. In a preamble it affirms that even as late as July 1933 the constitution of the German Evangelical Church had been legally stated to be the gospel of Jesus Christ as revealed in scripture and expressed in the Reformation creeds; that the various branches of German Protestantism with their particular confessions were united in this basic affirmation; and that now their unity was threatened by the so-called German Christians. 'In view of the destructive errors of the German Christians and the present national church goverment', the Declaration then stated its six theses, the first of which, with its solemn affirmation of Christ alone as the church's source of revelation, has been quoted in full already. Each thesis followed the same pattern of scriptural text, affirmation of truth now to be taught and practised, and repudiation of error.

In summary the remaining five paragraphs ran thus. The second affirmed 'God's mighty claim on our whole life' and repudiated the notion that 'there are areas of our life in which we belong not to Jesus Christ but another Lord', areas in which we do not need Christ's justification and sanctification. The third thesis affirmed the church as the community in which Christ works through word and sacraments by the Holy Spirit, and exists solely by and for the comfort of his word of forgiveness. It repudiated the claim that 'the church can turn over the form of her message and ordinances at will according to some dominant ideological and political convictions'. Thesis four emphasized that the office of leadership within the church is not of rule by one over others, but 'the exercise of the service entrusted and commanded to the whole congregation', so leading to a clear repudiation of the *Führer*-principle within the church. The fifth (and longest) thesis acknowledged the God-given responsibility of the state 'to provide for justice and peace in the yet unredeemed world' by human means including the threat and use of force, but equally affirmed the church's calling to remind people of 'God's kingdom, God's commandment and righteousness, and thereby the responsibility of rulers and ruled'. It repudiated as false the teaching that the state might expand beyond its special responsibility 'to become the single and total order of human life' and so fulfil the church's commission — and equally the idea that the church could take on the functions of the state and so itself become an organ of the state. Finally, the sixth thesis declared that the church's freedom consists in fulfilling her commission of serving all people through word and sacrament with the message of God's free grace, and repudiated the claim that the church 'can put the word and work of the Lord in the service of some wishes, purposes or plans or other, chosen according to desire'.

Those participants who later recorded their impressions of the Barmen Synod speak of an almost unbearable tension as, after hours of debate and all-night re-drafting sessions, the final, sober reading of the Declaration took place and the vote was called for — followed by the jubilation and relief which burst into a spontaneous rendering of the hymn 'Now thank we all our God'. After months of wavering and confusion, the church — or at any rate a major part of it — had at last spoken, publicly, clearly and courageously. Still today, it is hard to read the document with an eye to its context without catching something of the drama of that moment, and as a Christian to feel glad to have been alive in the same century.

But *what* had Barmen declared? It was a very public statement, in a highly-charged political context, but was it actually a political statement, or even addressing political issues? In one sense it was plainly no such thing. One looks in vain in Barmen for any reference to any of the major issues on the German political scene: no mention of one-party rule, or the police-state, or the concentration camps, or the persecution of the Jews. This was basically a statement by the church and about the church, not about society as such. It was the church saying that it was not prepared to lose its identity as the possession of Jesus Christ and become an arm of the Nazi state. It did not criticize that state as such, and in fact a good many of those present at Barmen were equally willing to affirm, as citizens, their loyalty to Hitler's government. Indeed it was probably only because the young Hans Asmussen, whose responsibility it was to present the proposed Declaration to the Synod, insisted on a clear distinction between what the gathering was saying as church, and what each of the participants might feel about the political scene as individual citizens on the basis of their personal 'world-views', that there was such marked agreement. If the document had attempted to pass comment on the secular, political scene there is no doubt that the whole exercise would have foundered and the Confessing Church would have disintegrated from the start. In this respect, therefore, far from illustrating how wonderfully the Christian community can and should weigh into the political scene, the Barmen Declaration signally demonstrates the sheer difficulty of the church corporately addressing specific political issues. This misunderstanding of Barmen is not due solely to the passage of time. Within days, it was being equally misunderstood among church circles outside Germany, especially in the western democracies, where people had been eagerly awaiting signs of Christian resistance to what was clearly a repressive and oppressive dictatorship. Liberal English observers, for example, welcomed Barmen as an impressive utterance on behalf of 'religious liberty'.[4] This was at best a half-true perception. Barmen was calling not for an open society, tolerant of any belief, but for a church closed against error. It was not about the freedom of the conscience, but, as Barth was to say, about the bondage of the conscience to Christ; not about freedom to preach, but freedom *in* preaching the gospel. It was all about the church being truly the church.

Is the Declaration therefore to be criticized as a-political, wilfully ignoring the distressing realities of the time, and to be

---

[4]See 'Religious Liberty or Christian Freedom? Bonhoeffer, Barmen and Anglo-Saxon Individualism', and 'The Freedom of the Church: Bonhoeffer and the Free Church Tradition', in K.W. Clements, *What Freedom? The Persistent Challenge of Dietrich Bonhoeffer*, Bristol Baptist College, 1990.

dismissed as irrelevant if we want an example of witness in the political realm? This, equally, would be a superficial judgment. The statement is heavy with political significance even if not directly expressed.

In the first place, in a totalitarian context it is virtually impossible for any event or statement in the public realm to be devoid of political meaning, simply because of the assumption by the regime to total rights in that realm. For the church to declare that it had its own identity to affirm, independent of the new Reich, its own doctrine and order to maintain, its own gospel to proclaim and its own style of servanthood to follow, in other words to resist *Gleichshaltung*, meant denying a certain space to the claims of the state. It meant affirming, as Karl Barth put it, the church as the frontier of the state. In practice the children of this world saw things more clearly than the children of light, for the Nazi authorities and the Gestapo certainly regarded the Confessing Church as a politically-motivated opposition, despite the many disclaimers from pastors who continued to declare no political interest and to affirm their loyalty to the state. The Confessing Church, whatever else may be said about it, survived to the end of the Second World War as almost the one public area of life in Germany where the Nazi writ did not completely run, and was thus an embarrassing thorn in the flesh of the Reich. As such, its very existence, and that of the Barmen Declaration on which it was based, was of no mean political significance.

Second, the inspiration behind the Barmen Declaration was primarily and deliberately theological, not in order to deny Christian political responsibility but precisely in order to clarify the basis on which a Christian political judgment was to be made. Karl Barth had repeatedly criticized the 'Young Reformation' movement for jumping into the fray against the German Christians as one church political group set against another in a sheer power struggle. Barth called for *theological* existence, commitment to the confession as the basis of the church's life, before all else. The church was not first to align itself with one political position over another, but was first to place itself under the cross where all human enterprises, including all political ones, come under the judgment of God.

Then, and only then, would one be in a position to enter into practical and political issues. Barmen thus did not pretend to be a direct political statement, but it was a clearing of the decks for authentic Christian political vision, the identification and affirmation of the place (the sole lordship of Christ) from which such judgments could be made. In face of all the pressures from the contemporary excitements of 'national renewal', the seductive and turbid racial mythology, and the dazzling political leadership of a seemingly magical genius crowned with one success after another, all of which were laying claim to be direct indicators of the will of God, such a fundamental task was the first theological imperative. As Klaus Scholder puts it, 'the church did not allow any political themes — whether appropriate or inappropriate — to be forced on it'.[5] Barmen may not have been directly political but it certainly was not apolitical either. It is best described as *pre*-political, locating the theological point from which authentic political witness could be made.

Third, there are more than hints in the actual contents of Barmen, especially in theses two and five, that God's command and grace extend into the political realm, and that the church's commission, while not being confused with that of government itself, includes reminding the state of the righteous claims of God on ruler and ruled alike. It has to be said that, with the exception of one or two notable occasions, the Confessing Church itself was not able in the subsequent months and years to fulfil concretely what is implied here. It did not cry out against the oppression of the Jews in society at large, nor oppose preparations for war. Karl Barth himself, after his enforced return to his native Switzerland in 1935, was to lament that the Confessing Church, whenever it did speak out, spoke only for itself, and after the Second World War he was to declare that a political word should have been uttered more quickly. Dietrich Bonhoeffer, the most loyal servant imaginable of that Church, was to be even more trenchantly critical in his prison writings, and demonstrated in his life and death the fullest implications of Barmen.

[5]Scholder, *Requiem*, p. 80.

In short, Barmen was certainly the church speaking, but not speaking directly to specific political issues of the day.

Kairos 1985

'The time has come. The moment of truth has arrived. South Africa has been plunged into a crisis that is shaking the foundations and there is every indication that the crisis has only just begun and that it will deepen and become even more threatening in the months to come. It is the KAIROS or moment of truth not only for apartheid but also for the church.'[6]

There is no mistaking that, in contrast to the Barmen Declaration, these opening words of the *Kairos Document* herald a very direct political comment indeed! 1985 saw South Africa plunged into deepening civil strife as the youth of the townships once more rose up against the apartheid system that had oppressed their parents and grandparents in their turn, and had massacred many of their older sisters and brothers in Soweto in 1976, and as the international community at length began to threaten more compelling economic sanctions, so sending shudders through the financial corridors of South African commerce. President P.W. Botha's only response was to make a speech of meaningless rhetoric declaring that South Africa had 'crossed its Rubicon' of change — and to impose a still more repressive state of emergency across much of the country.

Those responsible for issuing the document were a group of radical, mainly black, theologians in Soweto, closely associated with the Institute for Contextual Theology but drawing on a wide range of collaborators. South Africa, a country where some 80% of the population are estimated to claim some form of Christian affiliation, had over the years witnessed the use of Christianity both to legitimate the apartheid system (above all

[6] *The Kairos Document. Challenge to the Church: A Theological Comment on the Political Crisis in South Africa.* Produced by the Kairos Theologians, and published in UK by Catholic Institute for International Relations and British Council of Churches, 1985.

in the Afrikaner theology of the white Dutch Reformed Church),
and to oppose it, often at great cost, as in the testimony of such
courageous figures as Beyers Naudé, Desmond Tutu, Allan
Boesak and the communities of resistance which they led.
Since 1961 and the famous Cottesloe Statement, which led to
the parting of the ways between the Dutch Reformed Church
and the ecumenical family both inside and outside South
Africa, there had been a number of impressive declarations
condemning apartheid as a sin, or as a heresy, and calling for
a radical change for justice. This Christian opposition to
apartheid owed not a little for its inspiration to the struggle of
the Confessing Church in Germany, and nowhere have Barth
and Bonhoeffer been read more keenly than in South Africa,
and there is therefore more than an accidental link in the
historical backgrounds to Barmen and *Kairos*.

Nothing, however, that had preceded it in South Africa had
quite the immediate and wide-ranging impact of *Kairos*, both
nationally and worldwide. Much longer than Barmen (it runs
to a thirty-page booklet), it is nevertheless ruthlessly terse and
to the point, and the ominous drum-beat of that opening
paragraph is maintained without let-up to the very end. In part
its impact is due to the infusion of the notion of 'Kairos' itself
on every page, 'Kairos' being the biblical Greek word for time
in the sense of 'season' or 'opportune time', as distinct from
chronological time: time of critical importance when great
developments for good or ill may be expected. It was, said the
document, such a Kairos now, not just for South African society
but for the church, and especially the church, as well: 'The
Church is divided and its day of judgment has come.'[7]

The document trenchantly criticizes 'state theology', that is,
that reading of the Christian faith which emphasizes one-
sidedly the duty of Christians to obey the authorities without
question (Romans 13), and which allows the state to claim
divine sanction for even the most brutal policies in the name
of 'law and order'. The god whom the South African state
invokes to justify its authority, and to whom pious appeal is

[7]Ibid., p. 5.

made even in the preamble to the country's constitution, is nothing but an idol, 'as mischievous, sinister and evil as any of the idols that the prophets of Israel had to contend with ... a god who is historically on the side of the white settlers, who dispossesses black people of their land and who gives the major part of the land to his "chosen people"'.

The document's real fire however is reserved for 'church theology', that is, the version of the gospel evidently favoured by the mainline churches in South Africa, even by those who declare themselves opposed to apartheid. Here the keyword has become 'reconciliation' at the expense of *justice.* 'In our situation in South Africa today it would be totally un-Christian to plead for reconciliation and peace before the present injustices have been removed.'[8] Equally seductive had been the condemnation of all 'violence' without distinguishing the violence of protest and self-protection from the primary aggressive violence of the state. 'Church theology' lacks any social analysis, and it is this which the *Kairos* authors insist must be part of a genuinely 'prophetic theology'. Such a theology will combine realistic perception of what is going on in society, identifying the structures and processes of oppression, with a drawing upon the biblical resources of faith in a God who takes the side of the poor and oppressed against tyranny. A tyrannical government is an enemy of the people, and cannot help but become more violent. There can be no doubt that the apartheid minority regime is such a tyrant, and irreformably so. The conclusion is as explicitly and politically prescriptive as can be: the church must take sides with the poor and oppressed, not only refusing to collaborate with tyranny but mobilizing 'its members in every parish to begin to think and work and plan for a change of government in South Africa' to the point of civil disobedience if necessary.[9]

So, then, a pungently political statement from a theological standpoint. But, though its authors and 120 signatories were all Christians, is it accurate to describe this as *the church* speaking? The document was never officially owned by any of the churches

[8]Ibid., p. 8.
[9]Ibid., p. 26f.

in South Africa, nor even adopted as a statement by, for example, the South African Council of Churches on whose premises it was publicly launched. Relatively few church leaders put their names to it, even from among those hitherto most associated with the opposition to apartheid. One could of course argue that in *Kairos* we hear the voice of the *authentic* church, and that thereby the location and membership of the 'true church' in South Africa were being redefined. That would certainly put the document on a par with the Barmen Declaration which was, indeed, clarifying who did now truly constitute the Evangelical Church of Germany. But the *Kairos* document never claims this intention of redefining the true church. The clue to its real intention is given in its title: *Challenge to the Church.* Note, *to* the church, not by it or from it. Here was a prophetic voice, certainly from within the church, addressing the whole community which claimed to be Christian with the sharpest of challenges to recognize its true calling in the hour of crisis.

Barmen and *Kairos* then are two remarkable statements produced by Christians in a time of political crisis. That common background, however, must not allow us to blur the real difference between them as in the publishers' statement on the cover of the British edition of *Kairos*: 'Like the Declaration of Barmen in Nazi Germany, it defines the demands of the Gospel at a time of great political crisis, as Christianity is used to justify an intolerable, oppressive system.' Taken each by itself, neither document in fact demonstrates the church corporately addressing specific contemporary political issues. In Barmen the church spoke powerfully — but essentially about being the church. In *Kairos* a powerful political message was uttered — but not by the church as such, rather to the church by a group within it.

Whether the church as a body can speak in a convincing way to the contemporary political scene is a real challenge still left to us by both Barmen and *Kairos*. It would be a counsel of despair to opt for a final choice between corporate statements of ecclesiastical blandness on the one hand, and sharp, challenging thrusts by radical minority groups on the other. Both will be overcome by the rush of worldly events themselves.

What has to be clarified is the significance, potential and actual, of the church itself making a political witness by the kind of community it is, regardless of what statements it makes. In fact, at local level it was a highly political witness which was made by a Confessing Church parish when it refused to dismiss its 'Jew-pastor' as demanded by the local Gauleiter. And for all its trenchant thrusts, it is a weakness with *Kairos* that throughout its emphasis upon prophetic speech and action the question of what kind of church community might be expected to speak and act in such a way, and thereby lend authenticity to what could otherwise be little more than gestures and slogans, is not addressed. For this reason, much more recognition than has generally been accorded it is merited by a document which followed soon after *Kairos* from another and somewhat unexpected quarter in South Africa: *Evangelical Witness in South Africa.*[10] Here, evangelicals (mainly black) took up the challenge laid down by *Kairos* but, rather than merely transposing the critique of apartheid into an evangelical key, the authors subjected their own church and mission-organization structures to a devastating critique, exposing much of it as white-led paternalism and thus the consolidation of apartheid within the church itself. The document ranks as one of the most honest Christian self-assessments from within South Africa, or anywhere else for that matter, in recent times.

If Barmen and *Kairos*, properly understood, caution us against assuming too great a capacity for the church to speak concretely to the political situation, that is not entirely the end of the matter. If I have reached a somewhat negative conclusion it is because so far in this chapter I have been guilty of following precisely the approach against which I warned earlier, that of concentrating almost exclusively on the verbal · statements themselves. If we look more closely at just how the two statements came about, and at the contexts in which they arose, and what else was happening in their preparation, we shall in fact find out a good deal more about what it means for the church to 'speak'. The problem with such famous statements

---

[10]*Evangelical Witness in South Africa. A Critique of Evangelical Theology and Practice by South African Evangelicals Themselves*, Evangelical Alliance, 1986.

is that naturally we tend to see them only as finished products, documents now totally extracted and divorced from the processes which created them. An unreal impression is conveyed that one fine day, a number of brave and concerned souls sat down, the fire for justice in their hearts and the light of truth in their eyes, and, knowing what had to be said to combat evil, said it. Why cannot one's own church or council of churches or whatever organization be as clear-cut and radical as that? The temptation then is to want to produce, if not carbon-copy statements, then documents of similar ilk in one's own or neighbouring contexts, and to generate quite unreal expectations about the capacity of one's church leadership to 'speak'. Following the South African document, 'Kairos' suddenly became a vogue-word in many parts of the world, and all sorts of Kairos groups and statements began to appear. One has similarly heard calls from time to time for a 'British Barmen' statement in the face of social injustice, militarism and so forth. But there are no short-cuts to genuinely prophetic positions, and there are responsibilities which can be at least as important as making statements. That, as we shall see in the remaining part of this chapter, is in fact one of the most important lessons of Barmen and *Kairos*.

A history of speaking

The Cathedral of Ulm in central Germany boasts the tallest spire in the world, soaring more than five-hundred feet above the Danube. A look inside the building too, however, well repays the visitor seeking a sense of history. Not only does the chancel display a remarkable set of figures from the bible and classical antiquity — remarkable not least because for once it comprises equal numbers of women and men — but the late medieval wooden pulpit has an unusual feature. Its builder was clearly a theologian as well as a craftsman, for in addition to the usual sounding-board set just above the preacher's head, higher up there is another one, slightly smaller. This is for the Holy Spirit, the invisible preacher in every genuine sermon.

Never, perhaps, did that pulpit seem so appropriate a place from which to speak as on Sunday 3 April 1934, when from all over Germany, at very short notice, there gathered representatives of the growing movement for a new confession of faith in opposition to the 'German Christians'. The previous evening there had been intense discussion about a declaration which would claim that only such confessing groups could call themselves the legitimate Evangelical Church of Germany. Now, at the Sunday morning service, a congregation of over 5000 filled the vast nave and stood to hear Theophil Wurm, Bishop of the Lutheran Church of Württemberg, preach on the text: 'Honour all men, love the brotherhood, fear God, honour the king' (I Pet. 2.17). But the tension grew even greater as Bishop Hans Meiser of Munich took his place beneath both sounding-boards and read what became known as the Ulm Declaration. It declared that only a church which held fast to the confession was a church. A body might possess all offices and intruments but if it abandoned the confession it was no longer a church of Jesus Christ. This was nearly two months before Barmen, and the Ulm Declaration, rather than that made at Barmen, might be said to have heralded the actual birth of the Confessing Church.

The fact is that Barmen arose out of a long and sometimes confused process of speaking, or of efforts to speak. It did not suddenly arrive complete in itself. For one thing, there had been several previous attempts to construct a new confession to meet the crisis, which would unite all the Protestant traditions. The most concerted such project was the 'Bethel Confession', so-called because the work on it was carried out in the famous Bethel pastoral centre for the handicapped during the summer of 1933, by a group of younger theologians led by Dietrich Bonhoeffer.[11] Bonhoeffer's original draft was significantly sharper at some points, especially on the relation between church and state, than Barmen itself was to be. But the text was subjected to a considerable amount of sandpapering by committee in the winter of 1933-34, by which time the exercise was overtaken by events anyway. But most notable was how the movement towards a new confessing of the faith, while it

[11]See Bethge, op. cit., pp. 231-234.

culminated in the central, national event of Barmen, received its primary impetus from a wide variety of local initiatives, local not simply in the sense of the different *Land* churches, but truly local, that is, even at parish level.

Indeed, the germ of the whole idea of a renewed confession can be located in an incident in the summer of 1932, six months before Hitler came to power, in Altona on the outskirts of Hamburg. On Sunday 17 July, known thereafter as 'Altona Bloody Sunday', a vicious street-battle flared up between Nazi storm-troopers and local communists, right outside the main church as the afternoon service was being held. At the end of the day, 17 people lay dead and many were seriously wounded. The local pastors held emergency church services a few evenings later, each following the same liturgy, and each issuing a solemn statement to the congregations. This statement, instead of the usual anodyne expression of concern that might have been expected, was a stark confession that in the confusion of the times only the name of Jesus Christ could help, and equally that the church had to confess its own solidarity of guilt in what was happening. The primary fault lay in the divisive wish for self-righteous glorification, of party against party. '... We confess before God as the Holy One that it originates in the fact that we are no longer willing to be sinners together, before God, with all the brothers and sisters of our people, irrespective of social status and party. Each one wants to claim his own righteousness. But we bear witness to our congregations that all that is evil arises out of this self-righteousness.'[12]

It was one of the younger of those Altona pastors, Hans Asmussen, who nearly two years later was to read to the assembly at Barmen the great Declaration. The confessing movement was thus 'from below', and from the local edges towards the centre, not a single grandiloquent declaration from above. Martin Niemöller, soon to be the acknowledged knight-gallant of the cause, won his spurs as preacher and pastor in his own parish in Berlin-Dahlem. It was a movement in which parishes and local synods discovered a new purpose and strength in community, and preachers found they really

---

[12]Scholder, *The Churches*, Vol. II, p.179

had something to preach about — and congregations had something to listen to after all. It is true that the greatest single inspiration behind the Barmen declaration was Karl Barth himself, and that most of the wording was due to him. It may even be true, as he was wont to claim mischievously later on, that at the crucial drafting committee at Frankfurt two weeks before Barmen, his two Lutheran colleagues had a siesta after lunch while he, fortified with coffee and cigars, produced the actual text — 'The Lutheran church slept, the Reformed Church stayed awake!' he quipped. But Barmen was truly a collaborative effort to which many sermons and other pulpit statements (remembered or forgotten), many drafts, (used or torn up), many arguments (won or lost), many figures (famous or unknown) made their contribution.

The case was very similar with *Kairos*.[13] What came to be a critically important national event began in one place at the heart of the struggle, Soweto. In July 1985 the group of theologians associated with the Institute for Contextual Theology held their first discussion group. Individual members of the group were then assigned specific themes on the current crisis and the various responses to it by the churches, in order to prepare material for the next session. At the next meeting the draft material was subjected to a thorough critique and still more problematic areas were identified for investigation. At the third meeting, more than thirty theologians, lay-people and church leaders discussed at length the collated material. A committee was appointed by the group to expose the document to still more criticism and comment by Christian groups throughout the country. This working committee was consequently flooded with responses from many quarters, and comments were still coming in when the document was sent to the printers on 13 September. In fact, it was made clear that the document itself was not to be regarded as final, but a basis for continuing discussion.

Barmen and *Kairos*, then, can be seriously misunderstood if we read them only as finished products in isolation from the

[13]See *Kairos* p. 2f.

people and events from which they emerged. Significant declarations do not come cheaply.

Not by words alone

If Barmen and *Kairos* must not be read out of context with a much wider process of speaking, at many levels, then neither must the whole attempt at voicing a Christian judgment be divorced from the totality of confession which, in both cases, included far more than verbal statements. Barmen would have been little more than theological rhetoric, had not there already been costly decisions and actions undertaken in obedience to the truth, leading to the genesis of a *confessing community* of the church. Already in the summer of 1933, to come out openly against the flooding tide of nationalist and *völkish* religion involved more than expressing a contrary theological opinion: it meant risking abuse, intimidation and perhaps one's job. However innocently non-political a pastor may have felt his motives to be in saying 'No' to the German Christians, the Nazi propaganda machine certainly saw him as a threat to the closed ranks of German national feeling behind Hitler. Before Barmen came innumerable personal and costly decisions. In September 1933 the infamous 'Brown Synod' of the Prussian Church took place in Berlin — so-called because the majority German Christians all wore Nazi uniforms — and demanded the imposition of the 'Aryan paragraph' on the church. The church opposition solmenly and publicly withdrew from the synod after President Karl Koch of Westphalia had attempted to read a statement of protest, against a barrage of abuse from the brownshirts. In opposition to the dictatorial methods and decrees of Reich Bishop Müller, the Pastors' Emergency League led by Martin Niemöller was formed in September 1933, soon to number 7000 members, providing networks of fraternal assistance and support and encouraging renewed study of scripture and the confessions. Again, to join it meant obloquy and intimidation. By the time of the Barmen Synod, not a few members of the League had known imprisonment. And at Barmen itself, it is important to note, while the Declaration did not explicitly refer to the 'non-

Aryan' pastors in the church, the Synod in fact resolved with particular seriousness to accept non-Aryans for theological training.

The confession was not just a matter of words, therefore. In fact, from the earliest days of the church struggle there were warnings given about placing too much emphasis on statements. Immediately after the Ulm Declaration of April 1933, a small group of young Reformed theologians in the Württemberg church pointed out that simply to attack the German Christians provided no guarantee of the rightness of the existing church. The 'church as it is' had itself to repent and undergo rebuilding from the foundations upwards: 'So we would do better first of all to dispense with all great public confessions. They are too dangerous, because they can all too easily delude us and others about the true state of our church.'[14]

Early on, the confessing movement almost unconsciously tapped another dimension of Christian existence. At the height of the struggle in early July 1933, Martin Niemöller with other pastors held a service of repentance and prayer in the Dahlem church. For once, prayers, unison recitation of the confession, scripture readings on the lordship of Christ, and congregational hymns, far outweighed in length the pastors' addresses which were kept to a minimum. 'Here the church had found its own form of resistance — more impressive than proclamations, declarations and speeches could ever be.'[15] It was to become typical of much of the Confessing Church's style, a new discovery of spirituality for resistance. Ordinands at Dietrich Bonhoeffer's seminary at Finkenwalde, expecting to be taught only how to preach, learnt how to pray and meditate at great length, and to sing in unison, and to regard these activities as of at least equal importance to the ministry of the word.

In South Africa, once again, there are certain parallels between the movement which generated the *Kairos Document* and the confessing communities in Germany. Here too, the priority of action and of prayer over statement is apparent.

[14]Scholder, op. cit., Vol II, p. 87.
[15]Scholder, op. cit., Vol I, p. 371.

Among the Sowetan theologians were those who themselves
had known imprisonment and torture. In calling for costly
resistance to tyranny they were simply putting words on the
already existing substance of their committed lives. Perhaps
that is why, as one who was present at the actual launch of the
document in Khotso House in September 1985, I was struck by
the matter-of-fact, almost flat, delivery of those who addressed
the microphones and cameras. It sounded like a postcript to
what they had been living for a long time, even though the
content of what they were saying was potential dynamite. It is
therefore ironic that even in South Africa one of the results of
Kairos was to generate a good deal more speaking and writing.
As one South African theologian, commenting upon it some
months later, said 'So many words! Any further comment must
be reluctant. The document is actually calling for action!'[16]
Equally ironic is that one of the signatories of *Kairos*, an
academic, came under criticism from some quarters during
the security clamp-down in 1986 for apparently staying quiet
and for not joining protest marches in the streets. His critics
did not — indeed could not — know that in fact he was putting
Kairos into action by hiding student activists, on the run from
the police, in his home.

Here too there has been an emphasis on corporate
spirituality. In South Africa, resistance has been sung as well as
acted, prayed as well as declared, wept for at funerals. In fact,
just prior to *Kairos* in 1985 there had taken place the almost
equally contentious campaign of 'Prayers for the End to Unjust
Rule', which generated as much upheaval in the mainline
churches as any previous theological statement, and apparently
also provoked extreme anxiety among the state authorities
who had hitherto assumed that it was the duty of the churches
to pray only for the continued well-being of the government of
the day. Designed to commemorate the victims of the massacres
in Soweto on 16 June 1976, and of earlier atrocities, the
'Theological Rationale' stated: 'We now pray that God will

[16]C. Villa-Vicencio, 'A Reluctant Response: Has the Challenge Been Heard?',
Journal of Theology for Southern Africa 55 (June 1986), pp. 56f.

replace the present structures of oppression with ones that are just, and remove from power those who persist in defying his laws, installing in their place leaders who will govern with justice and mercy.'[17]

Statements such as Barmen and *Kairos*, therefore, should not be read as if they constituted the only, or even necessarily the most important, form of witness in their contexts. By the same token, witness in our own contexts should not be obsessed with statements.

Beginning to learn all over again

The issuing of declarations might give the impression of assured knowledge of all that has to be said, the fruit of study and learned deliberation resulting in clarification. One of the notable features of both Barmen and *Kairos*, however, is the way in which they *initiated* renewed study by the Christian communities into the basis of their beliefs and their concrete application for that hour. They were declarations less of what the church understands, than of what it needs to understand and seek to know. I well recall as a student opening Dietrich Bonhoeffer's *Cost of Discipleship* and being surprised by his first words: 'Revival of church life always brings in its train a richer understanding of the scriptures.'[18] My evangelical background wanted me to say that Bonhoeffer had got it the wrong way round, that bible study comes first and renewal of Christian life, individual and corporate, follows from that. Bonhoeffer probably would not have demurred, but would have pointed out that it was precisely the earthquake events of 1933-34 in the German church, and the dramatic decisions that people found themselves having to take in obedience to the truth, that shook them into realizing their need of a fuller and more vital knowledge of the bible and their own churches' traditions of belief. 'Behind all the slogans and catchwords of ecclesiastical controversy, necessary though they are,' Bonhoeffer continues,

[17]'Prayer for the End to Unjust Rule. A Theological Rationale and Call to Prayer', *Journal of Theology for Southern Africa* 52 (September 1985), p. 58.
[18]D. Bonhoeffer, *The Cost of Discipleship*, SCM Press, 1959, p. 29.

'there arises a more determined quest for him who is the sole object of it all, for Jesus Christ himself.' In fact the renewal of bible study in lay groups, pastors' sermon-preparation meetings and suchlike, was one of the most important features of the Confessing Church. At the Barmen Synod itself, it was a lay-person, Reinhold von Thadden, who amid all the talk of confessing and declaring the true faith, stood up and called for greater recognition that such proclamation was not the prerogative of the pastors alone, but the responsibility of the whole Christian community. Twelve years later, amid the ruins left by the Second World War, von Thadden was able to begin realizing his dream of an educated Christian laity with the first of the Kirchentags, the great gatherings of Christians from all over Germany for bible study, theological reflection on the pressing public issues of the day, and celebration in worship. The two-yearly Kirchentag, now increasingly with an international constituency, is today the largest regular Christian gathering in Europe.

In 1933-34 this emphasis upon a renewal of education for both pastors and people was not incidental to confessing the faith, but stemmed right from its heart. 'Confession' carries a number of overtones. It does not mean just stating a view of things, but consciously placing oneself in relation to the truth which is stated, and owning it in the most solemn way. But Christian confession can never be wholly unambiguous. In the very first recorded 'Christian' confession Simon Peter confesses Jesus to be the Son of the living God, but in the next breath has to be rebuked for trying, like Satan himself, to prevent Jesus from treading the way of the cross (Mk. 8.31–33). Christian confession is of the righteousness of God, not the rightness of our beliefs and action. Hence the common notion of confession as meaning the admission of sin does come into play here. Christian confession says 'We declare this to be the truth' but also 'We admit that as of now we ourselves are not in this truth.' We both confess Christ as crucified and risen Lord, and confess our own hand in his crucifixion. Confession therefore belongs together with repentance, repentance which acknowledges that the faith has to be learned all over again for the sake of the kingdom, requiring that we become like little children (Mt.

18.3). As we have seen, this was recognized right at the start of the confessing movement in Altona.

Equally, a link between the declaration and a renewed search for understanding the critical relation of Christian belief to society was found with *Kairos*. In fact, as we have seen, the document itself claimed to be no more than the initiator of a great debate throughout South Africa for all Christians, bringing together their bibles and their daily experience of what was happening in their country. It called for theology to be prophetically renewed by taking seriously the need for social analysis — a challenge indeed to traditional seminary thinking. It was an invitation to relearn. As such, *Kairos*, for all its sharpness of language, did not claim itself to be the truth. In a way surprisingly reminiscent of those rubrics attached to Puritan confessions of the seventeenth century, humbly asking the reader to notify the authors if in any respect the confession might be in error according to scriptural standards, *Kairos* commended itself as 'a people's document which you can also own even by demolishing it if your position can stand the test of biblical faith and Christian experience in South Africa'.[19]

The church's genuine witness, therefore, requires that it be prepared to exhibit itself as a learning community, itself needing instruction in the truth it claims to declare. We shall return to this theme repeatedly. But in concluding this chapter, one final warning needs to be given against falsely romanticizing these two notable Christian declarations of modern times and hence obscuring their truly profound significance. They were great and courageous statements indeed, but precisely as such they pointed up the longer-term *failure* of the church. Barmen was only necessary because for so long the Protestant churches had allowed themselves to become part of bourgeois German society, unable any longer to distinguish between, on the one hand, what was apparently good for Germany, and on the other hand what actually being the Christian church in Germany meant. *Kairos* was deemed to be necessary because the South African churches in large measure were still shielding

19 *Kairos*, p. 18.

themselves from looking at their complicity in the ugliest happenings around them. Barmen and *Kairos* are indeed great examples of what the church can and should do — when things get that bad. The real question, the less glamorous question, is how the church, in any context anywhere in the world, should through its continual ministry and witness in society seek to prevent things getting that bad in the first place.

The Chattering Culture

A parable

The large industrial plant which is the main employer in a certain town is bitterly locked in a labour dispute. For weeks, then months, the dispute drags on, management and union seemingly ever more dug into entrenched positions. There is deepening despair as the livelihood of the whole community drops into sharp and perhaps irreversible decline, families are on the breadline and the town becomes a national byword for economic suicide. At length, the bishop in whose diocese the town lies, and who has long pressed the need for the church to proclaim 'a socially relevant gospel', comes to believe that since all else and everyone else has failed so far, he might have a role to play in mediation. So he makes personal calls to senior figures on both management and union side and invites them to meet him confidentially, first separately and then together. The result is a series of clandestine meetings which, in fact, enable the negotiators eventually to produce a formula giving both sides something without losing too much face in compromise. On the morning of the day when the agreement is to be announced the bishop is sitting in his study contemplating with no little satisfaction the kudos which will accrue when it becomes known just how crucial a part has been played by the church in saving the situation. He is turning over in his mind the telling phrases to be used when, as will surely happen, the reporters and TV cameras roll up to interview him — '... as always the church is here to serve the community ... relevance of Christianity even in, or perhaps I should say

51

especially in, a complex modern industrial society ...' — when the telephone rings. It is the union leader, saying that for various tactical reasons one last condition has to be observed if the deal is to be taken to the workers: there must be no publicity given to the bishop's role in reaching the agreement. Not even the hint of a mention, and only if the bishop solemnly promises not to allow any disclosure of his role will it stand. Not surprisingly, the bishop is somewhat crestfallen. After all, his press officer is standing by putting the finishing touches to a public statement. The bishop says he will think it over and call back shortly.

The reader is invited to complete the story for him- or herself. Perhaps the bishop will call the union leader's bluff and tell him not to be so childish. Consequently the agreement may well fail, but if so the public can relish the exposure of yet more industrial bloody-mindedness and be made to see just how (nearly) effective the church for its part can be. One or two feathers will be added to the cap of social relevance. Even the diocesan officer for evangelism will be impressed at the 'talking point' now offered in the community by the bishop's daring and compassionate venture. Or, perhaps, the bishop will comply with the request for secrecy. The agreement will stand, the factory will re-start production, the town's economy will revive, children will wear new shoes again and all will be, more or less, well. The bishop, however, for the rest of his life will be known as little more than a well-meaning but impractical man, and his obituary will express mild regret that 'during the protracted and bitter industrial dispute at ———— in 19— he never seemed to involve himself beyond the utterance of moral generalities'.

The gospel and secrecy

'... Let your light shine before others, so that they may see your good works and give glory to your Father in heaven' (Mt. 5.16). There are certainly plenty of biblical encouragements to public action and witness. But in the Sermon on the Mount there are also those sayings which enjoin absolute secrecy: 'Beware of practising your piety before others in order to be seen by them, for then you have no reward from your Father in heaven' (Mt. 6.1). Alms-giving, prayer, fasting, are to be done so secretly that we ourselves do not know what we are doing (Mt. 6.2–18): the picture of the left hand not knowing what the right is doing describes a catastrophic breakdown in the nervous system. So the heart which is set solely on pleasing God and seeking God's kingdom is one where normal modes of consciousness and control are superseded. The reward will come from God alone, who sees in secret. Indeed, this is the sternest test of genuine commitment, whether we are prepared to do what is right and good regardless of it being noted, or not, by others. If, as Søren Kierkegaard said, purity of heart is to will one thing,[1] then the final clinging impurity is most likely to be a desire for being known to be pure in heart.

Jesus' commands on secrecy rank among the hardest of 'hard sayings' in the gospels because, like the requirement to forgo riches in order to enter the kingdom of God, or the demand to leave family for Christ's sake, they run clean counter to everyday human assumptions. Our natural impulses resist them utterly. The commands on hiddenness are of a piece with the requirement to leave self behind and take up the cross (Mk. 8.34), for they signify nothing less than a crucifixion of what we take for granted as our rights and our 'need for recognition'. For this reason they comprise the least expounded and the most neglected element in the gospels. When did any of us last hear (or for that matter preach) a sermon on them? They certainly sit uncomfortably with the conventional wisdom that 'there's no such thing as bad publicity'.

In fact this aspect of the gospel teaching has not gone entirely neglected in Christian tradition. In the early centuries of the church it was realized that in certain cases there *is* bad publicity. The innermost mysteries of Christian belief as embodied in the sacraments of baptism and eucharist were not for wanton public display. They were to be preserved from profane misunderstanding. Even catechumens were not allowed to witness the eucharistic climax to worship. The meaning of the rite of baptism was fully explained during the long period

---

[1] S. Kierkegaard, *Purity of Heart*, Collins Fontana, 1961.

of preparation for the Easter vigil, but what actually happened was closely guarded for the occasion itself. Basil of Caesarea (*c.*330-379) justifies such custom thus:

> Well had [the Fathers] learnt the lesson that the awful dignity of the mysteries is best preserved by silence. What the uninitiated are not even allowed to look at was hardly likely to be publicly paraded about in written documents ... Moses was wise enough to know that contempt attaches to the trite and to the obvious, while a keen interest is naturally associated with the unusual and the unfamiliar. In the same manner the Apostles and Fathers who laid down the laws for the church from the beginning thus guarded the awful dignity of the mysteries in secrecy and silence, for what is bruited abroad at random among the common folk is no mystery at all.[2]

Tertullian, Cyril of Jerusalem, Origen and Ambrose speak similarly. To our modern ears it may all sound élitist and obscurantist but in fact there was at work here a profound sensitivity to how spiritual truth is communicated. These pastors and teachers were not opposed to evangelism. Far from it, they were outstanding public communicators of the faith (for example, Ambrose's preaching in Milan helped to convert a certain young North African called Augustine, and he excommunicated the emperor Theodosius for a massacre at Thessalonica). But they knew that there are stages in apprehension, and that not everything can be conveyed, or received, at once.

This 'secret discipline', as it was termed by church historians of later times, was recalled by Dietrich Bonhoeffer in his prison letters, as was the fact that the Hebrews were reluctant even to take the name of God upon their lips. It may be no accident that shortly before taking up this theme Bonhoeffer had been reading the early church fathers again.[3] Bonhoeffer's concern

---

[2]Basil of Caesarea, *De Spiritu Sanctu.*, XXVII.66, in H. Wace and P. Schaff (eds.), *St Basil: Letters and Select Works,* Library of Nicene and Post-Nicene Fathers, James Parker, 1895, p. 42.

[3]D. Bonhoeffer, *Letters and Papers from Prison,* SCM Press, 1971, pp. 135f.

was 'Who is Jesus Christ for us today?', in a world which increasingly seems to get by without 'God' and 'religion'.[4] His concern was equally that the church should not rush prematurely to answers for this question, or the result was likely to be a trivializing of the message, indeed a 'profanation' of it. The time would surely come, Bonhoeffer held with conviction, when once again Christians would be able to speak with truth-compelling power even in a 'religionless' world.[5] In the meantime we need a new secret discipline which preserves the great mysteries of faith, neither jettisoning them in embarrassment before the modern world nor profaning them in our over-anxiety to 'communicate'. A humble period of re-learning is required by the church itself — the whole church in effect becoming its own catechumenate — where the rule will that of 'prayer and righteous action' out of which the new words will be born.[6]

Bonhoeffer's remarks on secrecy and silence have been the least regarded elements of his thought, just as the gospel commands to hiddenness of piety have largely been ignored. How ironic that especially in the radical theologies of the 1960s, instead of resulting in a *pro tem* moratorium on speaking about God, Bonhoeffer's prison letters were quickly co-opted into yet more verbose programmes to make God 'meaningful' in secular society. The fact is that the injunction to be seen and heard less, whether it comes from the bible or from Bonhoeffer or anywhere else, is intolerable to us and meets with the utmost resistance from what we feel is both our instinct and obligation to 'communicate'. Such feelings of instinct and duty, however, may have as much to do with the conditioning induced by our present culture in the modern west, a culture in which *publicity* is an unquestioned value in almost every department of life.

The relationship between Christianity and its cultural context at any one time and place is a complex affair. In the course of history the gospel has variously been seen to be totally

[4] Ibid., pp. 279-282, etc.
[5] Ibid., pp. 299f.
[6] Ibid.

antithetical to all human culture *per se,* or indifferent to it, or
called to take charge of it, or to interact with it critically in a
transforming way, to name but some options.[7] Today, after
more than two centuries of western missionary enterprise and
its aftermath, the whole question of the 'inculturation' of
Christianity in non-western contexts provokes lively and at
times fierce debate, as it did at the Canberra Assembly of the
World Council of Churches in 1991.[8] What has been given less
attention, until comparatively recently, is the question how far
western forms of Christianity themselves represent legitimate
or illegitimate assimilations of the gospel to the contemporary
climate of post-Enlightenment culture. 'Gospel and Culture'
has certainly become an important theme of debate in Britain
in the past decade.[9] The field of enquiry here is vast, but for the
purposes of our present study the key question is: what factors
in our present culture may be conditioning the church to
assume 'speaking out' to be an unqualified public duty whenever
and wherever possible?

In this regard three features of our contemporary western
consciousness merit special scrutiny. These do not represent
particular systems of thought or ideologies so much as basic
perspectives on 'how things are and what should happen' in
human affairs and the world at large. They are culturally-based
presuppositions of our perceptions and behaviour-patterns.
They may be called, respectively: reality-publicity; problem-
solution; instant-value.

Reality-publicity

I well recall a few years ago having to go to Newport in Gwent
to collect my new passport. There had been a national go-slow
by passport office staff over new working procedures, and the
combination of both the procedures and the industrial action

---

[7]The classic study of such alternatives is H.R. Niebuhr, *Christ and Culture,* Faber
& Faber, 1952.

[8]Cf *Signs of the Spirit. Report of the Seventh Assembly,* WCC Publications 1991, esp. on
the presentation by Chung Hyun Kyung and the ensuing debate.

[9]The debate has been stimulated in particular by the writings of Bishop Lesslie
Newbigin: *The Other Side of 1984,* WCC, 1984.

produced a huge back-log of applications. Needing my new passport within days, I was advised to go personally to Newport and collect it. There I found an already quarter-mile-long queue, which for several hours shuffled slowly round the streets towards the office entrance. Mercifully it was a fine day, and most people put up with it all as a tedious necessity with reasonably good humour. Suddenly, a television news crew arrived on the opposite side of the road and went into action. It was impossible now not to feel somewhat differently about the whole business. It wasn't just a break in the tedium, nor was it an excitement about being one face in the crowd on millions of screens that evening. It was, rather, that something was happening which raised the whole status of what we were doing. What had previously been, for each of us in that queue, an irksome waste of time, a personal inconvenience, suddenly seemed more important: it had been declared to be of public, indeed national, significance by the descent of the cameras and sound-booms.

Do the mass media communicate what is significantly real? Or is it that the significantly real is, by definition, what they happen to choose to communicate? Around these questions swirl some of our sharpest contemporary debates, which are not just about the media taken in themselves but embrace everything to do with the nature of democracy and the location of power in our societies. The temptation at this point is to launch into the familiar diatribe against the modern media, especially television and some elements of the press, for the way in which they over-simplify, sensationalize and trivialize, not to say distort, truth in the cause of governing political and commercial interests. The counter-case is readily to hand. There is serious investigative journalism both in the press and in broadcasting. As well as the game-show there is the documentary. As well as superficial soap-opera there is probing drama, and so on. But this kind of debate often does not touch on the issue of media as media, and what the pervasive power of the media means for our very existence and consciousness as human beings in society today. The media are no longer just a fact of life, they are deeply part of the very way we all live and move and have our being today. If by nothing else, this is shown by the fact that virtually the only way we feel we can have any impact on the media is — via the media themselves. The phrase which Marshall McLuhan gave us over a quarter of a century ago, that 'the medium is the message',[10] may have become the cliché of clichés but that cannot disguise the truth that not only do the media have immense power by the very fact of creating a new, electronically interdependent world of awareness, but also that 'the formative power in the media are the media themselves'.[11] That is, they have a life of their own, imposing their own requirements and standards on their field of activity and beyond. The media have become a subject of intense, sometimes narcissistic, interest to themselves. One of the main 'stories' of the British General Election campaign in 1992 was how far the result was determined by the media, especially some sections of the press.

Complaints about the power of the public media, it must be admitted, are frequently an exercise in nostalgia for the ways of life they have deposed. New forms of media have always created a sense of loss. Few of us today can really envisage, for example, what the development of printing must have meant for those academics who regarded the medieval method of oral disputation as the pinnacle of human intellectual achievement. Not surprisingly, serious commentators including those with a theological interest, are arguing that 'the modern mass media, rather than the Church or the academic theologians, are redefining faith in the twentieth century'.[12] Angela Tilby, a writer and producer of religious programmes for the BBC, describes television as 'becoming a vital cradle of meaning for most of Western society',[13] and another commentator, James Curran, states that 'the mass media have now assumed the role of the Church, in a more secular age, of interpreting and making sense of the world to the mass public'.[14]

---

[10]M. McLuhan, *Understanding Media. The Extensions of Man*, McGraw-Hill, 1964.
[11]Ibid., p. 21.
[12]D.C. Weber, *Discerning Images. The Media and Theological Education*, University of Edinburgh, 1991, p. 79.
[13]Quoted in Weber, op. cit., p. 79.
[14]Quoted in Weber, op. cit., p. 98.

Out of this cradle of meaning for western culture has sprung, among other progeny, the assumed rights and requirements of public communication. What is real has to be made public. What cannot be publicly communicated is not real. To be real, to be taken with absolute seriousness, requires that it be aired abroad. And what is aired abroad is what must be taken seriously: the legitimating role of the TV cameras. Quite justifiably, this culture suspects secrecy in high places, and 'cover-up' is rightly a dirty-word since it marks the self-seeking motives of those with vested interests in keeping untoward facts out of the public gaze, whether in government, industry or wherever. But is 'the right to know' limitless? Recently the reviewer of the biography of a British composer who had died the previous decade complained bitterly that the author had not revealed more about the personal life and sexuality of his subject. The assumption behind his complaint was that knowing every detail mattered as of right and necessity. Secrecy is *ipso facto* wrong.

But to increase publicity does not necessarily mean increasing knowledge, and it is the tendency of this culture to equate knowledge with publicity which is so striking. Hence the seeming paradox that it is precisely our societies which are seemingly so open, and so dominated by the mass media, which at the same time get most frustrated at being 'kept in the dark' by powerful political and economic interests. We can be swamped by 'news' and 'information' while government and other powers can devise yet more ways of obscuring how, when and why vital decisions affecting our lives are made. A classic case occurred during the Gulf War in 1991, when radio and television provided virtually round-the-clock 'coverage' of the events for weeks on end. The coverage amounted to a great deal of desert footage, studio discussion, maps and models, yet very little was revealed of what was actually going on, certainly as far as damage and casualties on the Iraqi side were concerned. The line between 'coverage' and 'cover-up' can become dangerously blurred.

There is a further feature of the 'news culture' which enables it to generate its own momentum still further. It lies in what Marshall McLuhan describes as the 'mosaic' form of the

newspaper as distinct from the linear structure of the book.[15]
It is precisely in presenting to our eyes the appearance of a
patchwork of items simultaneously competing for, if not
meriting, our attention that the appeal of the press lies; as does
that of the television news bulletin with its fast-moving parade
of scenes with speech limited to (at most) ten-second sound-
bites. The criticism to be made of this treatment of 'news' is
well-known: it encourages a simplistic, superficial perception
of what is going on in the world and discourages reflective
analysis on where the 'truth' may actually lie. That may be
answered by pointing to the the role of the documentary. The
most telling point about the mosaic image, however, is that
whereas in a true mosaic, such as we may view on the floor of
a Roman villa or a Byzantine church, the picture is viewed and
appreciated as a whole (almost without realizing that it *is*
composed of individual pieces of stone), the modern news
mosaic is essentially a jumble of unrelated pieces which are
admired for their individual colour or glister, one by one.
This means either that only those stones will be selected
which seem to have an especial glister at the moment, or that
there will be no limit to what may be included and almost
anything can claim a right to be there. Questions of
correspondence with reality and of significance defer to
those of immediate effect. And the question of 'the whole'
may not even be asked at all.

The nature of the publicity-culture has wide implications,
not least for artistic creativity. Strikingly a British novelist,
Philip McCann, also invokes the mosaic image to explain why,
for the time being at least, he has given up writing:

> I didn't want to go the way many others have done, away
> from the priority of newness and the individual, towards
> a kind of post-modernist craft work, social art: to me,
> many contemporary novels are like pieces in a mosaic that
> stands in the marketplace as a symbol of culture. There's
> praise to be passed around each artisan; anyone, so long
> as they work hard to add another bit, can be person-of-

[15]McLuhan, op. cit., pp. 210f.

the-minute. The dumbest thing they can do is to linger over detail, try to cut their bit more finely, get it more resplendent: it's just going to sit there with all the others.[16]

The market-place is seductive and its appetite is voracious. There is unlimited scope, and demand, for item after item of news and opinion to be aired. Some social critics declare a nightmare vision of a media-and-consumer society where reality disintegrates altogether into images — where TV is the world, where 'people are caught up in the play of images that have less and less relationship to an external "reality". Concepts of the social, political, or even "reality", no longer seem to have any meaning and the "gooey, sticky, blurry omnipresent and ubiquitous media-saturated consciousness" ... destroys the concept of meaning itself, which depends on stable boundaries, fixed structures, shared consensus.'[17] Such a milieu engenders the assumption that publicity is a *sine qua non* of effective action. One has to be seen and heard to be taken seriously, one *has* to be legitimated by visibility and audibility above all. When in September 1992 polytechnic colleges in England and Wales achieved the status of universities, the staff at one such institution almost immediately received an expensively produced, glossy brochure illustrating, with stern instructions, exactly how the new logo of the institution was to be used on letter-headings. The fact that many lecture-rooms still lacked such mundane apparatus as whiteboards for staff to write on, and chairs for students to sit on, seemed to matter less. The logo is indeed the symbol of an age where instant recognizability is everything. Note too how 'ikon' has become a fashionable description for those figures in the public eye who are held up as typifying the aspirations and attitudes of the current generation, drawn from royalty, football stars, pop singers or whoever. Unlike the genuine ikons of Byzantine worship, however, which point to a realm transcending their immediate appearance, these cult figures are unashamedly recognized as being no more than

[16]Philip McCann, *The Guardian*, 23.2.93.
[17]R. Billington et al, *Culture and Society. A Sociology of Culture*, Macmillan 1991, pp.191f.

reflections of the frustrated lusts and ambitions of those who create them. Hence they can be lifted up in mawkish adulation one week and dragged down in leering contempt the next. For many of them, at least, it is true that there is no such thing as bad publicity, for without publicity they are nothing.

In such a culture, where publicity is a good in itself, with one group after another seeking to be the most prominent piece in the ever-expanding mosaic, to 'speak out' becomes a perilous exercise if it is not to be just one more form of self-advertisement, another voice to be added to the general chatter.

Problem-solution

It would be instructive to know how many times in a single day any one of us refers to a 'problem'. The word is so much part of our way of life and thinking that even to consider the question may seem — problematical. But its daily usage to describe tasks and difficulties seems to be a relatively modern phenomenon. The King James Bible, for example, does not know the word.

To a degree we like having problems to deal with, else we would not while away boring long journeys, or spend our leisure time, trying to solve them in the shape of crossword puzzles, or cards, or chess, or snooker, or detective stories or whatever. Further, many people actually relish the challenge of the intellectual or practical problems posed in their daily work and find real satisfaction and fulfilment in solving them. There are limits of course. Beyond a certain point the number of problems facing us becomes overwhelming, and there is the kind of problem, of such depth, where one by itself threatens to swallow us up. But we talk not only about personal, but public and social problems too. At the moment of writing there is great public concern in Britain over the 'problem' of an inexorably rising rate of juvenile crime. There is the perennial 'problem' of economics which every government has to face, of controlling both inflation and unemployment. We see 'problems' on the world scale also — the environment, population growth, the international trade in arms and suchlike, are all frequently spoken of as 'problems'. To see the whole range of life's responsibilities, from the most personal to the global, in terms of problems requiring solutions, is fundamental to our contemporary western mind. Concomitantly, the assumed criterion for the worthwhileness of our various enterprises is whether they manage to 'solve the problems'. Perhaps, though, the fact that the same term can be applied to so many different kinds of issues, and at so many levels, from the child's puzzle-book to 'the problem of human survival', should make us pause to ask quite what is going on here. A method of genuinely coming to terms with reality or a vast oversimplification?

A brief look at the origins of the words 'solve' and 'problem' can be illuminating. The verb 'to solve' hails from two Latin roots: *se*, apart, and *luere*, to loosen. Its root meaning is therefore to untie, loosen, unravel. It denotes a rearrangement of items that are awkwardly fused, as in the closely-related physical meaning of a *solution* of a solid substance in water or some other liquid. The noun 'problem' stems from the Greek *pro*, forward, and *ballo*, to throw. Literally, it is something thrown forward: a question or matter tossed by a teacher to the class, or the ruler to counsellors, for discussion. Historically, it has chiefly denoted questions in logic, mathematics, affairs of state — and games such as chess. Only relatively recently has it acquired its almost universal application to matters that tax heart and mind at all levels of life. What is significant about a living language is that root meanings are rarely shed completely in the course of their history, and it is not accidental that it should be in the society so dominated by scentifically-based engineering and technology, that reality should be seen so universally as 'problems to be solved'. For what is notable about the root meaning of 'solving problems' is that they denote quasi-mechanical, or mathematical, situations that need sorting out by rearrangement of what is there. The knot needs to be untied, the equation needs to be balanced, the constituent parts need to be separated and put together in some appropriate way, perhaps with the addition of one or two items as necessary.

There is, however, a further feature of 'solving problems'. The nature of a problem is that it appears to confront us, 'thrown before' us for consideration. The teacher puts it up on the board. It engages us as something apart from us.

The triumph of the scientific-technological treatment of the world about us, and its utilization for human benefit, needs no elaborating here. In the industrialized world nearly all of us live in it and by it, and just as one can only attack the media by using the media, so one can hardly criticize the technological age without using technology itself. There is irony in the spectacle of passionate critiques of technological culture being written on word-processors, delivered at international conferences using simultaneous translation facilities and closed-circuit television, and attended by participants nearly all of whom have journeyed there by jet aircraft. The question is whether the scientific-technological culture, quite apart from the ambiguity of its own direct achievements, has nurtured a fundamental mind-set which assumes that the whole of the realities which call for us to make decisions, can be viewed as 'problems seeking solutions'. If it has, then it is deeply misleading, and will promote by turns a false optimism and an equally false despair.

A student visits his tutor and tells her his 'problems' with the course he is doing. There is far too much group-based course-work, he feels, and he is not satisfied with the other members of his group in the current term's project. Much of the course is, he tells her, a waste of time and he could learn as much if he were to be excused some of it and be left to read it up for himself. In other words, he has a problem which he thinks would be solved by a rearrangement of his timetable. In the course of their conversation, however, it becomes clear that such a rearrangement will not work. For one thing, no exceptions can be made to anyone on the course for having it restructured to suit their personal wishes. Chaos will result if first one, then another, and so on, are granted such dispensations. For another, the student knew very well in advance of starting the course what the demands would be. But then the conversation moves to a deeper level, about why the student actually feels as he does. The tutor begins to open his eyes to realize that here is something much deeper than a 'problem' for him. If there is a 'problem' it lies not so much 'before him' on the timetable, but within him as a human being. He has come to college believing that education is about being given information for him to use directly. He hasn't yet seen that he is being educated not just to take notes and reproduce the thoughts of others, but both to think for himself and work with others. He hasn't yet quite grown up enough to realize this, but he walks away from the tutor's office with the dawning realization that what he thought was a problem of timetabling, was in fact a matter for fundamental change in attitude on his own part.

Counsellors in many fields will be familiar with like cases where people bring 'problems' to them centring upon other people at home, or at work, or work itself and wanting to know 'what is to be done about them'. They come seeking a re-arrangement of the life about them and advice on how to achieve it. In some cases there may well indeed be need for such restructuring. Some young people *are* better off away from home. Some people do need, and deserve to be allowed, to relinquish a burdensome office. But the notion that all pain and threat can be removed by a rational rearrangement of external circumstances is deeply built into the problem-solution culture, preventing people from realizing that they are bumping up against the points where they are being challenged to radical reappraisal of their abilities, motivations and expectations.

That mind-set takes hold of much perception of the public and international sphere. Single 'answers' are sought to 'problems' as entrenched as 'the Irish problem', juvenile crime, the global population explosion and third-world poverty. What is looked for is some single, simple policy which can be 'applied' to 'it'. Often, significantly, that 'solution' is quasi-mechanical in nature, if not literally so. Juvenile offenders need 'locking up' or worse. The third world simply needs birth-control methods. The ultimate in 'solutions' is of course the most mechanical of all, that is, the use of military force which is becoming ever more technological, and ever more costly in every way. All such approaches externalize and distance both the problems and the solutions, in the belief (or hope) that something will be found to remove the pain and instability threatening us. The world will be rearranged more comfortably — with minimal change to ourselves.

For a generation it has been argued by social philosophers like Herbert Marcuse[18] that western industrial society, at almost every facet of its life from the most personal sphere to the most public areas of policy, is imbued with the motivation of *dominance*, the dominance rooted in the scientific exploitation of nature which carries over into a rationalistic, instrumental approach to all things human. Humanity has become 'one-dimensional', something to be *managed* in a rational way which secures the dominance of the already-powerful over the less-powerful, and over nature. All other considerations, whether art for art's sake or the right to internal privacy, count for nothing in a materialistic, media-fed race to secure this dominance. Marcuse graphically depicts the consequences of this rationally-based one-dimensionality:

> Invalidating the cherished images of transcendence by incorporating them into its omnipresent daily reality, this society testifies to the extent to which insoluble conflicts are becoming manageable — to which tragedy and romance, archetypal dreams and anxieties are being made susceptible to technical solutions and dissolution. The psychiatrist takes care of the Don Juans, Romeos, Hamlets, Fausts, as he takes care of Oedipus — he cures them. The rulers of the world are losing their metaphysical features, Their appearance on television, at press conferences, in parliament, and at public hearings is hardly suitable for drama beyond that of the advertisement, while the consequences of their actions surpass the scope of the drama.

> The prescriptions for inhumanity and injustice are being administered by a rationally organized bureaucracy, which is, however, invisible at its vital centre. The soul contains few secrets and longings which cannot be sensibly discussed, analyzed and polled ...[19]

Marcuse of course writes with a note of irony. Deep down we

---

[18]H. Marcuse, *One Dimensional Man. Studies in the Ideology of Advanced Industrial Society*, Routledge and Kegan Paul, 1964.
[19]Ibid., p.70f.

know that the heights and depths of the human condition, as depicted in the archetypal figures and in the tragedies of our time, are *not* susceptible to 'solution' as so often advertised. But it is a comforting illusion to imagine that they are, or that at least a 'solution' is just around the corner.

Our age is still a child of the Enlightenment with its belief in progress and the rationality of life, and in the confidence of scientific instrumentality, of seeing persons and institutions as means to definable ends, above all the utilitarian end of the greatest happiness for the greatest number. It has become the age of *management*, where matters are defined as problems to be solved and ways of solving them, and there is no greater accolade than to be called 'an effective manager'. That has resulted in many benefits, but also, as Marcuse perceives, the effective denial and hence trivializing of what cannot be solved by such rationality. From a very different quarter to Marcuse has come another criticism of the notion of 'management', by the philosopher Alistair McIntyre who calls in question the very status of the 'manager' as a totem of our age, a status relying on managerial 'expertise' and 'effectiveness'.[20] McIntyre argues that there is a severe contradiction in modern culture between, on the one hand, the prizing of the autonomy of the individual human person as a moral agent, each of us defending our freedom against the intrusions of others, and on the other hand our esteem for the 'good manager' who in fact acts by manipulating other human persons for bureaucratic goals.[21] Further, and more provocatively, McIntyre suggests that the whole concept of 'managerial effectiveness' could turn out to be a complete fiction because it is essentially unproveable. That is, one can argue in general terms that to take decisions in certain ways and to adopt certain kinds of procedures should lead to improved performance for the company or institution in question, better industrial relationships and so on, but it is very difficult actually to prove, in a particular instance, that it was the application of such measures which led to a perceived

[20] A. McIntyre, *After Virtue. A Study in Moral Theory*, University of Notre Dame, 1981.
[21] Ibid., p. 71f.

improvement. Could not such claims be based on chance association, just as the parson who prayed for rain could claim an answer to prayer if it did rain shortly afterwards? Claims to managerial effectiveness, McIntyre points out, will normally be made by managers themselves, and may be as much a means of disguising manipulative social control as of actually promoting 'efficiency'.

Such arguments illustrate just how deeply problem-solving has become a basic frame of reference for us, and how much kudos attaches to claims to be able to provide answers and achieve results in the 'problem areas' of life. It is therefore extremely difficult for any who would address the public domain, not to adopt the style of problem-solving: of suggesting means of rearranging, indeed manipulating, human affairs so as to remove the threat of pain and chaos in a way that is as comfortable as possible to ourselves. To appear on platform or screen or in the press without any such 'solutions' on offer risks appearing not to have anything worth saying at all.

Instant-value

It has become a truism that modern western societies value instant productivity, the usually-cited tokens of this being instant coffee and instantly-available money from computerized cash dispensers. As with criticism of the scientific-technological culture as a whole, it can become a somewhat cheap and hypocritical observation to inveigh against all this when so few of us would be prepared actually to give up the convenience such devices offer. Taken in association with the two cultural assumptions already mentioned, however, instant-value points to a deeply significant feature of our mental culture. It relates both to reality-publicity and problem-solution, and indeed each of these mind-sets both feeds upon and encourages the others.

People have always eagerly devoured 'news'. But whereas Oliver Goldsmith's *Deserted Village* was a place

> Where village statesmen talked with looks profound,
> And news much older than their ale went round,

today in the satellite age even the remotest village pub expects 'news' to be genuinely 'new', that is, bringing accounts of events on the TV screen virtually as they happen. Soon after Terry Waite's release from captivity in Beirut in late 1991, a London evening paper was able to advertise itself by recalling its headline 'Terry Waite Free Today!' in smart comparison with the national dailies which next morning could only announce it as yesterday's news. Unless we have kept it for a particular purpose, there is a sense almost of unreality when we glance at a paper even just a few days old.

To justify itself on the crowded platform of the instant, news must be 'real news'. This, rather than human morbidity, to a great extent accounts for the fact about which complaint is so often made, that most news seems to be 'bad news'. Disasters like plane crashes and earthquakes, precisely because they happen with such brutal suddenness, literally in an instant, are easily capturable as stories, as are massacres and other atrocities. Confrontations and disputes in political life 'erupt' and can be snappily summarized in a few seconds of snarls and ripostes. Marriage break-ups of royalty and other celebrities can be conveyed in a single picture of people — literally — going their separate ways. By contrast, stories about development of safety-devices for aircraft, or the slow rebuilding of communities after disasters, may be interesting but they are hardly 'news', and the same applies to the building of relationships and co-operative ventures among people. Hence, too, the way in which one disaster can soon be displaced in public consciousness once it has ceased to be 'news' — even though the aftermath of suffering may continue and even get worse.

Solutions to problems, likewise, need to be rapid or they are not considered to be real solutions at all. There is of course a healthy distrust of justifications for undue delay — jam tomorrow, economic recovery still just around the corner — but expectations are short in a consciousness imbued with technological rationality. Things 'ought to be made to work'. Political life, in particular, is subject to the demand for results, and not least results which will keep the politicians themselves as popular as necessary to remain in power. Hence the criticism that in the late twentieth century we need to make profound long-term changes in our social and economic affairs if humanity is to sustain a worthwhile existence, yet political leaders cannot look beyond the next election, or perhaps even the next press conference. Short-term aims and long-term needs militate against each other, and at present the former prevail.

It was Jeremy Bentham (1748–1832) who first expounded what many today would regard simply as commonsense, the philosophy of utilitarianism or, more specifically, 'hedonistic utilitarianism'.[22] Baldly stated, this argues that the the driving force of human moral behaviour is the desire for 'pleasure'. Later, as applied to social morality, utilitarianism was often summarized as the principle of providing for the greatest happiness of the greatest number. Bentham attempted to list several dimensions of 'pleasure', such as the intensity of its sensation, the certainty of its occurrence and, very significantly, its *propinquity* or nearness: we value most those pleasures that follow soonest from our chosen actions. Accordingly, we value most those 'solutions' which promise the quickest results.

This is fine when we are dealing with essentially mechanical and physical processes. But, as has been argued earlier, difficulties arise when the assumptions of physical rationality are transferred to the areas of human relationships, whether on the more intimate inter-personal level or on the wider, more public level where people relate as collectivities. Here in fact could lie one of the most significant contributions of the so-called 'green' thought and politics which have entered the western scene in the last two decades or so. Emphasizing the interconnected, organic nature of life and its support systems on this planet, and the way in which we are both inheritors of the past and preservers or destroyers of the future, it has brought about a highly necessary emphasis on wholeness instead of individualism, on nurture instead of dominance. In its emphasis on natural life-processes it stresses growth in a deeper sense than what is often meant by 'development'. It has encouraged us to see the importance of *fruits*, the outcome of natural growth, rather than *results*, the product of mechanical

[22] J. Bentham, *A Fragment on Government and An Introduction to the Principles of Morals and Legislation*, ed. W. Harrison, Basil Blackwell, 1948.

activity. What has been lacking, however, is the ability of 'green' thinking to pervade and influence the political areas and issues other than those of its immediate concern such as the environment. Even where as in Germany the Green Party made some inroads into parliamentary power it remained largely a single issue party and as such eventually of very limited effectiveness. It has been unable to transpose its 'organic' emphasis into other issue-areas where it could have been decisive, such as education, industrial relations and the economy generally. Meanwhile, the tide of quick-result thinking flows on. Education becomes the acquisition of 'skills' rather than growth in understanding and perception — even theological education for ministry comes under pressure to concentrate less on 'theology' (!) and more on giving ordinands the 'tools for the job'. And clergy all too frequently are judged, by themselves as by others, on the 'results' they produce in their congregations. The pressure to produce inflicts itself on the arts too. In a radio interview in 1984 the conductor Christoph von Dohnanyi commented on the hurry of younger conductors to produce 'their' recordings of the great classical symphonies as soon as possible, whereas if they had anything genuinely new to say through Beethoven and Brahms it would only grow in the course of time, testing and experience. The sense of history, communal and personal, has largely broken down.

The culture of reality-publicity, problem-solution and instant-value puts those who have a sense of public responsibility under an almost irresistibly seductive pressure to conform to its mores. The church is no exception here, and in fact for a number of reasons is especially vulnerable. Faced with questions as to its credibility and relevance in an increasingly secularized society — that is, a society in which religion is of less and less social significance — and when it is in numerical decline (not actually the same thing as secularization but often concomitant with it), then the temptation grows acutely to 'speak out', to seek legitimation by being seen and heard whenever possible. When an ecumenical delegation of British church leaders returned from visiting the conflict-ridden former Yugoslavia in 1993, one church press officer commented that little interest had been shown by the media because 'You didn't condemn anyone'. Above all, the temptation is to seek accreditation by proffering 'solutions' to the 'problems of society', to be seen as the all-knowing manager (perhaps now retired but still available on a consultancy basis) of the world with its problems. The peril, though, is that at exactly this point when the church thinks it is challenging or leading the world, it may simply be falling in with its ethos, and adding one more voice to the chattering culture.

At this point, the church's first task is to rediscover its own true identity, and to chart where the distinctiveness of its message really lies. The rest of this chapter sketches how even a cursory look at the bible, and the gospels in particular, points us towards an ethos very different from the cultural features we have been examining.

Gospel counter-culture

Reality-publicity culture is contradicted by the gospel requirement to be in the truth rather than in the limelight, and the warning that if we seek the limelight we shall not be in the truth. There is a publicity proper to the disciples, but it is not one that they seek or create for themselves. It simply happens, as a light set on a stand or a city built on a hill cannot be hidden (Mt. 5.14–16). Righteousness is to be practised regardless of its being seen or not. It is to be done because God's own self is righteous, and it is God who sees, even in secret (Mt. 6.18). Legitimation comes not from public awareness and approval, not from the cameras, but from God.

Within the gospel sayings there lies the whole biblical emphasis upon the *hiddenness* of God — 'Truly you are a God who hides himself, O God of Israel, the Saviour' (Is. 45.15) — which is not a contradiction of God's reality but the deepest affirmation of God's holiness and majesty. Jesus manifests both the presence and otherness of God. It is a very public world in which Jesus operates, the world of fishing boats and synagogues, crowded houses and bustling streets. But he can never be totally comprehended by the public world of his day. He is not somebody because he is talked about, he is talked about because he is somebody — but who? 'Some say John the

Baptist, but others Elijah ...' (Mt. 16.14). He addresses the crowds, but also withdraws with his innermost group of followers; and sometimes even from them, to pray alone. There are the strange, strict injunctions to keep secret certain of his most wonderful deeds of compassion, as with the healed leprosy sufferer (Mk. 1.44) and the girl brought back to life (Mk. 5.43). After Simon Peter's confession of Jesus' sonship of God at Ceasarea Philippi the disciples are sternly told 'not to tell anyone about him' (Mk. 8.30). Certain of the parables of the kingdom and their interpretation are meant for their ears alone, at least for the present (Mk. 4.11). The time will indeed come when what is now hidden will be brought to light (Mk. 4.22) but that day must not be prematurely anticipated. The reality of God's reign is not dependent on its visibility. For the time being it is as hidden, and as real, as the seed growing secretly in the earth, the yeast in the dough. Some religious leaders demand from Jesus 'signs', straightforward, directly visible and public demonstrations of heavenly power, but these are refused (Mt. 12.38–42). He resists the tempter who suggests that he should establish his credentials by performing a spectacular public feat of self-preservation from off the pinnacle of the temple (Mt. 4.5–7).

The signs of the kingdom are there for those who can see with the eyes of faith what is happening among the most needy and humanly hopeless in society (Mt. 11.4–5). Jesus certainly was a public figure, but controversially so because he was concerned to turn the light not on himself but upon those in the shadows. What offended many of the self-consciously righteous was the way in which the presence of Jesus resulted in the sudden, centre-stage visibility of those who seemingly had no business to be there at all. Tax-collectors, outcast or 'unclean' women, little children, the foreign centurion, are all illuminated as bearers and exemplars of the kingdom. The very man whom the crowd told to be quiet as Jesus' entourage left Jericho, blind Bartimaeus, is brought from his roadside begging-bowl and asked by Jesus, 'What do you want me to do for you?' (Mk. 10.51). It is Bartimaeus, not the the official religious leaders who enjoyed and sought so much high-profile for themselves (Mk. 12.38f.), who is highlighted as the role-model for faith.

The publicity which Jesus facilitates for those in the shadows prefigures the final kingdom where nothing and no-one will be hidden, a hope with which the whole of the New Testament is translucent. In the Revelation of John it is seen as a city which indeed cannot be hidden, whose gates are open to all four quarters of the earth, whose street is pure gold 'transparent as glass' (Rev. 21.21), a city flooded with light not from the rising and setting sun or moon 'for the glory of God is its light, and its lamp is the Lamb' (21.24). Here in this utter transparency no-one needs to seek publicity for themselves, for the light of the divine presence floods all without reserve, and reflects from each to each in mutual love. There is indeed a publicity proper to the kingdom, and it is one against which the world's current mores, and the church's tendency to follow them, must be held up for examination.

Problem-solution culture is not at home with the thrust of the biblical message, either. The New Testament proclamation is not about 'solving' problematic situations by rearranging human affairs, but about a critical confrontation and transformation of the human condition through death and resurrection. 'Solutions' deal with restructuring what is already there, perhaps also by removing or adding some parts to the machine. The bible however speaks not of 'restructuring' but of re-creating, not even of improving things, but of a quite new and other world emerging within the old. It is no accident that the very words 'problem' and 'solution', though emanating from the ancient world, hardly if at all figure in the scriptures. Certain matters brought to Jesus for his opinion admittedly have the character of 'problems' but it is striking that they are given short shrift. 'Friend, who set me to be a judge or arbitrator over you?' replies Jesus to the man whose brother needed persuading to settle the family inheritance (Lk. 12.13f.); and immediately Jesus goes on to confront the real need of that man and everyone else within earshot, in the parable of the rich fool.

Even more striking is the way Jesus deals with the 'problems' brought to him by the would-be intellectuals. The lawyer who wants to know what he must do to inherit eternal life, is not wholly satisfied with his own answer, which is, to love God wholly, and 'your neighbour as yourself' (Lk. 10.27). However he now presents Jesus with a real problem with which to justify his initial enquiry and asks 'And who is my neighbour?' Thereby is prompted the story of the Good Samaritan. The man lying beaten and dying on the road certainly presents a 'problem' to the priest and Levite who successively come along. For one thing, if they stop to give him aid they may well be delayed on their journey, and this would expose them to danger themselves on that bandit-ridden road. They would also be hindered from reaching Jerusalem in time to carry out their cultic duties. Worse, if they so much as touched a bleeding and possibly dead body they would become ritually unclean, and this for a time would certainly debar them from officiating in the temple. They solve their problem quite neatly by rearranging their route and passing by on the other side. The Samaritan however does not see a problem but a fellow-human being in direst need. How carefully it is said that 'he came near him; and when he saw him, he was moved with pity'. In other words, he allows himself to be changed through encounter with this person as his neighbour. Instead of viewing him as a problem to be solved, or even as having a problem requiring a solution, he becomes bound up with him in a relation of compassion, at one with him in his need and peril. In taking care of the man, the Samaritan does not solve a problem — in fact he creates even more problems for himself. He has become so caught up in relation with the stricken man that such 'problems' are relativized.

Dietrich Bonhoeffer in his *Ethics* makes the point forcefully:

> Jesus concerns himself hardly at all with the solution of worldly problems ... His word is not an answer to human questions and problems; it is the answer of God to the question of God to man. His word is essentially determined not from below but from above. It is not a solution, but a redemption... Instead of the solution of problems, Jesus brings the redemption of men, and yet for that very reason he does really bring the solution of all human

problems as well ('All these things shall be added' (Mt. 6.33)), but from quite a different plane.[23]

'Not a solution, but a redemption'. Bonhoeffer's words will surprise many who look upon him simply as the prophet of Christian secularity. Bonhoeffer however does not deny, in the section from which these words are taken, that 'on the basis of Christianity there is something definite to be said on the subject of worldly matters'. But he was highly critical of the tendency he found, especially in Britain and the United States, to view the Christian mission as one of sorting out all problems in the socio-political sphere. For one thing, some of these problems are so intractable there simply are no solutions and they may well just have to be lived with. For another (and more provocatively), he suggests that the unsolved state of some problems may be more important to God than their solution 'for it may call attention to the fall of man and to the divine redemption'.

We may take Bonhoeffer's words as a call for all Christian public action and speaking to be grounded within the fundamental categories of biblical understanding. Hence the emphasis on redemption rather than solution. Redemption means liberation into a new relationship with God and others, and the church's first calling is to celebrate and announce that the decisive act effecting this has taken place in Jesus Christ, from God's side. And whereas 'solutions' are so often offered in detachment from the 'problem', redemption is deeply costly to all concerned. Through Christ 'God was pleased to reconcile to himself all things, whether on earth or in heaven, by making peace through the blood of his cross (Col. 1.20). The cross as the central sign of Christian faith puts the severest question-mark against any idea that the human condition can be seen as 'problems' to which there are 'solutions' as we normally understand them. Rather, there is a crisis which has to be met, as the Samaritan met the stricken man on the Jericho

---

[23]D. Bonhoeffer, *Ethics*, SCM Press, 1955, p. 324.

road, and made the victim's need his own burden, in utmost risk, solidarity and self-giving. For Christian faith, the cross marks both the way which God has taken in judgment and solidarity with humankind, and the way in which faith likewise is called, in response to that grace, to enter into closest solidarity with others rather than seeking 'solutions' for them.

In a culture so beset with the problem-solution mentality, a church which does not discipline itself with these biblical categories will lose any sense of a distinctive voice and action as it is faced from all sides with the questions 'What has the church to say to this?', 'What is the Christian answer to that?'. The assumption that there has to be a 'Christian solution' to *everything*, far from enlarging the mission of the church in fact leads to its death by distraction and exhaustion: 'Martha, Martha, you are worried and distracted by many things; there is need of only one thing' (Lk. 10.41). The decisiveness and radicality of the Christian message is not to be dissipated in a welter of comments on first this, and then that, 'issue' which happens to be the headline-catcher of the moment. 'Problems' in our media-age, it should be noted, do not just occur. They have a habit of endlessly generating new progeny to occupy the feature pages of our newspapers and the topical slots in television schedules: the mosaic again, in which questions of interrelatedness, fundamental causes and *priorities* are lost in a proliferating agenda, sensationalizing and trivializing by turns. Again and again, in facing the world in its need it is 'the one thing needful' — or at any rate most needful — which the church is called to attempt to discern.

Finally, the world of *instant-value* is confronted by the fact that in the bible, while there is an undoubted note of urgency in the call for decision, there is equally an emphasis that the crucial developments in human destiny cannot be programmed according to human wishes. We have noted already the use by Jesus of the images of hidden *growth*, the seed growing secretly and the yeast fermenting the dough. The former parable is especially striking in its picture of a process entirely beyond human comprehension or control: 'The kingdom of God is as if someone should scatter seed upon the ground, and would sleep and rise night and day, and the seed would sprout and grow, he does not know how. The earth produces of itself, first the stalk, then the head, then the full grain in the head. But when the grain is ripe, at once he goes in with his sickle, because the harvest has come' (Mk. 4.26–29). Closely related to this theme is the contrast between the small beginnings of the kingdom here and now, and its final, huge fulfilment: like a mustard seed, smallest of all seeds on earth yet when full grown a great shrub big enough for birds to nest in (Mk. 4.30–32). The wheat and the tares must be left to grow together until the final harvest (Mt. 13.24–30).

The fundamental biblical category is not that of a mentally-conceived solution which can be 'applied' to a situation as quickly as possible. It is rather that of a history which is being made, at great pain and cost, and in the making of which we are invited to be partakers, at no less cost to ourselves yet with the assurance also of participation in its glorious fulfilment. The emphasis is upon the potential, as yet barely glimpsed, of small, seemingly insignificant things like seeds. That is the real significance of the doctrine of providence. That doctrine is not intended to provide a justification for things as they are now, a claim that the *status quo* has been ordained by God (as for example in the constitution of the late Republic of South Africa) and therefore to be maintained by all means possible. Quite apart from its obvious sanctioning of rank injustice, that view is purely past-oriented. Providence, however, literally means fore-seeing, the belief that God envisions what is yet to be. It is future-oriented, underwritten by what Dorothee Sölle calls 'revolutionary patience'.[24] It persists with nursing and nurturing possibilities, however humble, which have the germ of Christlikeness in them, entrusting their future to the God who chooses 'what is low and despised in the world, things that are not' (I Cor. 1.27), who brings life even out of the grave. With Paul, it looks at the universe as pregnant with new life in Christ, and painfully awaiting its deliverance: 'For in hope we were saved. Now hope that is seen is not hope. For who hopes for what is seen? But if we hope for what we do not see, we wait for it with patience' (Rom. 8.24f.). In fact patience, long-

---

[24]D. Sölle, *Revolutionary Patience*, Lutterworth, 1979.

suffering, faithfulness, are among the most frequently enjoined qualities in the New Testament. Love, the supreme gift of the Spirit, is the greatest of all precisely because it embraces these qualities. 'Love is patient ... It bears all things ... hopes all things, endures all things' (I Cor. 13.4, 7). So too in the gospels there is the call 'to pray always and and not to lose heart' (Lk. 18.1–8), and the parables spelling out the need to keep awake, to keep lamps trimmed, to keep on fulfilling the tasks of faithful servants however long the bridegroom or master seems to be delayed in coming.

All this goes against the grain of a culture where publicity-conscious politicians look for quick-fix solutions, whether in Somalia or former Yugoslavia, or in dealing with unemployment and crime at home, and where the temptation for churches is to jump in with advice on which such remedies are likely to be the most effective. The bible is at quite another game altogether, and the true vocation of the church may have to lie in querying the assumptions of the instant-value mentality wherever it is manifested; to plough more deeply, if more slowly. If that is so, then that true vocation is itself something which the church for its own part has to learn over and over again. That is our theme for the next two chapters.

4

The Way of Prophecy

Apart from its continued use by fundamentalists who wish to inform us of the precise timetable for the end of the world, the adjective 'prophetic' has in our time become almost the sole monopoly of the advocates of 'speaking out' for social justice. In fact 'prophetic' has come to mean virtually any outspoken or critical stance in relation to contemporary society, and usually the contemporary church as well. So, a 'prophetic witness' is called for against every form of injustice and oppression, from apartheid to the international arms trade, from mass unemployment to environmental pollution. Behind this usage stands the image of the apparently typical Old Testament prophet: 'Ah, you who make iniquitous decrees, who write oppressive statutes, to turn aside the needy from justice and to rob the poor of my people of their right, that widows may be your spoil, and that you may make the orphans your prey!' (Is. 10.1f.).

Far from wishing to debunk the idea of prophetic witness I wish to strengthen it and give it more content. 'Prophetic' can indeed mean courageous speech with a real cutting edge. The witness of people like Bishop George Bell during the Second World War, protesting in the House of Lords against the saturation-bombing of civilian populations in Germany, or the soaring oratory of Martin Luther King in the fight for racial justice in the United States, is ample testimony to that. (Though note that both examples illustrate further the point made in earlier chapters, that such verbal witness has its authenticating ground in costly actions. Bell had been tirelessly working for justice for German *émigrés* and refugees interned in Britain, as well as keeping in close touch with the German resistance to Hitler and pleading its cause before the British government. King's actions as leader of the civil rights movement, which involved far more than speeches and in the end meant his death, hardly need underlining.) But 'prophetic' as applied to lesser mortals can too readily be a euphemism for a strident exercise in denunciation which achieves little beyond a self-righteous glow of satisfaction for the speaker. Biblical warrant can apparently be claimed for the sweet pangs of self-induced martyrdom in face of opposition or indifference: 'for in the same way they persecuted the prophets who were before you' (Mt. 5.12).

The basic weakness of this use of the 'prophetic' motif is that, just as the verbal utterances of more recent movements and figures are abstracted from the living context of their history, so the words of the biblical prophets are wrenched from the life in which they were generated. Their words become disembodied statements, resulting in a grossly truncated understanding of the prophet and prophecy as a whole. Thereby much of the actual power of the prophetic motif is lost, and instead of a sustaining nourishment and strength for the church's witness, it degenerates into a set of 'examples' to follow, or a style of speech to adopt. Under such formidable judgment, local congregations and national church leaders alike will be berated for never being prophetic enough. Amid their feelings of guilt and demoralization the question remains unanswered and indeed rarely, if ever, asked: How does one *become* a prophet?

Indeed, what does it mean to *be* a prophet? Typically, our modern view of the 'prophet' is of one who critically addresses the community of society, or church, or both. It concentrates on the prophet as addresser of the community. That is not untrue to the biblical picture of the prophet but as it stands is severely reductionist. The fundamental, if naive, fact of biblical prophecy must not be overlooked, namely, the belief that through the prophet it is *God* who addresses the community. As well as the prophet-community relation there is the prophet-God relation, or perhaps one should say the God-community relation *via* the prophet. The biblical prophets cannot be understood simply as people who for one reason or another expressed a righteous dissatisfaction with the present state of society. They were first of all gripped, possessed, overcome, by the divine claim: 'O Lord, you have enticed me, and I was enticed; you have overpowered me, and you have prevailed' (Jer. 20.7). This possession was not exhausted by the impulse to social righteousness.

This is a very general statement, which presently will be fleshed out in some detail. Suffice it for now to say that the prophet-community address is bereft of meaning if divorced from the prophet-God relation. At this point, however, certain questions must be faced concerning the appropriation of the Old Testament prophets by present-day Christianity. What are we actually doing when we cite as particularly authoritative texts for today, certain passages from the last third (or somewhat less) of the Hebrew bible? Are we simply putting their words on our lips to add an aura of sanctity to our convictions? How do we actually make the link between prophecy then and 'being prophetic' today?

The prophetic past and the Christian present

Any present-day Christian usage of the Old Testament prophets has to answer three main questions.

First, is it not naive to imagine that we can be at home with the prophets, and they with us, when there is such a vast cultural gulf between their world and ours? Even the most exacting scholarship has had to admit that, as a matter of historical information, there is much we simply do not know about the conditions under which the biblical prophets lived and spoke. What does seem clear, however, is that their behaviour would have seemed distinctly odd, even alien, to modern westerns. Even those whose literary deposits seem quite sophisticated, suitable material for our lectionaries, almost certainly would have delivered their oracles in states of trance or ecstasy, possibly induced in frenzied cultic activity, and on occasion exhibiting symptoms indistinguishable from severe mental illness: a world far removed from deliberative committees, consultations and report-editing, not to mention Sunday morning worship and sermonizing. The biblical world is not in fact so far removed from what many cultures in present-day Africa and Asia would recognize as their own, where spirit-possession is recognized as a normal phenomenon. Any rationalizing complacency which assumes a smooth continuity between the prophets and ourselves needs to be shaken at this point, and perhaps encounter with contemporary spirituality in much of the two-thirds world can serve precisely this need. (For various reasons I do not think that 'charismatic' Christianity in the modern western world quite fits this bill.)

The question can, I believe, be answered if we are prepared to admit that in any culture there can be an interruption by the extraordinary, an invasion of the routine and accepted pattern of 'normal' thinking and behaviour by a transcendent imperative, the arousal of a 'beyond' in our midst. This need not be limited to particular phenomena of trance or possession characteristic of eighth-century BC Israel or contemporary Uganda. But it always appears out of the ordinary.

The second question is sternly theological. Orthodox Christianity accepts the whole of the scriptures as authoritative for faith and life, but *the* way, truth and life is Jesus Christ himself (Jn. 14.6). In placing so much emphasis on the 'prophetic tradition', are we placing the Hebrew prophets on a par with Jesus, if not higher? This is a particular form of the perennial question about the relationship between the 'old' and 'new' covenants, which has taxed Christianity ever since Marcion in the second century alleged that the 'God' of the Old Testament has nothing to do with the God and Father of Jesus Christ. Under the new dispensation, the Hebrew bible can be consigned to the waste bin. If, however, we are to reject both that view, and the belief that the prophets are significant only as predicting the arrival of Jesus as the Messiah (a view which would render the greater part of their written desposits as totally irrelevant or incomprehensible), there clearly have to be some ground rules for their continued usage in Christian teaching and liturgy. The alternative is a totally arbitrary, free-wheeling plunder of the Old Testament simply to add weight to whatever contemporary enthusiasm we wish to promote. A proper drawing up of such rules is too big an exercise to be undertaken fully here, but some guidelines can be identified and sketched.

The basic need is to affirm Jesus Christ as the fulfilment of Old Testament prophecy in a way which does not in fact render obsolete a continued reading of the prophets in their own right. The starting point for this must surely be the ministry and teaching of Jesus himself. Jesus was not only perceived by the people as a 'prophet' (Mk. 8.29, Mt. 21.11) but clearly spoke as one in his critical and decisive message: 'The time is fulfilled, and the kingdom of God has come near; repent, and believe in the good news' (Mk. 1.15). Luke's account of the opening of Jesus' ministry at Nazareth makes the prophetic linkage even more explicit as Jesus takes to himself the words from Isaiah 61: 'The Spirit of the Lord is upon me ... to proclaim the year of the Lord's favour' (Lk. 4.18ff.). Of course the gospel writers interpret Jesus as being not just 'in line with' the prophets but in a unique sense their 'fulfilment': here, now, in this Jesus of Nazareth the reign of God which had been proclaimed by the prophets is indeed coming to pass! 'Today, this scripture has been fulfilled in your hearing' (Lk. 4.21). But fulfilment does not mean leaving behind, in the way a butterfly discards the shell of the chrysalis in which it has pupated. Jesus makes clear that in fulfilling the law and the prophets he does not abolish them (Mt. 5.17). His teaching underwrites that of the law and the prophets, and he summarizes their basis and centre in the two great commandments of the love of God and love of neighbour — 'On these two commandments depend all the law and the prophets' (Mt. 22.40). The gospel narratives thus present Jesus focusing the prophetic witness as the culmination of God's dealings with his people and the continuing guidance for how they are to live in the here and now.

There is however another linkage made in the New Testament between Jesus and prophecy. The Fourth Gospel is a theological reflection, in narrative form, on Jesus as the Son of God who reveals the glory of the Father in his human life and death. Here there is depicted controversy among the Jews, on whether Jesus is a true prophet or not, or indeed whether he is *the* prophet who is to come into the world (Jn. 4.19; 6.14; 7.40, 52 etc.). However, the evangelist deepens the picture of Jesus as a prophet and moves on to another plane: 'The one who comes from heaven is above all. He testifies to what he has seen and heard, yet no-one accepts his testimony ... He whom God has sent speaks the words of God, for he gives the Spirit without measure' (Jn. 3.31–34). This might almost be said of any of the prophets 'sent by God' and inspired with his Spirit. In the next sentence however it is seen to apply to Jesus in a new sense: 'The Father loves the Son, and has placed all things in his hands' (4.35). Throughout this gospel it is reiterated that Jesus speaks as the Son who speaks as the Father bids him; who does what he sees the Father doing; who gives his followers the word which he has received in a unique way, not simply as an inspired man, but as the Son whose being from all eternity has been with the Father (Jn. 17.4). But the word he gives to his followers is ultimately himself, by his death. He himself *is* the word, God's own definitive self-communication, through whom all things were made, as a human being (Jn. 1.14).

Elsewhere in the New Testament, the Letter to the Hebrews begins with a statement of the finality of the revelation in Christ, which at first appears to be set over against the provisionality of the prophets: 'Long ago God spoke to our ancestors in many and various ways by the prophets, but in these last days he has spoken to us by a Son, whom he appointed heir of all things, through whom also he created the worlds ...' (Heb. 1.1f.). But while this epistle does indeed see Christ in terms of substance as against shadow, of completion as against beginning, the Old Testament remains a crucial source for the writer's teaching on present-day faith and obedience. Those who have run their course stand as the great cloud of witnesses for us who are still running (12.1).

We may say therefore that in the New Testament Jesus is 'prophet', one who mediates God's word to the world, in a sense which both *includes* the 'old' form of prophecy and goes beyond it. Later Christian theologians, especially in the Reformed tradition, sought to do justice to this by naming 'prophet' as the first of the titles of Christ in his three-fold office, along with 'priest' and 'king'.

However summarily, this gives us some guidelines on the

Christian appropriation of the Hebrew prophets. Jesus, in his own affirmation of their teaching, by his summary interpretation of that teaching as love of God and neighbour, and by his own unique ministry as word of God through his life, death and resurrection, both requires and enables us to listen to the prophets. Jesus and the prophets are not to be divorced from or set over against each other. It is by knowing the prophets that we shall know Jesus more fully — in effect we shall know more of 'what was in his mind' in concrete detail. And it is by knowing Jesus that we shall keep our reading of the prophets focused and directional. We check our reading of the prophets against Jesus' teaching and the totality of his witness in life, death and resurrection. Jesus without the prophets is less than the Jesus of the gospels, a truncated Jesus, often spiritualized and sentimentalized out of his incarnate Jewish humanity altogether. The prophets without Jesus simply become mouthpieces for any subjective whimsy and enthusiasm on our part, suppliers of texts for every occasion. We therefore have to maintain a reciprocal relation between the prophets and the Christ of the New Testament.

The third question is both cultural (or historical) and theological. By what right do we talk of a 'prophetic ministry of the church', a *corporate* witness of the church as a community, when Hebrew prophecy was a matter of *individuals* uttering the word of the Lord? The same seems to be true of the New Testament also, where particular prophetic figures are mentioned in the churches of Antioch, Caesarea and Jerusalem (Acts 13.1; 15.32; 2.17; 21.9). Paul expressly commends the prophetic gifts of those whose Spirit-given words build up the community (I Cor. 12.10 etc.). It does appear therefore that the biblical testimony is to a category of individuals who speak prophetically within and to the rest of the community, rather than the community as a whole being 'prophetic'. Is it wrong, therefore, to demand that Baptists as a whole be prophetic, when God gives only a Martin Luther King? Or for the Church of England to prophesy, when only a Bishop Bell can stand up in the House of Lords?

To this is may be said, first, that the whole point of prophets is that through their particular insights and words the wider community might in turn catch their vision. Second, it can be pointed out that the Bible in fact contains more than hints *against* prophecy being necessarily confined to an élite corps of individuals. 'Would that all the Lord's people were prophets!' exclaims Moses when the Spirit descends, in not entirely tidy fashion, on a group of Israelite elders (Num. 11.29). The prophet Joel foretells a time when God's Spirit will be poured out on all humanity, 'your sons and your daughters shall prophesy, your old men shall dream dreams, and your young men shall see visions' (Joel 2.28), and it is precisely the fulfilment of this promise that is claimed at Pentecost, the birth of the church (Acts 2.16ff.). And while Paul warns against presuming that all will be uniformly gifted within the diversity of the body (I Cor. 12.29), he nevertheless wants all his readers to 'strive for the greater gifts' (v. 31).

Bearing in mind such qualifications, therefore, it is not amiss to ask what it means to be a 'prophetic' church. At the very least it means that the community will own the ministry of such people and seek to incorporate what they have heard and seen in its collective consciousness. The lordship of Jesus will mean recognition of him as *primus* in the college of prophets, and recognition of the prophets as the college to which Jesus belongs. Old Testament prophecy is thus a legitimate resource for Christian witness.[1]

The prophet as God-related

'What has come over the son of Kish? Is Saul also among the prophets?' Such was the reaction of those who observed what happened soon after Samuel anointed Saul as the first king of Israel (I Sam. 10.1–13). What they saw was Saul's behaviour as he went on to Gibeah, and a band of prophets met him: 'and he fell into a prophetic frenzy along with them ... When his prophetic frenzy had ended, he went home' (I Sam. 10.10, 13). Much of what that 'frenzy' would have involved can only be guesswork, but presumably it meant intensely emotional

---

[1] For a fuller discussion of the possible interpretations of the prophetic motif in relation to contemporary theology, see John W. de Gruchy, *Theology and Ministry in Context and Crisis. A South African Perspective*, Collins, 1987, esp. Chapter 3.

behaviour 'out of the ordinary', an indication of possession by
a power not of the person's own choosing or even desiring,
which came and went of its own will. If we prefer the somewhat
more refined term 'ecstasy' to 'frenzy' in describing such
behaviour (or symptoms, some may wish to say), we still have
to admit that we are talking about a state of mind and
consciousness quite other than the normal patterns of everyday
life. At root, 'ecstasy' means 'to be put out of', or 'to stand
outside of' — to be translated on to a plane of experience and
awareness other than the routine and predictable. We cannot
pretend to imagine just what the companies of prophets such
as met Saul near Gibeah experienced and thought when
possessed in frenzy or ecstasy. Perhaps they themselves would
have been hard put to it to convey what happened to them, or
would not even have seen the point of trying to do so. To have
known that they had been intoxicated, overcome, by the
energy of Yahweh himself would have been enough.

As has been hinted earlier, it would be a mistake to assume
that the great canonical prophets whose written deposits form
so significant a part of the Hebrew bible, and whose 'books'
have become so familiar in Christian liturgy and teaching, were
any less ecstatic in their utterances than those prophets whose
seemingly 'primitive' behaviour is recorded in the historical
books of Samuel and Kings. The evident sophistication which
often marks the final literary product may be very misleading
as to its genesis. In any case we can, for example, hardly
imagine Jeremiah to have been exhibiting an urbane equanimity
when he exclaimed: 'My joy is gone, grief is upon me, my heart
is sick ... O that my head were a spring of water, and my eyes
a fountain of tears, that I might weep day and night for the slain
of my poor people!' (Jer. 8.18; 9.1). And when Isaiah felt the
thresholds of the temple shake at the sound of the heavenly
seraphim, the sense of his own dissolution in face of the Lord
of hosts must surely have been relayed in a shaking of his own
knees, if not his whole physique (Is. 6.4f.). When the prophet
speaks of the strong hand of the Lord being upon him (Is.
8.11), the very physicality of the expression signifies a need to
account for some form of observable behaviour quite other
than normal.

It is worth, once more, spending a moment on etymology. The word prophet is of course from the Greek, *prophetēs*. Ancient Greece was itself familiar with those who delivered oracles on behalf of the gods, but the precise original meaning of this compound word is not exactly clear. The verb *phemi* certainly means 'to speak'. The prefix *pro* means 'before' — but in at least three possible senses. It can mean 'before' in a temporal sense, in which case prophecy refers to a speaking predictively, *fore* telling events yet to take place. It can also mean 'before' in a spatial sense, in which case an obvious reference is to speaking before the hearers, a *forth*telling of what they have come to hear. It is this meaning which has in modern times been emphasized by those commentators wishing to distinguish prophecy from crude notions of soothsaying and fortune-telling. There is however yet another possible direction to which the 'before' refers, namely that of the divine being whose communication to humans is to be mediated. The reference is thereby to the *before-god* status of the speaker, a relationship which indicates the true profundity and the disturbing challenge — both to the hearers and no less to the prophet him- or herself.

It is not easy to ascertain which of these meanings, if any, predominated in Greek-speaking culture by the time the Hebrew bible was translated into its Greek version, the Septuagint, during the last three centuries BC. The word *prophetēs* was at any rate the term believed to be most appropriate for translating the Hebrew *nabi*. What is significant is that that Hebrew word in turn is ambiguous in its origin. The root is probably an Akkadian verb meaning 'to call, to announce or to name', and those who spoke in the name of Yahweh obviously 'called out' on behalf of him, and called the people to listen to his word. But scholars are not agreed that as applied to the *nabi* the sense is entirely active. In fact on the basis of the Akkadian evidence the reference is probably passive: one who *is called by* Yahweh to be his mediator.[2]

[2]Robert R. Wilson, *Prophecy and Society in Ancient Israel*, Fortress Press, 1980, pp. 136f.

It is certainly the case that the Hebrew prophets felt themselves to be primarily under an obligation to, and indeed a possession by, Yahweh. For the prophets of the northern kingdom (Ephraim) the relation to Yahweh was characteristically expressed as one of *hearing*: 'The word of the Lord that came to Hosea son of Beeri ...' (Hos. 1.1). For the prophets of Jerusalem the relationship was visionary rather than auditory: 'The vision of Isaiah son of Amoz, which he saw concerning Judah and Jerusalem in the days of Uzziah ...' (Is. 1.1). Not that the southern prophets never 'heard' Yahweh or that the northern prophets never saw visions, but the emphasis upon hearing and delivering the words of Yahweh as Yahweh gave them was an especial emphasis of the northern prophets, and moreover of those writers who finally shaped the historical record of both kingdoms in the books of Samuel and Kings, the 'Deuteronomists'. For them, the true prophet was one who spoke the word given directly by Yahweh, that and no other. For this tradition, the classic prophetic figure was Moses himself, and it is therefore worth looking at his portrait as given in the Pentateuch.

Regardless of its historical basis or otherwise, the picture of Moses as we now have it is a picture of authentic prophecy for those who edited the Hebrew bible in its later stages. His history as a prophet begins with an experience which, significantly, is both visionary and auditory, at the burning bush on Horeb: 'When the Lord saw that he had turned aside to see, God called to him out of the bush, "Moses, Moses!" And he said, "Here I am"' (Ex. 3.4). It is quite clear in this story that the initiative lies with God. The burning bush almost acts as a lure set by God to draw Moses to himself. Indeed, the story is told so as to emphasize that it is really God's story, God being the chief actor. It has begun even before this incident, as God hears the groaning of the Israelites in slavery and 'remembered his covenant with Abraham, Isaac and Jacob' and 'took notice' of his people (2.23–25). Having told Moses that he is the God of his ancestors, it is the disclosure of this prior turning in compassion towards his people which is the first substantial part of God's communication: 'I have observed the misery of my people who are in Egypt; I have heard their cry on account of their taskmasters. Indeed, I know their sufferings, and I have come down to deliver them from the Egyptians, and to bring them up out of that land to a good and broad land ...' (3.7f.). Then follows the commission: Moses is to go to Pharaoh and obtain the release of the Israelites. In this call and response, therefore, Moses is caught up into God's own liberating action, as agent and spokesperson.

It is crucial, however, that it is the liberating action of God which is primary here, and not a general idea of liberation which is raised to some absolute status. Moses is faced with the liberation of God, not the divinization of liberation. Moses had already known such an ideal of liberation when he killed the Egyptian whom he found beating his fellow-Israelite (Ex. 2.11–15), and shortly afterwards fled to Midian. Now, however, comes not liberation as an ideal, but a new historical moment when it will become possible and actual through the intervention of God. So begins the long trial and agony of Moses, as one set between God and the people. He speaks to the people on God's behalf, and to God on behalf of the people. And it is his relation to God which both sets him as leader of the people, yet also makes him so problematic to the people. For this God remains the one who can only be named as 'I am who I am', or 'I will be who I will be' (Ex. 3.13). As such, God, the one who is utterly free in his compassion for his people, subverts the entire static system and thought-world of Pharaoh's court — and equally shatters the self-enclosed world of the Israelites who were mentally as well as physically enslaved to their circumstances, who could imagine no other world, no other life, than that to which they had been born, in which they toiled, and in which they would die. In the wilderness wanderings, Moses' role is to keep the people open to the claims and promises of God. Sometimes they would rather go back to Egypt, or simply lie down and die. It was too much to live forever solely by such promises as had led them out of bondage. They needed a golden calf as a tangible deity, for at times Moses disappeared into the cloud with his God and 'as for this Moses, the man who brought us up out of the land of Egypt, we do not know what has become of him' (Ex. 32.1). The prophet is no more at the disposal of the people than is the God he knows.

'Thus the Lord used to speak with Moses face to face, as one speaks to a friend' (Ex. 33.11). 'Never since has there arisen a prophet in Israel like Moses, whom the Lord knew face to face' (Dt. 34.10). Even to such an intimate friend God does not reveal his face as he passes by in his glory, but only his back (Ex. 33.18–23). But it is clear that Moses' vocation, from beginning to end, is to be caught up into the presence and activity of God, and as such to be accountable to God before the people and to represent to the people the claims and the freedom of the One who is liberating them. As such he represents, continually, both an assurance and a disturbance, the *basis* and the *crisis* of the people's existence.

Such a role may be recognized as the core of so many of the canonical prophets' ministries. It is not just that they deliver God's oracles to the people—and moreover intercede with God on the people's behalf (a feature often overlooked in modern interpretations of 'prophetic witness'). By their very existence, as those called to listen to God and to see what he is doing, they serve as a kind of perpetual rent in the communal life of Israel, a wounded openness to the transcendent claims and possibilities of their history with God, a refusal to allow their society to settle down into a self-enclosed existence either of complacency or despair. This is so whether, as recent attempts at historical probing into their social settings have indicated,[3] they belonged to religio-social groups operating on the periphery of society, or to the central 'establishment' and its more conservative cultic and political apparatus. Examples of the former are many of those who functioned in the northern kingdom such as Elijah and Hosea (and Amos, though he was from the south). Prime examples of the latter are Nathan, who operated within the court of David and Solomon, and Isaiah who may well have belonged to the cultic life of the Temple and was at home in the royalist circles of Zion.

The prophets as called

Of greatest significance for a proper theological understanding of the prophets, therefore, are the stories of their *call-experiences*.

[3]See Wilson, op. cit., for a survey of the whole question.

These accounts of their initial, extraordinary encounters with God who wills that they speak in his name, varying in their telling from the almost unspeakably dramatic to matter-of-fact sobriety, are recorded not simply to register the prophets' claims to be genuine spokespersons of Yahweh in contrast to the 'false prophets', though undoubtedly that is part of their import. Each such story is vital and integral to the whole testimony of the prophet in question. As in the story of Moses — whose encounter with the burning bush is not just a moving religious experience, an encounter with the 'numinous' that might in principle occur anywhere, at any time, but a revelation that the God of the ancestors is here and now active in his people's history — so it is with the other recorded vocation-experiences. We may take three examples.

Amos describes his call in the briefest terms possible: 'I am no prophet, nor a prophet's son; but I am a herdsman, and a dresser of sycamore trees, and the Lord took me from following the flock, and the Lord said to me, "Go, and prophesy to my people Israel"' (Amos 7.14f.). This however is far more than an interesting little piece of biographical background on Amos. It is given in reply to Amariah, the priest of the royal shrine of the northern kingdom. Amariah has reported to King Jeroboam that Amos is 'conspiring' against him 'in the midst of the house of Israel', and now bids Amos depart back south to his native Judah and prophesy there, and never again in the royal temple of the north. In his terse reply, Amos is not simply providing his credentials to be a true prophet. In fact he appears to be distinguishing himself from being a prophet in the accepted sense — a 'prophet's son' probably refers to a member of a prophetic community rather than someone physically parented by a prophet. Rather, he is using his call-experience to underline the drastic nature of the crisis in the north which he has been addressing. Israel's blindness to its condition is both personified and brought to its head in the attitude of Amariah himself, the priestly guardian of the royal cult where God is supposedly to be known in the north. That Amos, a rural labourer in the south, was called by God and sent to the north is itself an indictment of the religious situation in the northern kingdom, and is part and parcel of the stark message: 'Fallen, no more to rise, is maiden Israel' (Amos 5.2). The prophet's calling is itself part of the divine activity upon the people.

Isaiah provides us with perhaps the most dramatic and certainly the most well-known account of vocation-experience (Is. 6.1–13). The awesome vision of the Lord of hosts high and lifted up, his clouds of glory swirling through the trembling temple echoing to the cry of the seraphim, has deeply influenced Christian theology and liturgy alike, and comes to mind in such diverse ways as Trinity Sunday, the *Sanctus* in Bach's B Minor Mass and in ordination services for ministers and missionaries. Once more, however, it is a vision which should be seen in the context of the total ministry of the prophet. The real actor in the story is God, not the prophet. It is the unseeable God, whom to see is to die, who is actually seen. It is the God of unbearably burning holiness who sees to the cleansing of the sinful mortal with the fire from the altar. Isaiah with his 'Here am I, send me' answers the heavenly question 'Who will go for us?' but it is the King, the Lord of hosts whose glory fills heaven and earth, who would appear to have no need of frail humanity to carry out his purpose, who actually commissions and sends. Isaiah's whole ministry is to affirm that this God, 'the Holy One of Israel' (5.18, etc.) is actually at work in the history of his people as their security and their judgment. The prophet's call-experience was both a revelation of this activity, and part of it. What happened to the prophet in that encounter is what God intends to do in and with his whole people, and is its beginning (Is. 1.10–17). It is the fact that this holy One is present and active in the midst which makes oppression and violence so offensive, cultic activity a damnable substitute for the practice of righteousness and justice, and alliances with foreign powers a breach of faith.

Ezekiel tells of his call-experience — 'I saw visions of God' (Ezek. 1.1) — at greater length than any other prophet, and what he saw and heard is described in uniquely complex detail: the stormy wind out of the north, the cloud and flashing fire, the four living creatures, the wheels whirring like a divine dynamo driven at will by 'the spirit' in any direction it chose, the crystal firmament surmounted by a rainbow-encircled throne occupied by a magnificently human form. 'This was the appearance of the likeness of the glory of the Lord. When I saw it, I fell on my face, and I heard the voice of someone speaking' (Ezek. 1.28b). Ezekiel however is brought to his feet empowered by the Spirit and commissioned to go and speak God's words to the exiles in Babylon, 'a nation of rebels who have rebelled against me' (2.3). The Spirit presently lifts him up and thither he goes, overwhelmed by that power (2.12–15). Again, there is the closest possible connection between this vocation-encounter and all that the prophet in due course says and does among his people. His message is on the one hand that the people are indeed totally unacceptable to their God and must bear his rejection, his glory having departed from the profaned and polluted holy place in Jerusalem; and on the other, that this same holy God will create a new people by the power of his Spirit which goes where it wills, which can cleanse the polluted and make new hearts of flesh to replace hearts of stone (36.26), and can even bring life out of death (37.1–14). The prophet's ministry is that of extending to his whole community that which he has experienced of this God in his own initial overwhelming encounter. All that he has to say stems from that encounter and the relationship in which he stands to God in the Spirit. And apart from that relationship he has nothing to say, and would be nothing as a prophet.

God's alternative history

It is the before-Godness of the prophets which is therefore paramount in their community-relatedness, and in what they have to say. To detach their 'message' from this Godward relationship is to do violence to the message, and certainly to reduce it, for their being called to be prophets is itself a key instance of the dynamic activity of God which they proclaim. It is equally important, however, to note the direction in which this God-relatedness leads them. Their encounters are not with an undefined divine presence felt as a general kind of 'numinous'. What they see and hear is certainly other than the ordinariness of the everyday world, but it is not another realm distant from this world which they enter. They remain very much in this world, the world of groaning slaves in Egypt, of bloody power-politics in the northern kingdom, of royalist decision-making in the courts of Jerusalem, of despairing exiles by the river Chebar. They are not taken out of history, but enter ever more deeply into history. For the otherness of God to which they are brought and by which they are overwhelmed is apprehended by them as *another, alternative history* seeking to challenge and transform the assumed everyday perception of history from within. It is God's own history, God's own dynamic purpose contending for acknowledgment against the people's illusory understanding of what they think their history is, which grips the prophet.

For the Hebrew slaves in Egypt — and those who enslave them — it is in fact doubtful whether history means anything at all. The Nile rises and falls, year in, year out. Pharaohs are born and die. Life, the universe itself, is essentially static. Life's business is to maintain the world as it is, where the ultimate ambition is to build solid cities to last forever, where bricks have to be made without straw, and backs have to be broken so that the rulers may remain rulers and the given order may continue. There is no future other than that which is now and always has been. Not even beyond death does anything really change and so the kings must take their treasures with them into their tombs to keep them happy in the after-life. But Moses returns to Egypt from the burning bush on Horeb bearing news of a totally different scheme, one where there really is a *future* other than the perpetuation of the present. The Israelites need no longer be slaves to the Egyptians, the seasons, the Nile. Their groanings and cries have been *heard* by the One who is going to act on their behalf, who will call them to participate in his action and march out according to his promise into a future. God will be what he will be in freedom, and in attachment to him the people will be correspondingly free. The old static order is subverted, a road opens up along which the people can travel — and even the sea is a barrier no longer. An alternative history blazes into being with God and undreamt-of possibilities stand out in the shadows.

The later prophets similarly confront their contemporaries with accounts of what is really going on in their life and world, radically different from the accepted and popular versions of society. What that current public wisdom was, and what the alternative prophetic history was in each case, of course differed markedly from one historical context to another. In the eighth-century northern kingdom, prior to the Assyrian conquest, the accepted version of events was that material and social security for Israel was ensured by a performance of the cult of Yahweh — and preferably of the local fertility deities also for good measure. The future was therefore one of assured stability. It is this complacent wisdom which Amos attacks with his stark alternative: '"The end has come upon my people Israel; I will never again pass them by. The songs of the temple shall become wailings in that day," says the Lord' (Amos 8.2). The accepted wisdom of smooth, continued existence (especially for the rich and privileged) legitimated by traditional religious observances is undercut by a vision that all is about to collapse under the judgment, not the protection, of Yahweh: 'Alas for you who desire the day of the Lord! Why do you want the day of the Lord? It is darkness, not light; as if someone fled from a lion, and was met by a bear; or went into the house and rested a hand against the wall, and was bitten by a snake. Is not the day of the Lord darkness, not light, and gloom with no brightness in it?' (5.18–20). What is really happening is *not* the guaranteeing of a satisfactory life under Yahweh's benevolence, but the build-up to a catastrophic judgment. Yahweh is already setting his plumb-line against the leaning walls of Israelite life, and soon the high places will be made desolate, the sanctuaries laid waste and the house of Jeroboam will be riven with the sword (7.8f.). The only hope, if there is one, is for a radical repentance (5.14f.), to let justice roll down like waters and righteousness like an everflowing stream (5.24).

Nowhere is the struggle for an alternative history more intense than in the life and witness of Jeremiah, in the final years of Jerusalem's independent existence in face of the Chaldean advance. What Jeremiah faced was not simply a conventional folk-religious belief that 'all will be well', but, especially in his later years, a deliberate and sustained attempt in official quarters to promote a patriotic and nationalist ideology of invincible Jerusalem under the hand of Yahweh. As he looks at the rod of almond blossom (*shaqed*) which would normally be hailed as a reassuring symbol of new springtime life, Jeremiah hears the word *shoqed*, 'watching'. The Lord is watching over his word to perform it — in a judgment to be performed against Jerusalem in imminent history, with foreign tribes setting up their thrones against the city and all the towns of Judah. The conventional religious interpretation of current events is that '[The Lord] will do nothing; no evil will come upon us, nor shall we see sword or famine ...' (5.12, cf. 14.13). In the last days of Jerusalem before the final Chaldean onslaught there is a bitter feud between Jeremiah and Passhur the priest, chief officer in the Temple (Chapters 19–20). Jeremiah continues to prophesy that God has turned against Jerusalem on account of its religious apostasy and social unrighteousness, and will give the city into the hand of Nebuchadnezzar. Obedience to God therefore requires surrender to the Chaldeans — a message which lays Jeremiah under the charge of treason for 'weakening the hands' of the people and military alike (38.4). Jeremiah does not deny hope — in fact he expressly affirms hope amid the darkening scene by purchasing his family inheritance of land at Ananoth (32.1–15). It is a hope, however, which lies on the far side of military defeat and exile, not (as the popular and official patriotism wants) a hope that such disasters will not occur. It is precisely from the exiles that a new community will be born and Jerusalem will be restored (Chapter 24). The popular and official history is that such disasters as military defeat and the loss of political independence are so unthinkable that they must not even be mentioned publicly. God must act as the preserver of all that is. Jeremiah's vision is of a history in which God is the destroyer in order that he might be the restorer. For this reason Jeremiah (as Amos before him) is a classic instance of what Walter Brueggemann describes as a key role in prophecy — the bringing to expression of grief and mourning at the fears of death and disaster which are normally buried and numbed by the 'all is well' philosophy of public life.[4] The prophet adopts

---

[4]Walter Brueggemann, *The Prophetic Imagination*, Fortress Press, 1978. If space were no consideration, the whole of this seminal little work would merit citation as an extended footnote for this chapter!

a rhetoric 'that engages the community in mourning for a funeral they do not want to admit. It is indeed their own funeral.'[5] Conventional versions of history do not permit grieving, because they cannot bear to contemplate endings. Only victories, real or imagined, are permissible. Jeremiah for his part does not simply call for lamentation (9.10, 17, 19), but incarnates that sorrow in his own uncontrollable tears and anguish (9.1), a 'grief beyond healing' (8.18), an almost ineffable pain: 'For the hurt of my poor people am I hurt. I mourn, and dismay has taken hold on me' (8.21). In such language, word of God and word of prophet are indistinguishable. Jeremiah, caught up into God's own history, shares God's grief and sheds God's tears.

But as Brueggemann says, the prophetic imagination is one which calls for celebration as well as mourning. In fact it is those who mourn who can truly celebrate, those whose numbness has been broken who can be open to healing:

> This tradition of biblical faith knows that anguish is the door to historical existence, that embrace of endings permits beginnings. Naturally kings think the door of anguish must not be opened, for it dismantles fraudulent kings. Kings know intuitively that the deception, the phony claims of prosperity, oppression and state religion will collapse when the air of covenant hits them. The riddle and insight of biblical faith is the awareness that only anguish leads to life, only grieving leads to joy, and only embraced endings permit new beginnings.[6]

Thus it is in the utterances of Deutero-Isaiah (Is. 40–55) that we find exultation unsurpassed in the Hebrew Bible. Here, among the exiles in Babylon, the alternative prophetic history runs counter to what has become a pathological culture of despair, among a people in mourning for itself for over a generation. The prevailing notion of history is that for Israel it has come to an end, his way hidden from the Lord and his right disregarded by his God (Is. 40.27). There is only a long and at times great

---

[5]Brueggemann, op. cit., p. 51.
[6]Ibid., p. 60.

past to contemplate, for all that the future offers is an insignificant existence in a pocket of the Babylonian empire. The prophetic message on the other hand is that there has been more than enough mourning, that Jerusalem's warfare is ended, her iniquity pardoned, and a double account has been paid for all her sins (40.1). The time has come to come out of confinement back into the responsibilities of world history. The alternative future offered by the prophet is as strikingly different as his portrayal of God is in contrast to the idols of Babylon: the incomparable God who stretches out the heavens, brings rulers to nought, calls out the stars by name, neither faints or grows weary but strengthens with infinite energies those who wait for him (40.18–31). Such a God, creator and re-creator, can begin history again, and is doing so now. The One who redeemed Israel from bondage in Egypt long before will bring about a new and even more glorious exodus. Deserts are no obstacle to him, nor seas either:

> I am the Lord, your Holy One, the Creator of Israel, your King.
> Thus says the Lord, who makes a way in the sea, a path in the
>   mighty waters ...
> Do not remember the former things, or consider the things
>   of old.
> I am about to do a new thing: now it springs forth, do you not
>   perceive it?
> I will make a way in the wilderness and rivers in the desert.
>   (43.15–19)

The Lord who transcends heaven and earth in his majesty is known by the prophet as inviting his people to participate in a history transcending all the possibilities that meet the eye in the present. His ways and thoughts are not the ways and thoughts of humankind, and will be shown in his freedom to initiate a new exodus in which the people will go out in joy and be led forth in peace (55.8–12). Not that this history is totally hidden. It is emerging publicly in the rise of Cyrus of Persia, seen by the prophet as not just another emperor to strut across the Middle Eastern stage, but the chosen of the Lord, his anointed (45.1) whose way to conquest of Babylon will be cleared by God, in order to set the exiles free. This is therefore an alternative history to the prevailing one of grim resignation, and not at all obvious to the eye of reason or commonsense. The people are blind and deaf, seeing the events of their time but not truly discerning what they mean (42.19f.), still enslaved to the victim-role in which they have been cast by their recent past. The prophet, for his part, calls already for the jubilation of return and restoration to begin, for the waste places of Jerusalem to sing together (52.9).

Hebrew prophecy thus entailed a deeply personal, existential relationship of the prophet with the God whose otherness was made known in a historical purpose quite other to the conventional notions of society as to 'what was going on'. In critical judgment, or in hope, or both, the prophetic understanding of God's history with Israel and other nations subverted both 'popular' and 'official' accounts of what was to be feared and hoped for. Whether prophesying judgment or salvation, such alternative histories required a radical shift of understanding on the part of the hearers, nothing less than a repentant liberation of the imagination to see what the prophet was seeing, and a new directing of the will to a commitment to participate in the realizing of that alternative history. The prophets were thus neither simply predictors of the future nor just social moralists. Caught up into relation with God, they saw beneath the surface play of events the dynamic activity and goals of the living, holy God and therefore saw his future; and in the light of that activity and that future, called for the appropriate human response of justice and righteousness.

The same holds for much of what is said of Christian prophecy in the New Testament. The reign of God as proclaimed by Jesus himself was a radically alternative history to much conventional religion and public piety: God was acting *now* to forgive sinners, welcome outcasts, release the poor and welcome all from east and west, north and south, to the feast of the kingdom. Outrageous in its immediacy and inclusiveness, such a version of history contradicted the current notions of events as building up to a divine intervention on behalf of Israel and, above all, of the pious élite within that community. Jesus' own alternative vision called for both celebration in his table-fellowship with sinners, and for mourning as he wept over

Jerusalem, the city that knew not the things that made for her peace, as he saw the inevitability of her destruction. Prophecy in the New Testament church, like that in ancient Israel, combined a discernment of how God was working and of the appropriate ethical response. To take just one incident, Acts 21.10–14 describes how the prophet Agabus came down from Judea to Caesarea where Paul and his companions were staying en route for Jerusalem after his third missionary journey. In a typical act of prophetic symbolism he takes Paul's girdle, binds his own feet and hands and says: 'Thus says the Holy Spirit, "This is the way the Jews in Jerusalem will bind the man who owns this belt and will hand him over to the Gentiles."' Hearing this Paul's friends beg him tearfully not to continue his journey. Paul for his part affirms his readiness not only to be imprisoned but even to die for the name of Jesus. This act of prophecy, again, stems from an alternative history: not an ordered progress from success to success for the great evangelist of the gentiles, but the way of suffering and the cross yet again. Such is to be the history of the Spirit with the church. And on the largest possible scale the apocalypse of John is one great exposition of what, to those given glimpses of heaven's open door, is the history that is really taking place behind the smoke and bloodletting of imperial Rome. On earth is disaster after disaster, cruelty after cruelty, but God's judgments are being wrought, Babylon-Rome is doomed, the slain Lamb is already on the throne and the new, ever-open, ever-radiant City of life and light is descending upon earth. Therefore: 'Let the evildoer still do evil, and the filthy still be filthy, and the righteous still do right, and the holy still be holy' (Rev. 22.11).

The prophetic counter-culture

The prophet-community relation, we have argued, cannot be divorced from the prophet-God relation which is primary. The prophet is one called into the burden of possession by God and to that radical alternative history which is of God's creating. The prophet's primary accountability is to the One who calls and who remains sovereignly free in energizing his historical purpose, and the prophet is beholden to none other. In this light, we cannot in any sense take up the prophetic mantle (cf. II Kings 2.13) today without becoming conscious of a sharp contradiction between the demands of this calling and those pressures, outlined in the previous chapter, which our culture generates for those seeking successful public roles.

Reality-publicity. The prophets are inevitably public figures, but publicity is not for them a value in its own right. They do not speak for the sake of speaking. They are not bound to comment on each and every event, each and every day. They do not need a regular weekly column in the press. They say only what God gives them to say, and when he gives it. They know when they have to be assertive and strident, thrusting themselves before public gaze. Jeremiah is told to go and stand right in the gate of the Lord's house to confront the people of Judah as they arrive for worship, to warn of a fearful judgment against which there will be no protection by parroting pious phrases about 'The temple of the Lord' (Jer. 7.1ff.). But they know, too, when they can only wait in comparative helplessness for people to seek a word from them. Jeremiah is underground and in chains when King Zedekiah eventually enquires from him, 'Is there any word from the Lord?' (Jer. 37.16–23) — and by then the only word left to deliver is that which has been spoken already and rejected: 'You shall be delivered into the hand of the king of Babylon' — and that word is being made good as the city's defences crumble. Words are their armoury, but they know when further words serve no purpose and they hear the command to silence: 'Bind up the testimony, seal the teaching among my disciples. I will wait for the Lord, who is hiding his face from the house of Jacob, and I will hope in him' (Is. 8.16f.). In such a time any further communication of God's message must be left to the eloquence of actual events. Moses finally leaves the presence of obdurate Pharaoh saying 'I will not see your face again!' (Ex. 10.29). Ezekiel sits for a whole week with the exiles by the Chebar, overwhelmed and silent, until the Lord speaks to him again (Ezek. 2.15).

To be prophetic is not to be a compulsive talker, nor to have the facility to have something to say about almost anything. The prophet is not necessarily a good person to appear on TV's *Question Time.* The answers do not always come pat from

Yahweh to the prophet, as Jeremiah knew only too well. The prophet does not speak and act out of a desire to be heard and seen, not even for the sake of the church's 'image' and 'credibility' in the eyes of contemporary society. The prophet rather is motivated by the desire to let be heard and seen what emerges compellingly from encounter with God as the *basis* and *crisis* of contemporary society, that alternative history and future to which God's own self is pledged in holy love. How and when that utterance should be made before political rulers, and what its precise content shall be, cannot be fixed in advance or governed by some general principle. It occurs in the freedom of the Spirit (Mk. 13.9–11).

Problem-solution. 'Is it you, you troubler of Israel?' asks King Ahaz of Elijah (I Kings 18.17). The prophets hardly appear in the guise of trouble-shooters or problem-solvers as far as Israel's politicians are concerned, but rather as trouble-makers and problem-creators. Far from offering solutions to the perceived problems of society, they raise radical questions about what the real problems are. In the light of the alternative history by which the prophets are gripped, the 'problems' of living within the assumed history are relativized before the real crisis confronting the community. Amos disturbs the smoothly ordered cultus of Bethel by pronouncing attendance at the shrine a sin against Yahweh. Isaiah denounces the policies of security-by-alliance as inimical to trust in Yahweh. Jeremiah specifically identifies the sins of priests and false prophets as peddling superficial remedies for the ills in the body politic: 'They have treated the wound of my people carelessly, saying "Peace, peace", when there is no peace' (Jer. 6.14). What Israel needs is not just some tightening up of social discipline, not just some reform of temple worship, but a radical transformation, a social repentance where the cause of the poor and needy is judged, where there is no longer dishonest gain, and where oppression and violence are at an end, for there Yahweh is known (Jer. 22.15–17). Quite justifiably from within the conventional perspectives, Jeremiah is virulently accused of not helping the critical situation as the Chaldeans lay siege to Jerusalem. His own 'answer' to the crisis, that of surrender and acceptance of exile, is so radical as to seem no answer at all, simply treason.

To be prophetic is thus to stand at that boundary where, on the one side, people demand answers to their problems, and on the other side God's own radical question is thrust forward requiring an answer. Jesus is asked by the mother of James and John to sort out questions of precedence among the disciples. His answer is that in God's kingdom such questions are inappropriate: true greatness lies in being a servant, and whoever would be first must be slave of all (Mk. 10.43–45). James and John are invited to forego their personal histories of would-be greatness which reflect the norms of this present world, and participate instead in the alternative history, the cup and the baptism, of the Son of Man who has come to serve and give his life for all. To be prophetic is, fundamentally, to be a sign that this boundary is always there. Prophecy can never be co-opted simply into providing answers to the problems which people define in their own terms. That is not to say that such problems are not real or important, or that it is not a Christian duty to meet them. But the primary task of a community that would be prophetic is that of exposing the fundamental crisis under which society stands before God, and of posing the alternative history of the reign of God amidst all the chatter about what is going on in the world.

As was stated in the previous chapter, part of the temptation in proffering solutions to problems lies in the prospect of the kudos of success and aura of the successful manager of events. Prophets, however, are again and again specifically denied any guarantee of such reward. The final criterion of their authenticity over against 'false prophets' is that their word does in fact come to pass (Dt. 18.21f.). But they themselves may well not live to see that day. Even Moses does not enter the promised land himself, but is granted only the view from Mount Nebo. Most of the prophets seem to disappear unsung in the tide of history. Moreover, not only are they not successful problem-solvers for others, the prophets are themselves landed with additional burdens of their own. Their call-experiences often resemble commissions for failure. The most that is assured them is that if they remain faithful to the word that is given them, come what may in face of indifference or outright opposition (Jer. 1.17–19, Ezek. 2.7), they will continue to be used by God as agents of his judgment. That part of Isaiah's call-narrative which speaks of his vocation to a ministry provoking blindness and deafness among the people for their judgment (Is. 6.9–13), is frequently omitted when the story is read in public worship. It sounds like a demoralizing put-down following the burning drama of what precedes. It is a sobering thought, however, that in the New Testament these verses are the most frequently cited of all Old Testament passages. As God-related servants the prophets are witnesses, and that to which they witness matters more than their own careers as witnesses.

Instant-value. The prophetic attitude to the speed of historical events does not as such manifest any single general principle. Jeremiah writes to the first generation of exiles in Babylon counselling patience and the expectation of a long sojourn, such as calls for the raising of families and promotion of the welfare of the city of their exile (Jer. 29.1–23). Talk of an early return is illusory. On the other hand, a generation later Deutero-Isaiah startles his contemporaries by announcing the imminence of that second exodus. Yahweh acts sooner than expected, indeed he *has* already acted decisively to redeem (Is. 44.21–23). It cannot therefore be said, for example, that the prophets always take the long-term view. What is crucial for the prophets is their notion of history itself, within which the personal will and purpose of God comprise the final, inner determinative power. But in a culture which prizes instant solutions and success, and in which the pressure is almost irresistibly towards short-term measures, the prophetic attitude will constantly be setting behaviour and decisions against the backdrop of wider and deeper considerations than apply at the instant and superficial level. It will point up the significance of decisions here and now for *the* crisis which must one day be faced and which cannot be deferred indefinitely. It will declare, for example, that the issues of peace and security cannot be settled by continuous short-term measures provided by military technology. Those who know of God's radically other history with the world will know that the key question is not how the already powerful may be made to feel more secure, but how the poor and vulnerable may be secure from want and be able to take charge of their own destinies, and unless that question with all its immense ramifications is faced, peace in this world will be an illusion. But neither will the prophetic attitude be under any illusions itself that such big questions will be easily answered or even willingly faced. There are those ominous warnings both in the Old Testament and in the apocalypses of the New, of earth being covered in darkness, of terrible confusion and struggle, of cosmic birth-pangs, before the day of the Lord comes. It is those who *endure* to the end who will be saved (Mk. 13.13).

The heart of prophetic consciousness: a radical learning

Retrieving the prophetic stance as a role for the contemporary church involves, we have seen, a recognition that to be prophetic means being called into a particular relationship with God, and therewith an awareness of that radically alternative history, God's 'wholly other' and dynamic purpose in and for the world. In Christian terms, the heart of that purpose is disclosed in the life, death and resurrection of Jesus Christ in whom the prophets are summed up, confirmed and seen in a yet new light. We have noted the dangers of too readily assuming an easy passage between the Hebrew prophets and ourselves, but have also argued for certain continuities between their roles and that of a contemporary community of faith witnessing in society. We have also criticized the tendency in some modern Christian circles to lose sight almost completely of the prophet-God relationship, in the understandable wish to stress the social dimension of prophecy.

It would be tempting at this point to leave matters by calling for a dual emphasis in our understanding of prophecy: the prophet as called and possessed by God, and the prophet as addressing society. This however would be less than satisfactory. It would still encourage endless debates as to which of these two emphases, in any situation, was getting more or less than its due. At the end of the day, it betrays a dichotomy in thinking which is foreign to the biblical world. The call-narratives of the prophets in fact portray the calling-and-sending as a single total experience. The prophet as prophet does not exist for any purpose other than that of addressing the community.

Conversely, the prophet is able to address the community only because called and possessed by God. We therefore do not have two identities, but one identity with two inseparable aspects or relationships. The one really fundamental relationship is that between God and the community, and the prophet exists to mediate that relationship. Is there a way of describing the prophet's mediating role which does justice at once both to the God-relatedness and the community-relatedness? In fact there is. It involves describing the role of the prophet in such an obvious way as to be usually overlooked, yet a way which offers what may potentially be the most significant line of continuity between the contemporary community of faith and the biblical tradition of prophecy.

To look for it, us turn to those four passages in Deutero-Isaiah where, in Christian tradition, Hebrew prophecy reaches its most profound and significant level: the 'Servant Songs'. In the first, Is. 42.1–4, Yahweh's servant is described as one chosen and endowed with Yahweh's Spirit, who will bring forth justice to the nations and will not fail or be discouraged until he has completed this mission for the whole world. Notably, he is not a voluble servant. 'He will not cry or lift up his voice, or make it heard in the street.' His ministry is to tend the broken reed and keep alight the smoking wick. Already, here, there seems to be a reticence — even a slight element of disillusion? — about prophecy as primarily utterance. The important thing about this servant is his carrying out of the commission to establish justice, come what may. In the second Song, Is. 49. 1–6, the servant himself speaks. God has called and prepared the prophet even from his mother's womb to be his servant in whom he will be glorified. But the servant confesses the difficulty and futility of his task, and can only cast himself on God for vindication: 'I have laboured in vain. I have spent my strength for nothing and vanity; yet surely my cause is with the Lord and my reward with my God.' God's answer is to widen the servant's commission still further, not only to restore Israel but to be a light to the whole earth. Here, there is an element of new discovery on the part of the prophetic servant, born out of his utter dependence on Yahweh who is his strength as much now as when shaping him in the womb.

The third Song, Is. 50.4–9, brings us to yet another aspect of the prophetic role, and for the purposes of our study the most significant:

> The Lord God has given me the tongue of those who are taught, that I may know how to sustain the weary with a word.
> Morning by morning he wakens — wakens my ear to listen as those who are taught.
> The Lord God has opened my ear, and I was not rebellious, I did not turn backward.
> I gave my back to those who struck me, and my cheeks to those who pulled out the beard; I did not hide my face from insult and spitting.

The poem moves on into a confident, indeed defiant, declaration of the Lord God's help in resisting his persecutors and in vindicating him. But what is striking is the emphasis *on being taught in order to be able to speak to others*. Three times it is stated: the servant is prophetic because he is himself first taught by Yahweh, and this being-taught is not a once-for-all course in divine oracles, but a repeated, daily occurrence in a relationship of complete dependence on God. Here is exposed what is implicit throughout the Old Testament prophetic tradition: prophets can only speak because they have themselves first received the word. They are its first learners. Indeed, they are first and foremost themselves learners. They are as those who are taught.

Finally, in the fourth Song, Is. 52.13 – 53.12, which has become so important in Christian tradition as a prefigurement of the suffering Christ, the servant is notable for his silence. He has nothing to say before those who oppress him and put him to death. But he still has everything to communicate. Now, as one who has been taught, he has a knowledge which will make many righteous (53.11). But his teaching is no longer a matter of words, rather a total act of self-giving in suffering. Moreover, while silent before his oppressors he is not silent before his God, with whom he intercedes for the transgressors (53.12). Prophecy has moved into redemption.

It is the insight of the third Song which is pivotal, and indeed according to one noted scholar it 'signifies the climax of prophecy in the Old Testament'.[7] It is only as the prophet is himself a *learner* before God that he can sustain a ministry which is other than futile and which in turn sustains the weary. That is the heart of all prophecy, the captivation of a human mind to discover and learn the radical otherness of the mind of God in a given historical situation, and thereby to learn of the alternative future lying before it. We usually talk of the vicarious suffering of the servant in the fourth Song. We need to recognize that the servant's acceptance of that way involves a *vicarious learning*, a learning for the sake of others. This is the element in prophecy which transcends its various particular cultural and time-bound manifestations, and by which we today can truly retrieve the biblical tradition for ourselves. It means the community of faith recognizing that before it can adopt a public didactic role, it must first itself be as one who is taught, daily, continually. It means an admission in utter humility that of oneself the prophet has nothing to say to the world, but only what has first been taught by God. It is here that the prophet-God and prophet-community relations are truly at one, for the insistence by the prophet on being open *to learn* from a source transcending the given situation, is in itself an address of enormous significance to the community. For often the community, whether of the church or wider society, will resist the idea that there is anything 'to learn' that is not known already. It offends the tyrannical self-sufficiency of assumed wisdom to be told that an interruption from an alternative perspective is due. In just such a way, totalitarian regimes are fearful and suspicious of painters, dramatists, poets and even musicians precisely because they demand the liberation of the imagination. By their very existence, unless they are made to toe the line completely, artists call in question the claim of the ruling ideology to prescribe in advance ways of looking at the human condition.

To be prophetic is therefore to be as one who is taught, whose ears are continually being opened. That is the primary identity of the prophet. To take this seriously will mean

[7]G. von Rad, *Old Testament Theology*, Vol. II, Oliver and Boyd, 1965, p. 69.

revolutionary changes for the contemporary church, in which prophecy has become equated purely with authoritative speaking. It means the church, in an exercise of radical humility, insisting on the space in which to carry out its own learning, before it rushes to the megaphone. This, after all, as seen in Chapter 2, was the true significance of Barmen in 1934: the church demanding the right to place itself under the word of God, and no other word, and therewith recognizing its own need of re-education. It was precisely this insistence which in itself had high political significance, in a context where nationalist enthusiasm was noisily claiming as obvious what the church should be saying and doing.

Prophets are indeed born where there is the openness to re-learn. Among white Christian leaders in the struggle against apartheid in South Africa, no name is more honoured than that of Beyers Naudé who founded the Christian Institute in the 1960s (modelled in part, incidentally, on the stance of the German Confessing Church) and who consequently suffered house arrest for seven years. The story of his pilgrimage from an upbringing in the heart of white Afrikanerdom and the Dutch Reformed Church, of which he became a minister, to becoming eventually such a vigorous opponent of the apartheid system is one of the great Christian sagas of our time. By his own account, the decisive factor in changing him was when, as never before in his life, he really encountered at first hand the black communities in the Transvaal. Here, he admits, he began for the first time to *learn* what his country was really like, and it was through that encounter that a new understanding of the role of the church dawned upon him. 'He went, he visited their congregations, he saw and he grieved.'[8] It was his openness to learning, and through his black sisters and brothers above all, that was decisive in turning him from an academically well-educated minister and eloquent preacher into a prophet.

---

[8]C. Villa-Vicencio, 'A Life of Resistance and Hope', in *Resistance and Hope: South African Essays in Honour of Beyers Naudé*, ed. C. Villa-Vicencio and J. W. de Gruchy, David Philip and Eerdmans, 1985, p. 8.

Hebrew prophecy, it is usually said, did not last long after the return from the exile in the sixth century BC, being superseded by the apocalyptic and the scribal traditions. But the motif of 'the one who is taught' remained and in fact deepened in Jewish life and thought. In the New Testament it emerges powerfully in the theme of discipleship, and it is to examine the bearing of this concept on the public role of the church that we must now turn.

5

The Way of Discipleship

Those who rightly fear that the over-use of 'prophecy' in our time may lead to a reducing of the church's role to that of rhetorical protest need not, it might first appear, be unduly alarmed. Waiting in the wings to counter any drift towards purely verbal declamations, bland or strident, against the wicked world is the motif of *discipleship*. Under this banner gather all the causes of Christian activism which call for concrete, practical programmes of action which will at least attempt to bend the present order of this age in the direction of the age to come. Actions speak louder than words. True Christians, long before Karl Marx, have known that the challenge is not so much to understand the world as to change it, and they will always do so. The proof-text of this emphasis is: 'Not everyone who says to me, "Lord, Lord," will enter the kingdom of heaven, but only the one who does the will of my Father who is in heaven' (Mt. 7.21). In the west at the moment, the discipleship motif is especially invoked by those calling for Christians, individually and corporately, to resist militarism in all its forms, and to promote both personal life-styles and governmental policies in line with peace, a just sharing of the earth's resources and the preservation of the integrity of the creation. Being Christian cannot be adequately embraced by the somewhat ambiguous idea of the 'good citizen', which almost inevitably leads to a highly conformist pattern of life, perhaps best summed up in the English Victorian ideal of 'manliness' (allegedly promulgated by that organ of muscular Christianity, *The Boys' Own Paper*): Shoot straight, keep clean,

113

fear God, honour the Queen. Rather, Christians are called to stand out from and stand against present polities and powers, and witness by their actions to a radically different way of living. It means actually putting into practice, at whatever cost, the way shown by Jesus in his own life, teaching and death. It is a genuine *following*, a radical, costly discipleship.

It is an entirely healthy and necessary emphasis. The question is whether, on its own terms, it has the resources to sustain itself.

Costly discipleship: the witness of Dietrich Bonhoeffer

Whenever in the last decade of our century of oppression and violence there is mention of 'costly discipleship', it is almost impossible not to hear echoes, direct or indirect, of Dietrich Bonhoeffer's matchless study *The Cost of Discipleship*,[1] and his own journey along the way of the cross which culminated on the gallows in the Nazi prison camp at Flossenbürg in April 1945. The book itself comprises lectures which Bonhoeffer delivered to his students in the illegal seminary of the Confessing Church at Finkenwalde during 1935–36. Expounding Jesus' teaching on discipleship, and the Sermon on the Mount, Bonhoeffer cuts to the heart of the malaise besetting much of his own German Protestantism of the time. Luther's doctrine that we are saved by grace alone, through faith alone, had been bowdlerized into a purely quiescent piety which could find hardly any room at all for 'works' in Christianity beyond that of being a dutiful *Bürger*. Anything more 'active' or distinctively Christian savoured of those dreadful 'enthusiasts', or those sentimental, liberal Christians in Britain and America who believed they could build the kingdom of God on earth by human effort; whereas the bible teaches (does it not?) that peace and justice will only be realized at the last day when God himself will bring in his kingdom in all its glory. Small wonder, then, that so many Christians were well content to hand over the running of Germany to Adolf Hitler with no questions asked.

[1] D. Bonhoeffer, *The Cost of Discipleship*, SCM Press, 1959.

Luther's original theological insight had been betrayed because in fact it had been reduced from its full dimensions: salvation is by grace alone, through faith alone, because it is through *Christ* alone. And Christ is not an abstract theological concept but the actual, living Jesus who calls people out of their present existence to be with him and to share his ministry. That means, asserts Bonhoeffer, that faith and *obedience* always go together, otherwise there will not arise an actual fellowship with Jesus. Peter and John could remain mending their nets and inwardly agreeing that Jesus was a great religious teacher, but unless they actually leave their nets and go with him down the road they will have no meaningful relationship with Jesus wherein faith is possible and their life is really changed. 'Only the obedient believe. If we are to believe, we must obey a concrete command. Without this preliminary step of obedience, our faith will only be pious humbug, and lead us to the grace which is not costly.'[2] That preliminary step of obedience will be followed by many others as the Sermon on the Mount makes clear — a discourse which, again, had been eviscerated of its challenge in Lutheranism by being treated as a description of what an impossibly ideal Christianity would be like, not a concrete direction for venturing by faith in the here and now.

Bonhoeffer thus re-anchors faith and salvation in the authentic 'by Christ alone' of the Reformation: the Christ of the cross, the Christ with whom fellowship means sharing the cross and whose grace is therefore deeply costly. Discipleship is costly because it is *his* grace, and it is *grace* because it is costly. By focusing on the exclusive allegiance with Jesus in the totality of his messianic calling which includes the cross, this understanding of discipleship resists any reduction to a simplistic, one-sided view of Christian life. In the last months of his life, while in prison, Bonhoeffer confessed to seeing some 'dangers' in *The Cost of Discipleship*, if it encouraged the notion that one could cultivate a 'holy life' for oneself, but at the same time he stated that he was prepared to stand by what he had written.[3] The continuity between what he wished to

[2]Ibid., p. 55.
[3]Bonhoeffer, *Letters and Papers from Prison*, SCM Press, 1971, p. 369.

affirm in the heat of the Church Struggle in the early 1930s, and his new exploration of what Christianity might mean in a 'world come of age' a decade later, is precisely this attachment to the person of Jesus himself: 'All that we may rightly expect from God, and ask him for, is to be found in Jesus Christ. The God of Jesus Christ has nothing to do with what God, as we imagine him, could do and ought to do. If we are to learn what God promises, and what he fulfils, we must persevere in quiet meditation on the life, sayings, deeds, sufferings, and death of Jesus.'[4]

Bonhoeffer's treatment of discipleship is a vital onslaught on a purely passive and conformist Christianity. The Christian community is indeed called to an 'extraordinary' type of righteousness in the world. But is it therefore a charter for activism pure and simple? Not if the focus upon the attachment to Jesus is maintained. While this fellowship must always include concrete obedience and 'following' in the sense of 'doing as Jesus would have done' it also includes as its fundamental presupposition, too easily forgotten, that the relationship between Jesus and his followers is that of teacher and taught. Much of the contemporary emphasis on radical discipleship in fact misses out on the basic meaning of *disciple* itself: one who is taught, one who is under the instruction, the discipline, of another. Disciples are not those who are simply eager to do as Jesus did and taught, but are those who, first, are prepared to come and learn what his actions and words are (Lk. 9.57–62). Bonhoeffer's own style of meditation in prison shows that this element was crucial to his own understanding of discipleship throughout, and became dominant again at the end.

Prophecy, we have seen, refers to those who are taught anew, whose ears are opened continually. That is where prophecy at its most profound, as in the Servant Songs of Isaiah, culminates. For its part, this is where discipleship, as the term itself implies, begins. But does it ever move beyond this fundamental position? The presupposition of much Christianity, historic and contemporary, Protestant and Catholic, is that it does: the

[4]Ibid., p. 391.

church is here to teach, to *make disciples* (cf. Mt. 28.19). But does that mean that Christians, individually and collectively, are no longer themselves in the position of having to learn? That they are now effectively in the authoritative place of Jesus himself? The importance of the discipleship motif is that it preserves equally both the indissoluble relation, and the distinction, between Jesus the Lord and his followers, between the head of the church and his body (cf. Eph. 4.15f). But it is the questionable presupposition that the church is no longer a learning community which lies behind so much of its unease in the contemporary world. Those who wilfully adopt an authoritative position not rightfully theirs are bound to be, by turns, nervously aggressive and defensive, making claims for themselves which cannot be substantiated. Or they will tend to become hyperactive in the attempt to justify those claims and indeed their very existence. The rest of this chapter is therefore devoted to a further biblical and theological examination of the discipleship motif as involving a willingness to be taught and to learn, and the profound implications of this for the contemporary church.

Learning and doing God's word: the witness of the psalmist

First, before turning to the gospels, let us briefly look at a passage in the Old Testament where the heart of Hebrew spirituality is laid bare. Psalm 119 has a significance far beyond its being, as everyone knows, the longest item in the Psalter. It is also, incidentally, a psalm which captivated and intrigued Dietrich Bonhoeffer from the time when in 1935 he heard the Mirfield brothers in the Community of the Resurrection praying it through in its entirety in the course of each day. At the beginning of the war, when his theological teaching was continuing in a clandestine and dispersed way in Further Pomerania, Bonhoeffer in fact set about writing a commentary on the psalm and encouraging his students to do likewise.[5] It is not just the length, but the intensity, of the psalmist's address to God which is remarkable. There is no let-up in the direct,

---

[5]Cf. E. Bethge, *Dietrich Bonhoeffer*, Collins, 1970, pp. 571, 580.

second person form of this prayer. After the opening three verses, not once does the psalmist slip into a third-person mode, or comments *about* God, other people or the world in general. Either 'you', or 'your', or both, occur in practically every verse to the very end. Everything is said directly to God.

The recurring theme of this address is the command, the word, the law, of the Lord. The psalmist believes that true joy is to be found in keeping and obeying God's word on this earth, despite all rival claims to allegiance, despite others' contempt for God's law and despite opposition and persecution from such people. 'I delight in the way of your decrees as much as in all riches' (v. 14). 'I rejoice at your word like one who finds great spoil' (v. 162). All the hope of the psalmist is centred on *this* joy, not a joy that might result in being taken from this earth, on which he is a sojourner or 'alien' (v. 19). There is more than one element in this joy. The supreme element is the joy of actually keeping God's commands. But the psalmist acknowledges his inexhaustible need to know and understand God's word — in order that he might keep it. 'Make me understand the way of your precepts, and I will meditate on your wondrous works' (v. 27); 'Teach me, O Lord, the way of your statutes, and I will observe it to the end. Give me understanding, that I may keep your law and observe it with my whole heart' (v. 33f.). The psalmist's joy is therefore joy in a God who promises not to leave his servant bereft of guidance — 'Confirm to your servant your promise, which is for those who fear you' (v. 36). This joy is not without pain, and at times the psalmist is almost desperate to know more of God's word — 'With open mouth I pant, because I long for your commandments' (v. 131). The psalmist gives thanks for all experience which can in whatever way lead to further understanding of God's law — 'It is good for me that I was humbled, so that I might learn your statutes' (v. 71).

So it goes on. The psalmist is wise through God's mercy, yet thirsts for still deeper and renewed understanding, for 'your commandment is exceedingly broad' (v. 96). The commandment is not some fixed, static statement which can neatly be possessed, but a living word which gives guidance for each step of the way (v. 105). The reason for the length of this psalm is therefore plain. It is not a matter or long-windedness, but the inherent nature of the situation of one who is placed before God in a relationship of trust and obedience. This requires an endless reciprocity between the knowing and the doing of God's will, between knowing and yet confessing the need to know again, and to know more. There is no graduation ceremony for one who has learnt God's decrees, but a wondering, hopeful and joyous recognition that the grace of being taught, and of being given life so that the word may be kept, is sure and certain. Such a prayer could literally go on for ever. It cannot be neatly rounded off with a pious flourish. The only appropriate way of humanly keeping it within the bounds of the Psalter is to confess abruptly, with what is indeed the concluding verse: 'I have gone astray like a lost sheep; seek out your servant for I do not forget your commandments' (v. 176). Faithfulness, so long as we are on this earth, begins and ends in the confession of the need to be taught, in trustful reliance on the One who comes to us in grace.

It should not be thought too fanciful, but of deep symbolic significance, that this prayer is located literally almost at the centre of the Bible. It lays out the basic paradigms of the situation of the believing community before God. With that in mind, and with like brevity, we turn to some key features of discipleship in the New Testament.

Learning to act and learning from acting: discipleship in the gospels

According to the gospels, Jesus calls certain people to become involved in a particular way with his ministry. 'He went up into the mountain and called to him those whom he wanted, and they came to him. And he appointed twelve, whom he also named apostles, to be with him, and to be sent out to proclaim the message, and to have authority to cast our demons' (Mk 3.13–15). Discipleship thus has a two-fold nature in its relationship to Jesus: being with him, and being sent by him. In being with him the disciples are enabled to be taught, sometimes in teaching which is explicitly for them as distinct from the multitude (e.g. Mk. 13.3–37), sometimes in private and further explanation to them of what he has declared to the people at large (e.g. Mk. 4.33). In being sent, they themselves announce the kingdom of God, heal the sick and cast out demons (Mk. 6.7–13, Mt. 10 etc.). But it is not as though their being sent in any way implies that they have learnt all there is to know about the kingdom and its impact, or that they themselves have no further need of being taught. In the first place, their dismissal for this mission itself provides the occasion for further teaching on how the world will resist the kingdom as represented by them (Mt. 10.5–42). Second, their return from the mission requires assessment and reflection on what has happened. According to Mark, on their return 'the apostles gathered around Jesus and told him all that they had done and taught' (Mk. 6.30) — the educational significance of 'de-briefing' should need no underlining. Luke's account of the sending and return of the 'seventy' is still more significant. They return with joy that even the demons submit to the name of Jesus (Lk. 10.17). Jesus confirms the reality of their victorious power over evil but adds: 'Nevertheless do not rejoice at this, that the spirits submit to you, but rejoice that your names are written in heaven' (Lk. 10.20).

In fact, as is well known, the gospels throughout are highly ambivalent on the spiritual standing of the disciples. They are never portrayed as omnicompetent, self-sufficient agents of the kingdom, however long and intimate their relationship with Jesus has been, however much experience they may have acquired through their own ministry. Their *lack* of understanding is repeatedly highlighted, from Peter's attempt to divert Jesus from the way of the cross (Mk. 8.32f.) to the quarrels over pre-eminence (Mk. 10.35–44, Lk. 22.24–27). The father of the boy riven by epileptic seizures complains to Jesus 'I asked your disciples to cast it out, but they could not do so' (Mk. 9.18), a failure which exposes the disciples to controversy with the scribes and makes clear their vulnerability. 'Why could not we cast it out?' the disciples ask Jesus privately, prompting his injunction to prayer (and, according to some versions, fasting). And all this is besides the culmination of their failure in face of the cross: betrayal, desertion and denial. The resurrection appearances, especially in the Lucan narratives, are educative experiences in which the meaning of the scriptures is unfolded anew (Lk. 24.13–27, 45–47), and the ministry of the risen Christ in the forty days between Easter and Ascension is alike one of instruction and 'speaking about the kingdom of God' (Acts 1.2, 4, 6–8).

The gospels' picture of discipleship is therefore, as in Psalm 119, one of continual interplay between being taught, acting on that teaching, and learning anew in reflection on that action, its successes and failures, and never moving beyond the position of being 'as those who are taught'. Being a matter of radical attachment to Jesus, discipleship has both educative and activist elements and cannot be simplistically reduced to one at the expense of the other. Discipleship is learning to act, and learning from acting.

A movement of learning: the New Testament church

What has been said about continuous learning and discovery remains true for the post-Pentecostal church as well. Luke's account in Acts makes clear that the downrush of the Spirit on the day of Pentecost, while it marvellously created the church as the vibrant community of worship, proclamation and common life, did not as such convey all the answers to the questions which were to arise as the church grew and spread. Those questions had to be discerned and faced as they arose in turn, whether that of how to ensure a proper distribution of aid among the different ethnic components of the community (Acts 6.1–6), or, much more searchingly, that of the claims of Jewish religious law upon gentile converts (Acts 15.1–21). The latter question provoked deep controversy, and scholarship over the last century or so has speculated whether in fact it ran even deeper than the New Testament records themselves explicitly record. Certainly Paul for his part makes clear the sharp confrontation between Peter and himself on the issue (Gal. 2.11–14). In fact the Acts account describes very clearly and dramatically a decisive learning experience for Peter in his rooftop vision at Joppa, wherein his whole background of assumptions about ritual purity were challenged (Acts 9.9–16). The mission to the gentiles demanded a radical rethinking on

the part of Jerusalem-based Christians, not simply on the
'strategy' of mission, but on the nature of the gospel itself. That
gospel was, as it had been from the beginning, the news that
God had acted for people's salvation in the life, death and
resurrection of Jesus. But *what* this salvation comprised — and
who this Jesus was for the world outside Judaism — demanded
a continual renewal of understanding. That renewal is
photographed in mid-flight above all in the letters of Paul, the
rabbinically trained scholar-turned-missionary who found
himself impelled to a re-reading of the Jewish scriptures
already so familiar to him.

In fact, the whole dynamic interplay in the New Testament
between proclamation and fresh understanding is foreseen
and captured in Paul's first response in encounter with the
risen Jesus on the road to Damascus: 'Who are you, Lord?'
(Acts 9.3). How odd this statement is, combining a recognition
of the lordship of Jesus and the wish to understand it. It is the
inherent paradox of knowing yet confessing the need to know
more truly, which is the hallmark of the genuinely *apostolic*
faith. The dynamic is also of course fully displayed in the
Johannine writings. Jesus foretells that after his departure
from them the disciples will continue to be taught through the
Holy Spirit, who will both 'remind you of all that I have said to
you' (Jn. 14.26) and 'will guide you into all the truth' (Jn.
16.13), for not all that Jesus has to say to them can be conveyed
in the present. The emphasis on this education being the work
of the *Spirit*, the breath of God which blows where it wills,
means that the believing community can never rest content
with what it claims to possess in understanding. This is not to
deny the belief that there is a fundamental, irreplaceable
givenness which can never be contradicted, namely, that the
Son of God has come in human flesh and dealt with the sin of
the world (I Jn. 1.1–4; 4.2 etc.). But the community will
continually need to understand what this means in terms of
actual living, the way of love, and that way continually needs to
be taught afresh (I Jn. 4.7–12 etc.).

A church that claims to be faithful to that of the New
Testament will therefore have to be marked by a certain
humility, a continual readiness to be taught new things about

the gospel by which it is constituted and which it proclaims. There is, however, yet one further challenge in this direction which must be faced.

The definitive model: Jesus the incarnate learner

The model for the church of faithful discipleship is Jesus himself. 'Jesus is Lord' is the foundational confession of the baptized (I Cor. 12.3, Phil. 2.11 etc.). The Lord is one whose lordliness, paradoxically, is shown in his freedom for lowly servanthood (Mk. 10.45, Jn. 13.1–16), and who calls his disciples to follow his example of humble service. Servants are not greater than their master (Mt. 10.24f., Jn. 13.16) — but have the implications of this been faced in all its dimensions? Was Jesus himself exempted from the need to learn? Truly, he 'taught with authority, and not as the scribes' (Mk. 1.22), but how did he come by such authoritativeness? One answer would be to say that as Son of God (in whatever precise sense, whether as the incarnate Logos or as one uniquely anointed by the Spirit at his baptism) he simply spoke as the mouthpiece of immediately given divine truth. The New Testament witness as a whole, however, does not so unequivocally suggest that Jesus was able to by-pass the conditions of full humanity. According to Luke, the young Jesus *increased* in wisdom as in years (Lk. 2.52). The Letter to the Hebrews, which brooks no doubt at all as to the unique status of Jesus in relation to God (1.1–14), repeatedly states the case for Jesus being as humanly vulnerable as any of us — 'like his sisters and brothers in *every* respect' (2.17) — to the decisive point of being able to say: 'Although he was a Son, he *learned* obedience through what he suffered …' (5.8). It was through the learning of that obedience to the point of the cross that he became perfect and the source of eternal salvation to those who obey.

Such a provocative scriptural witness need not be confined to this isolated saying in the Letter to the Hebrews, which has often in any case been taken to be a reference to Jesus' agonized trial of decision in Gethsemane (Mk. 14.36) when it was finally confirmed to him that the only way in which the cup of suffering would pass from him would be by his drinking it to the lees. It is not completely hidden elsewhere in the gospel narratives either. Jesus is finally *persuaded* by the Syro-Phoenician woman that her daughter has a claim on his healing ministry (Mk. 7.24–30). Equally instructive is the Marcan account of Jesus' return to his hometown (Mk. 6.1–6), an occasion which might have been expected to have provided a *fortissimo* of success to cap the crescendo of spectacular achievements in the early part of his ministry. Met by a refusal to believe that the local boy could be endowed with any special gifts, his impact is minimal, and Mark (by comparison with Matthew's account) does not mince his words in describing this as failure: 'He could do no deed of power there' (v. 5). The next part of the narrative is highly significant. He simply 'goes about the villages teaching' (v. 6b) and then, in what is clearly a quite new phase of his strategy, calls the twelve and sends them out on mission in pairs. The implication is that Jesus has read the experience of failure at Nazareth as a further sign of the critical urgency of the situation of Israel in face of the coming kingdom, and the need for a change in his mission strategy. That kingdom has now to be proclaimed more widely than ever, and not only by himself. The disciples, too, are given instruction on how to meet with rejection (v. 11). Jesus was indeed learning obedience through his suffering, and his authority as teacher was being strengthened accordingly.

This is not the place for an essay on incarnational christology. To develop fully this understanding of Jesus' humanity in relation to the doctrine of his divine sonship would be an exercise in itself which cannot be embarked upon here. Suffice it to say that such a view of his educability, far from being incompatible with the concept of his divinity, can be seen to be deeply consonant with it. Throughout the Johannine account of Jesus as the mediator of his Father's glory runs the refrain that he is communicating to his hearers what he himself has received from his Father. Nothing could be more explicit in this regard than: 'I do nothing on my own, but I speak these things as the Father instructed me' (Jn. 8.28). That saying, significantly, occurs in the context of Jesus' reference to the cross — his being 'lifted up' — as the point where it will be truly manifest that he has come from the Father and is in a unique relation to him. Again, therefore, there is the link between his being taught and his suffering. To be truly God and truly human in this world required a wholly and truly educable life. Jesus is the truth because of his utter openness to it. To the point of the cross.

If therefore the embrace of humanity in its fullness was the prerequisite of a sufficient salvation — the 'unassumed is the unhealed' to quote the fourth-century father Gregory of Nazianzus — and if to be human includes the capacity and requirement to learn, then the christological implications are clear. And if the marks of the church stem from that christology — the servant not being greater than the master — then the implications are equally clear for the authentic style of Christian and ecclesiastical life. The one from whom the church draws its life through the Spirit, and who is the supreme exemplar for its behaviour, is one who himself embodied the humility of the true learner, above all through suffering, and only as such is he the true teacher. He teaches, as he reigns, *ab ligno* — from the tree.

The gospel: freedom and requirement to learn

In the light of the above, the scriptural statement becomes even more pointed: 'Not many of you should become teachers, my brothers and sisters, for you know that we who teach will be judged with greater strictness. For all of us make many mistakes' (Jas. 3.1f.). It is surely in line with the strict, individual reference of this injunction to see it also as a warning to the didactic church as a whole. If it would teach, the church must itself always first be a learner. It never graduates beyond discipleship. Least of all can the Pauline teaching that by faith we are brought into an entirely new relation with God, be used as a pretext that our education is at an end. Paul's powerful statement in his Letter to the Galatians puts it thus:

> Now before faith came, we were imprisoned and guarded under the law until faith would be revealed. Therefore the law was our disciplinarian until Christ came, so that we might be justified by faith. But now that faith has come, we are no longer subject to a disciplinarian, for in Christ

Jesus you are all children of God through faith. (Gal.
3.23–26)

The Greek word rendered here as 'disciplinarian' is *paidagogus*:
the slave who in a comfortable and well-ordered household in
the Roman empire had the responsibility of seeing the son of
the family to and from school, sitting beside him in class and
making sure he paid attention to his lessons. He was not
himself the teacher, but made sure that the parents were
getting their money's worth out of their child's education. In
effect, therefore, Paul is saying that prior to Christ and faith in
him, the religious law acts as a disciplinarian to get us to God's
school, but that once faith in Christ comes, that function is
obsolete. He is *not* saying that no further education is necessary,
that schooling as such is not needed. The implication is that
faith itself provides the motivation to learn further, and external
constraints should not be necessary. It is as if the child has
become so infected with enthusiasm for his lessons that he can
be perfectly relied upon to get himself to and from school and
use his time there sensibly. If Paul had thought that 'teaching'
as such was no longer needed, he would hardly have spent a
good deal of the latter parts of nearly all his letters expounding
the ethical applications of the gospel to daily living.

The church as learner: retrieval of an identity

This chapter is being written in the ancient Spanish city of
Santiago de Compostela, and within sound of the great bells of
the cathedral chiming the hours and quarters day and night.
In that cathedral, according to tradition, lie the remains of St
James the Apostle. Today, as for centuries past, under the hot
Galician sun, through the narrow, paved streets pilgrims are
approaching the shrine to pray for forgiveness and inner
renewal. It is a powerful statement of the strength of spiritual
tradition across the ages. But perhaps it is also a sign of the
ambiguity of the role which the institutional church has adopted,
and not only in its Roman Catholic form. The very size and
grandeur of the cathedral, its solid romanesque interior now
encased with even larger baroque facades and towers, portrays

a church which is fixed and set firm in immoveable, splendid authority. It does not itself move, rather, it is up its great entrance stairway that people climb. It invites pilgrims, but is not itself on pilgrimage.

'They were on the road, going up to Jerusalem, and Jesus was walking ahead of them; they were amazed, and those who followed were afraid' (Mk. 10.32). One of the most searching challenges which churches of all traditions face, is that of continually recovering their proper identity as disciples *in via*, on a continual pilgrimage of learning after Jesus Christ. Only those on such a road of humility can qualify for the office of teacher in any respect. We would naturally much rather short-circuit this route, and straightway be those in robes of authority, to occupy places of honour, to be greeted with respect in the marketplaces (that is, in the public media) and to have people call us 'rabbi'. 'But you are not to be called rabbi, for you have one teacher, and you are all students' (Mt. 23.8).

In the eleventh century Anselm, Archbishop of Canterbury, taking a cue from Augustine seven centuries earlier, described his method of theology as *fides quaerens intellectum*, faith seeking understanding.[6] Significantly, the great archbishop and intellectual genius uttered this phrase as part of the *prayer* which introduced his adventurous exercise of demonstrating the reality of God's existence — and still more significantly the whole of his argument is cast in the form of an address to God:

> I do not endeavour, O Lord, to penetrate thy sublimity, for in no wise do I compare my understanding with that; but I long to understand in some degree thy truth, which my heart believes and loves. For I do not seek to understand that I may believe, but I believe in order to understand. For this also I believe — that unless I believed, I should not understand.[7]

Here was one who knew that, his ecclesiastical position and academic ability notwithstanding, he was but a pupil. We do a flippant injustice to the greatest medieval schoolmen when we

[6]Anselm, Proslogion, Chap. II, *Basic Writings*, transl. S. N. Deane, Open Court, 1982, pp. 6f.
[7]Ibid.

dismiss their intellectual endeavours as arrogant human attempts to scale the heights of heaven. Thomas Aquinas, the greatest of them all, was deeply aware of the earth-bound nature of all human rationality, and had a profound sense that Christians, theologians included, are *viatorum*, pilgrims, wayfarers; that faith is not sight, and that full knowledge will come only with the final, beatific vision when we shall know as we are known.[8] But the passionate attempts of the best minds to *learn* have all too frequently been seized, claimed and solidified by a church anxious, in the interests of power, to assume a divinely-assured didactic position.

Part of the reason lies in the fact that the specific role of *teacher* in the church — the caution in the gospels about adopting the title 'rabbi' notwithstanding — has from very early times been recognized as a necessity and indeed, according to the Pauline letters, a gift of the Spirit (I Cor. 12.28, Eph. 4.11). Once such a role is established, it almost inevitably becomes allied with — if not actually identified with — a position of authority. Greater attention is then paid to the requirement of the other members of the community to be under the authority of the teacher, than the need of the teacher him- or herself to be *in statu pupillari*, a student, in relation to *the* authority which transcends all human positions and institutions, namely, God's own self as made known in the gospel. Once an authoritarian relation is established, it shapes the entire style of the church in relation to its own members and to the world. The church not only has teachers, but is itself essentially a teacher without any further need for learning.

The need to learn: Calvin and education

The pattern continually recurs in Christian history. The recognition that the Christian community requires instruction in the faith and in faithful living becomes structured so as to ensure that what is taught is already known in its completeness, fixed and final, and simply to be handed out. Much of the

---

[8]Cf. *Summa Theologica*, Q. 17, Art. 2, in *Nature and Grace*, Vol. XI of Library of Christian Classics, ed. A. M. Forrester, SCM Press, 1954, pp. 295f.

liveliest theology, however, past and present, has struggled against such a static, self-enclosed ecclesiasticism, on behalf of a dynamic understanding, ever open to the Holy Spirit who is the real educator of the community. The tension is well seen in John Calvin who took the education of the community extremely seriously. 'We see,' states Calvin, 'that God, who might perfect his people in a moment, chooses not to bring them to manhood in any other way than by the education of the Church'.[9] For that purpose, God has instituted the teaching office in the church, and it is a Christian duty to attend to the public deliverances of the teachers rather than rely on private meditation. The teachers however are not self-appointed, but ordained by the church, and it is not their own doctrine which they teach but that to which God has opened their ears. Nor are the teachers necessarily authoritarian, commanding figures in their own right. 'Those who think that the authority of the doctrine is impaired by the insignificance of the men who are called to teach, betray their ingratitude; for among the many noble endowments with which God has adorned the human race, one of the most remarkable is, that he deigns to consecrate the mouths and tongues of men to his service, making his own voice to be heard in them.'[10] Calvin clearly discerned that the authority of the teacher of true doctrine derives from the teacher in turn being under the authority of the word of God in the Holy Spirit,[11] not inventing new doctrines but mediating the original teaching of the apostles. For that reason he argues that no teacher, however august, can claim authority for himself as an individual. Every claim must be subject to a more corporate judgment within the community. Thus:

> In regard to individuals, Paul certainly had been appointed as an apostle to the Corinthians, and yet he declares that he has no dominion over their faith (II Cor. 1.24). Who will now presume to arrogate a dominion to which the

[9]J. Calvin, *Institutes of the Christian Religion*, Book IV, I. 6, in edition of H. Beveridge Vol. II, James Clarke, 1957, p. 284.
[10]Ibid., p. 285.
[11]Ibid., IV, 8.8., pp. 394f.

apostle declares that he himself was not competent? But if he had acknowledged such licence in teaching, that every pastor could justly demand implicit faith in whatever he delivered, he would never have laid it down as a rule to the Corinthians, that while two or three prophets spoke, the others should judge, and that, if anything was revealed to one sitting by, the first should be silent (I Cor. 14.29f.). Thus he spared none, but subjected the authority of all to the censure of the word of God.[12]

Calvin was contending against what he saw as the individualism of enthusiast piety, and, equally, the claims of the Roman Church in its corporate self to complete, perfect possession of the truth of God. In face of both, he argued for a truly *communal* sharing of divine knowledge under the aegis of the Spirit who measures diverse gifts to each of the members, for the common advantage of all. But even this is qualified by Calvin: 'The riches of the Church ... are always of such a nature, that much is wanting to that supreme perfection of which our opponents [i.e. The Roman Catholics] boast. Still the Church is not left destitute in any part, but always has as much as is sufficient, for the Lord knows what her necessities require. But to keep her in humility and pious modesty, he bestows no more on her than he knows to be expedient.'[13]

That Calvin should have been the exponent of such a circumscribed understanding of Christian teaching — or, put more positively, of teaching as itself subject to authority — will doubtless surprise many who equate his name with sheer dogmatism and authoritarianism. Calvin himself, however, would have been surprised, if not aghast, at many of the forms that 'Calvinism' in due course assumed. The checks and balances which he had envisaged to keep teachers in their place, and to keep the teaching itself continually subject to the living word of God in its freshness and vitality, largely went by the board. A new scholasticism emerged, Protestant by name but as rigid and authoritarian as anything against which the

[12]Ibid., IV, 8.9, p. 395.
[13]Ibid., IV, 8.12, p. 397.

first reformers had inveighed. To quote Edwin Muir on the highland kirk:

> The Word made flesh is here made word again,
> A word made word in flourish and arrogant crook.
> See there King Calvin with his iron pen,
> And God three angry letters in a book,
> And there the logical hook
> On which the Mystery is impaled and bent
> Into an ideological instrument.[14]

A source of this inherent trend towards authoritarianism, is the way in which the relation of teacher to the community is seen as essentially one-way. God speaks to the teacher, the teacher speaks to the rest. The teacher's views may have to be checked against the judgments of other teachers. But the possibility that the Spirit may also be speaking to the rest of the community in a variety of ways is hardly considered, although it is clearly attested in the New Testament (cf. I Cor. 12.4–11 etc.). According to the gospels, the first definitive message, foundational to everything in the church, was announced not by, but to, the apostles: 'The Lord is risen!' And announced by women. Hence the description of Mary Magdalene as *apostola apostolorum*, apostle to the apostles. Those who would teach have therefore a prior calling to listen with discernment to what is being experienced and expressed in the believing community as a whole. This does not mean that teaching means simply being an amplifier for the community and reflecting back to the members their views (though that is often what congregations, consciously or otherwise, want from pastors). There has to be discernment of spirits (I Jn. 4.1). It does mean, however, that the wider experience, insights and committed activity of the whole people of God is a primary source of raw material for teaching, and therefore to be listened to with the utmost attentiveness. In this respect too, teachers have to be learners, and to embody the proper style of the whole church being a student.

---

[14]'The Incarnate One', *Penguin Book of Religious Verse* (ed. R. S. Thomas), Penguin, 1963, p. 55.

Learning by all: Karl Barth and the hearing church

If Calvin is a surprising choice for taking us part way in this direction, then equally the name of Karl Barth may at first be thought to be scarcely associated with promoting humility on the part of the church as a whole and teachers within it, and taking us further along that road. Both the title and the sheer length of Barth's *Church Dogmatics*, volume after volume of massive tomes produced over a thirty-year period of teaching (and even then unfinished), seem to typify all that is most forbidding about theology occupying the lecture podium, and talking, talking, talking. Before coming to the main point in refutation of this notion some preliminary remarks are in order. First, Barth did not begin his *Church Dogmatics* until he himself had been shaken through a series of turbulent upheavals of re-learning in his own experience and understanding. As a young pastor in Switzerland he had found his liberal theological education quite inadequate to equip him as pastor and preacher when the abyss of war and revolution opened up beneath European 'civilization' in 1914–18. In a world gone mad, he turned from preaching the innate human potentialities of religion and culture to the God who rejects the world in judgment, especially the pretentious religious world, yet who creates his utterly new world in the cross and resurrection of Jesus Christ. Second, during the 1920s and early 1930s as a professor in Germany, Barth repeatedly struggled to find a new way of expounding Christian belief to replace the old liberal optimism which he had demolished — theology cannot remain in negativities. He was never afraid to admit how hard he found this task. At least once, having laboured till the small hours, he had to cancel the next morning's lecture having come to the conclusion that what he had written was nonsense.[15] And he fully admitted that his initial attempt at a new exposition of doctrine, the *Christian Dogmatics* of 1928,[16] was a 'false start'. Significantly, it was through Anselm and his 'faith seeking

[15]E. Busch, *Karl Barth. His life from letters and autobiographical texts*, SCM Press, 1975, Chap. 4.

[16]*Prolegomena zur Christlichen Dogmatik. Die Lehre vom Worte Gottes*, Christian Kaiser Verlag, 1928.

understanding' that he was able eventually to feel on secure ground. Third, in the long course of the *Church Dogmatics* Barth had no inhibitions about changing his mind on important points and taking seriously the critical comments of others. His theology was indeed a theology *in via*.[17] That of course did not mean a trimming of his sails to whatever wind was blowing, rather, in addition to an awareness of his own fallibility, a recognition that particular historical contexts in turn require the emphasis to be put now here, now there. He never doubted that during the First World War he had been right to protest against the impotence of liberal theology to criticize the social system that had bred war, not to mention the war itself; still less, that in 1934 everything in Christianity stood or fell on the ability of the German church to speak — greatly influenced by himself — as it did at Barmen.

Fourth, we need to bear in mind the testimony of many of those who as young theologians went to study 'under' Barth — and were taken aback to find themselves invited to study *with* him. One such, Thomas F. Torrance, gave this contemporary account:

> Barth has an uncanny ability to listen which is accompanied by an astonishing humility and childlikeness in which he is always ready to learn. That is what overwhelms the student as he enters the great man's study for the first time. He goes in fear and propounds his questions with trembling, but soon finds that the Professor has turned the tables on him, and is asking him questions, drawing him out and listening to him as if he were the disciple and the student were the teacher. Few men are really able to listen like that, and fewer still are able to maintain a genuine listening attitude while posing such searching questions...[18]

Finally, there is the fact that for Barth true theology is marked not by grim aggressiveness or defensiveness, but *joy*, the joy of

---

[17]Cf. K. Barth, *How My Mind Has Changed*, St Andrew Press, 1969.
[18]T. F. Torrance, *Karl Barth: An Introduction to his Early Theology 1910–1931*, SCM Press, 1962, p. 21.

continually being amazed at the wonder of God's grace, a joy which for him was mirrored above all in the effortless beauty of the music of Mozart, the composer who does not force his self-expression on to us but simply conveys the music of creation as he has heard it.

For our immediate purposes however, Barth's most substantial contribution to an understanding of the church as a learning body is what he actually says about the way the revelation of God's truth is mediated to, in, and through the Christian community. First, it must be understood that by 'dogmatics' Barth does not mean formulae which have to be promulgated 'dogmatically' in our popular current sense of 'dogmatic', but, in accordance with the literal meaning of 'dogma', simply that which is to be taught. It is that thinking by which the church's preaching and witness (including its actions) are to be tested to see if they are truly in accord with the gospel. Next, basic to his understanding is that God's self-revelation really is the revelation of Godself, the act of his self-disclosure, and therefore not primarily a text whether of scripture or creed, but an event impacting upon human existence. 'Pure doctrine is an event.'[19] It was failure to maintain this insight, he holds, which led post-Reformation Protestants into a rigid dogmatism of fixed doctrinal formulae (as we might say, with contemporary fundamentalism also). The true teaching is the event of the grace of the word of God and of the obedience of faith created by this grace, in the dynamic vitality of the Holy Spirit. From the human side, doctrine is therefore always a task remaining before us. 'All the conclusions of dogmatics must be intended, accepted and understood as fluid material for further work.'[20] Barth goes on to emphasize that this requires that the first task of dogmatics, or Christian teaching, is to *listen*, critically, to what the church is saying in the whole scope of its activities[21] in the light of the word of God.

[19]K. Barth, *Church Dogmatics Vol. I, The Doctrine of the Word of God, Part 2*, T&T Clark, 1956, p. 768.
    [20]Ibid., p. 769.
    [21]Ibid., p. 775.

So far, Barth's exposition as a Reformed theologian is essentially along the lines of Calvin himself, though with a greater and more dynamic sense than had Calvin of the need for constant re-examination of the forms which Christian witness has acquired. Doctrine is not just the repetition of texts. But Barth advances in a still more radical direction in his chapter entitled 'Dogmatics as a Function of the *Hearing Church*' (emphasis mine), under the introductory rubric: 'Dogmatics invites the teaching Church to listen again to the Word of God in the revelation to which Scripture testifies. It can do this only if for its part it adopts the attitude of the hearing Church and therefore itself listens to the Word of God as the norm to which the hearing Church knows itself to be subject.'[22] Crucial here is Barth's emphasis that it is *the whole church* which has to listen, not just one class of members who have to listen to another class designated as 'teachers'. He draws attention to the distinction in Roman Catholic vocabulary between the teaching Church, *ecclesia docens*, and the hearing church, *ecclesia audiens*, but argues that the order should be reversed. The church is first and foremost a hearing church, and only then and as such a teaching church. Second, he criticizes what he sees as the traditional application of this distinction to two mutually exclusive classes of people: the ecclesiastical teaching office and the laity. Rather, in the totality of its members the church is both hearing and teaching, in a common responsibility and participation. The challenge is for the whole teaching church to be again a hearing church before attempting to teach, 'and the esoterics, theologians or office-bearers will ill understand their technical functions if they, of all people, try to elude this challenge'.[23] Theologians cannot teach except as the mouthpiece of the congregation of Jesus Christ 'which does not in any sense consist of listeners only, but of those who, as listeners, are themselves teachers'.[24]

[22]Ibid., p. 797.
[23]Ibid., p. 798.
[24]Ibid.

The church therefore, according to Barth, must 'seize the weapon of continually listening',[25] and in such a way that its whole life is put in question, in readiness for a convulsive revolution and reshaping of that life. This listening is not an openness to novelty for its own sake, but to its original starting point in the word of God. 'It takes place as the church which teaches Jesus Christ turns from teaching to hearing him.'[26] Barth recognizes only too well the pull of human loyalties, whether those loyalties are to time-honoured, traditional formulae and expressions or to new movements generating enthusiasms especially among the young. But in face of all such, the church must continually be pulled up short and questioned incisively, in order that 'Jesus Christ should again be heard in his church as the Lord of the church'.[27]

Barth takes us powerfully and further in the direction of the primacy of hearing and learning over that of teaching, and thus along the road of the community of discipleship in which all members are equals, or, more accurately, servants of one another (Mk. 10.43f.). His insights have yet to make their full and revolutionary impact upon the congregational life even of the Protestant churches which might have been expected to have been most receptive to them. His critique of the fatal distinction between a teaching office and a listening laity, it should be noted, was directed against all churches and not just the Roman Catholic communion in which the distinction was most explicitly articulated in technical language; though perhaps the Orthodox tradition, in which some of the most important teachers are recognized to be not the hierarchical clergy but the humblest monks, might have some pertinent comments to offer here. Of all Christian communities, it seems to be the Quakers who establish most firmly the identity of discipleship with learning, in the invitation given to each new member of the Society of Friends to become 'a humble learner in the school of Christ'.

[25]Ibid.
[26]Ibid.
[27]Ibid.

But while Barth takes us a long way, there is still much ground to be covered if the primacy of hearing and learning in the church is to be secured. Is it only to a listening to each other and the scriptural tradition that Christians are called in discernment of the word of the one Lord of the church? Mutual encounter between church members forms only one slice of Christian experience, and often only a small portion of the whole at that. The church is set in the world, and Christians live their lives as part of that world, the world of daily experience, of personal and public concerns, of work and leisure, political and economic pressures, scientific and technological developments, cultural creativity, national and international conflict, and struggles over human and moral values. In relation to this world, does — or can — the church only teach? Often enough that is the impression given. But that is to overlook the biblical witness that God is the Lord of all creation and all history, and that faith involves reading 'the signs of the times', from the prophets who saw in the world upheavals of their days the stirrings of divine judgment and eventual hope, to John of the Apocalypse who dared to look at, into and beyond Rome's imperial aggrandisement to the victory of the Lamb.

The church listening to the world: the Second Vatican Council

From the 1960s onwards the slogan 'Let the world write the agenda' was popularized among the churches, especially in ecumenical circles. It meant that issues such as racism, militarism, unjust economic structures and human rights were to become the priorities for Christian mission and obedience. Given powerful impetus by the Fourth Assembly of the World Council of Churches at Uppsala in 1968, it was an absolutely necessary and healthy call for 'conversion' of the church to the world, and it remains so. Left to itself, however, the slogan was too slick. It implied that if the world would write the agenda, the church could and would supply the answers.

In fact, in the matter of calling the church to take the contemporary world seriously, as far as statements of an official nature are concerned none are more thoughtfully framed than certain of the documents from the Second Vatican Council. That on the Pastoral Constitution of the Church in the Modern World, *Gaudium et Spes*, issued in December 1965[28] begins with an impressive statement of the solidarity of the church with the joy and hope, grief and anguish, of the whole human family at the present time. This is the context for the church's understanding of its task: 'At all times the church carries the responsibility of reading the signs of the time and of interpreting them in the light of the gospel, if it is to carry out its task. In language intelligible to every generation, she should be able to answer the ever recurring questions which men ask about the meaning of this present life and of the life to come, and how one is related to the other. We must be aware of and understand the aspirations, the yearnings, and the often dramatic features of the world in which we live.'[29] But if there are 'answers', the document is aware that there are no ready-made ones, no short-cuts to providing them:

> The people of God believes that it is led by the Spirit of the Lord who fills the whole world. Moved by that faith it tries to discern in the events, the needs, and the longings which it shares with other men of our time, what may be genuine signs of the presence or of the purpose of God. For faith throws a new light on all things and makes known the full ideal which God has set for man, thus guiding the mind towards solutions that are fully human.[30]

The implication of a necessary humility on the part of the church is fully drawn out still later, in the recognition that the church has much to receive from the modern world, just as it has been enriched by past ages. Most striking of all is the sentence:

> With the help of the Holy Spirit, it is the task of *the whole people of God, particularly of its pastors and theologians, to listen to* and distinguish the many voices of our times and to

[28]A. Flannery, ed., *Vatican Council II. The Conciliar and Post-Conciliar Documents, Vol. I*, Fowler Wright, 1980, pp. 903ff.
[29]Ibid., p. 905.
[30]Ibid., p. 912.

interpret them in the light of the divine Word, in order that *the revealed truth may be more deeply penetrated, better understood,* and more suitably presented.[31]

That is indeed a charter for a new kind of church, oriented to a servanthood of learning, a missionary discipleship in the fullest sense. The same spirit is breathed by the post-conciliar document *Religious and Human Advancement* of 1981,[32] calling for the traditional contemplative approach of the religious life to embrace secular matters within its purview, a caution against members of religious orders entering into political life notwithstanding. 'The story of the contemporary world, given flesh in the lives of men and women, becomes a book open for intense meditation by the Church and all its members, urging them to a radical renewal of life and of commitment.'[33]

To many within and outside Roman Catholic circles, much of the renewal promised by Vatican II seems to have been obstructed in a resurgent conservatism. Part of the reason may lie within some of the Council's statements themselves. The Dogmatic Constitution on Divine Revelation, *Verbum Dei,* issued in November 1965,[34] is a superb exposition of revelation as a continuing activity of the Holy Spirit in the church, in which the church continually has its ears opened to scripture and tradition in encounter with new situations. But an unassailable place is still carefully reserved for the *magisterium,* the teaching office of the church. Authentic interpretation of the word of God is entrusted to the *magisterium* alone,[35] under whose 'watchful eye' all study of the sacred texts is to take place.[36] In this respect, they may well be right who argue that Vatican II effectively consolidated the role of an established élite, however much liberalization may have been encouraged at other levels in the church. But the debate has gone on. Hans Küng in his

[31]Ibid., p. 946 (emphasis mine).
[32]Flannery, op. cit., pp. 260ff.
[33]Ibid., pp. 271f.
[34]Flannery, op. cit., pp. 750ff.
[35]Ibid., p. 755.
[36]Ibid., p. 763.

well-known critique of the doctrine of infallibility[37] argues that the very notion of a 'teaching office' in the church is comparatively modern. In a manner closely parallel to Barth's criticism of the distinction between the teaching and the listening church, Küng rejects the assumption of a distinction between *ecclesia docens* and *ecclesia discens*, which the church taught[38] — a distinction which was only introduced late in the seventeenth century, and became frequently used only after the beginning of the nineteenth century. The term *magisterium* itself, in its modern ecclesiastical technical sense, became habitual in the debates and documents of the First Vatican Council of 1870, in which the doctrine of papal infallibility was finally decreed. And like Barth, Küng calls for a genuinely communal understanding of Christian teaching. Still more recently E. Schillebeeckx has called for a democratic, non-hierarchical understanding of the church, in which 'speaking with authority' is partner with 'letting oneself be told', in a church which in its totality is subjected to the word of God.[39] Furthermore, according to Schillebeeckx, the proper understanding even of the saving lordship of Christ 'can only be understood in the totality of human history'.[40] It is surely also significant that such a creative Roman Catholic writer as Avery Dulles, in the most recent edition of his book *Models of the Church*[41] has added an entirely new final chapter on the church as 'A Community of Disciples'. In doing so he has picked up a passing comment of Pope John Paul II himself in his encyclical *Redemptor Hominis* of 1979, a description which has in fact also been welcomed in a number of subsequent episcopal statements.

The learning church: a paradigm of humility

We are therefore at a point in history where a decisive struggle is taking place for a new paradigm of self-understanding of the

[37]H. Küng, *Infallible?*, Collins, 1971.
[38]Ibid., p. 182.
[39]E. Schillebeeckx, *The Church. The Human Story of God*, SCM Press, 1990, pp. 214ff.
[40]Ibid., pp. 224.
[41]A. Dulles, *Models of the Church*, 2nd ed., Gill and Macmillan, 1988.

church, in both in its inner relations and its relation to the
larger human community, and indeed to the whole created
order. Teaching must be presupposed on the priority of
learning, including learning from those whom the teaching
would address, and from this requirement neither any
individual, nor any group within the church, nor the whole
community of the church, is exempt, 'for you are all students'.
It is the paradigm of discipleship — not just for individuals but
for the whole church, learning to act and learning from acting,
learning to serve and learning from those whom it seeks to
serve. As the deacon Isobel puts it in Joanna Trollope's *The
Rector's Wife*: 'You could not just say, Christ will help you bear
it. That was opting out. you had to show that you understood
the suffering, knew the price it exacted, as a fellow human
being, before you even thought of bringing Christ into it.'[42] To
repeat, this struggle is facing all churches, not just the Roman
Catholic. A *magisterium* of assumed authority is found in a
number of guises, not just in the papal curia. It is found
whenever a person or group mounts the podium saying, in
effect, 'We know what you need to know'. It is the stance of
assumed expertise. Ecumenical bodies as well as individual
churches need to beware of it, especially since, as was indicated
in an earlier chapter,[43] a hidden agenda of all such groups is
often that of wishing to demonstrate their relevance in a
secularized culture by being able to provide 'solutions' to
'problems'. At a recent gathering of British church
representatives in the field of social responsibility, called
together to consider Christian perspectives on the future of
the European Community, a proposal was urged that a special
working group be convened to formulate recommendations
on policies affecting workers' rights, migrants, minorities and
so forth. The result would be a paper which would then be put
to the government as 'the churches' point of view', in the
traditional didactic mode. A rather different strategy, however,
was also suggested. Why not seek to engage with the decision-
makers from the beginning of the process, which would then

[42]J. Trollope, *The Rector's Wife*, Black Swan, 1992, p. 88.
[43]See above p. 68.

be one of continuous critical dialogue? Why not be prepared
to admit at the start that we have much to learn from those
grappling at first-hand with the issues? That would at least help
us to discover the really crucial points which have to be
addressed and where pressure needs to be applied. This is not
to deny that there are occasions when the churches will be
called to take the initiative in speaking out on fundamental
moral priorities which they believe are being clearly violated in
the public sphere. The appropriate strategy to adopt is a matter
of discernment, of faithful discipleship, in each particular
instance, and to this we shall return in a later chapter.

In fact 'ecumenical learning' for a time did become
something of a vogue concept following the 1968 WCC Assembly
and, as Konrad Raiser points out, witnessed to the ideal that the
whole ecumenical movement should be considered as a
continual learning experience.[44] The vision was that of enabling
individuals and groups to learn responsibility through
encounters across cultural barriers, experience of conflict-
situations, and committed actions, so enabling awareness of
the wider human community. It was, especially, geared as
learning for empowerment to action. The trouble is, as Raiser
points out, that such projects tend to become programmes run
by pedagogic specialists, and, however well-intentioned, unless
there is real participation by those who are to be 'educated', it
'atrophies into transmission of information and knowledge
unrelated to people's own experiences'.[45] The concept of
'[t]he church as a learning community' by itself leaves
unanswered the question of who actually controls this learning,
and in whose interests it actually takes place. Or, as I would
phrase it myself, another *magisterium* of expertise arises, those
who presume to know best what people need to know, and
serving the interests of a particular power-structure.

For the moment, I would not wish to desert the notion of a
'learning community' without pursuing some biblical
reflections further. The willingness and readiness to learn
continually is not just a preliminary to witness, but an integral

---

[44]K. Raiser, *Ecumenism in Transition*, WCC, 1991, p. 21.
[45]Ibid., p. 23.

part of it. It is a sign that the lordship of Christ is being acknowledged, just as the picture of the disciples coming to Jesus on the mountain to hear his teaching (Mt. 5.1f.) is a sign that something quite new is on the way. The reign of God is breaking in, and space is being made for it by those who at least have ears to hear. The openness to learn what is new challenges and subverts the present order which is closed in upon itself with its conventions, power-structures and apparent inevitabilities. It puts a question-mark against the world (and the church) as it is, having seen the exclamation-mark of the kingdom, the alternative history of God and the new possibilities it brings. That strangeness of God's history, with its surprising direction, is the primary subject which the disciples are to learn and then be witnesses of before others. They are fundamentally eschatological students, learners of the *end* of all history which is the will of the Father, made known in Jesus and being anticipated even now in the power of the Spirit. If they are called to learn *that*, as followers of one who learned obedience by what he suffered and took the costly path of the cross in order that it might be learnt by all, they will not think themselves above being students in all things, and from all people.

Whatever is happening in the world and in human experience cannot in itself be read as a straightforward manifestation of God's kingdom. Catastrophic errors can be, and have been, made by Christians who see interesting and exciting developments in human affairs simply as messianic signs, 'Lo here!', 'Lo there!' (cf. Mt. 24.23), as with the Germans who saw the apparent renewal of their national life under the advent of Hitler as God's great intervention.[46] Until the last day, the world remains an ambiguous field of wheat and tares growing together. But it is God's field, under the ultimate lordship of Christ. On the other hand, neither can that ultimate lordship be used as a superior piece of wisdom on the part of the church to impose a particular ideology on the world in triumphalistic fashion. As Konrad Raiser has argued,[47] the intensely christocentric language which was the main theological

[46]See above, p. 26f.
[47]Raiser, op. cit., pp. 41–53.

vocabulary of ecumenical circles during the 1950s and 1960s, while it was important in giving an ultimate frame of reference for dealing with world affairs in the immediate post-war world of competing super-powers, also encouraged a certain monistic attitude. It was embodied in a single version of history, whether that of the world-wide triumph of the Christian west, or the universal spread of secularization seen as the final phase of biblically-inspired liberalization of all human institutions from false sacrality. Such single, all-embracing 'solutions' to the riddle of history have proved untenable in face of the collapsing framework of post-Enlightenment assumptions about universal norms and values. We are now in a world of highly competitive values and aspirations, resurgent nationalisms, passionately revived religious loyalties and real fears for the sustainability of the planet. Wheat and tares seem to be not only growing together, but to be hybridized in all kinds of confusing forms.

Christians indeed confess that in Christ, in the fullness of time, all things will be gathered up (Eph. 1.10); that he is the first-born of all creation, in whom and for whom all things and all powers have been created, and in whom all things hold together (Col. 1.15–17); that he is the one worthy to unravel the scroll inscribed with the mystery of human destiny (Rev. 5.1–5). But the *way* to apprehending these great claims cannot be by a direct trip to heaven. The fundamental New Testament confession is not simply the lordship of Christ, but the identity of the risen Lord with the crucified one, and therefore the confession of the ultimate lordship must continually take the road of the cross in this world.

There is therefore no route to understanding and effective responsibility except that of discipleship, ever humble, ready to listen and learn, even if this proves costly and brings suffering. There is great merit in the Catholic tradition which commends Mary, the mother of Jesus, as the supreme disciple in that 'she treasured all these words and pondered them in her heart' (Lk. 2.19). We might add, that she was also the first to be told that her son would suffer rejection and that a sword would pierce her own heart (Lk. 4.34f.). For his part, Jesus introduced to his disciples one model above all, of humility, openness and sheer receptivity to the kingdom, and sat him or her on his knee: the child (Mk 9.37f., cf. 10.13–16). This is not a pretext for sentimentality, but a witness that discipleship is a matter of continual openness to what is yet to be known, a readiness to re-learn to the point of *metanoia*, repentance. It is therefore appropriate to conclude this chapter, as we began, with a reference to Dietrich Bonhoeffer, who found in his imprisonment the opportunity to reflect profoundly on the simple yet most searching question, 'Who is Jesus Christ, for us today?' It is no accident that he too returned to the role-model of the child for a church which needs to begin all over again in its understanding of the gospel with meaning for the contemporary world. As noted in Chapter 3, it was precisely on the occasion of his godson's baptism that he described the situation of the church of the day as being like that of the child over whom the great words of the Christian tradition are pronounced — before he can begin to understand them.[48] They, like the modern world itself, are new and strange to us. Being prepared to admit this, rather than pretend to an authority and expertise we do not have, is in fact where new life and real hope begin.

[48]Bonhoeffer, *Letters and Papers from Prison*, pp. 299f.

6

What the Church Does Know

Nothing of what has been said in previous chapters is intended to countermand the Christian community's vocation to be a 'voice' for justice and peace in the contemporary world. It is precisely because that calling is so important a matter, and in order to safeguard its seriousness, that we have placed a number of qualifications against the notion of 'the church speaking out'. The truly prophetic church, the church faithful in discipleship, is not interested in speaking for its own sake — especially if speaking is a substitute for action — nor in speaking for the sake of publicity, nor for gaining a reputation for instant 'problem-solving'. Prophecy is not didacticism, whether conservative or radical, stuffily pious or trendily secular. It speaks in the political context, as at Barmen, by insisting on clearing a genuinely theological space amid the political pressures of the time, and so calling into question the worldly forces and assumptions of the hour. It speaks, as in the *Kairos Document*, less by providing answers than by asking even more difficult questions than have yet been posed. It does not therefore simply add to the self-advertising, self-justifying chatter of the market-place, nor add to the plethora of cut-price 'solutions' on offer for the world's 'problems'. Rather, it offers a vision, a fresh conceptual framework, within which those questions can be viewed. It speaks when it really does have something to say as the church before God. The prophetic church is one which lets itself be taught to discern God's alternative history in and for the world. It is as the church of discipleship, the continually learning church, learning to act and learning from acting, attending to the coming kingdom, that it speaks with integrity.

It has to be admitted that, taken in isolation, this emphasis on the primacy of the learning or hearing church over the teaching or speaking church might become a pretext for evading any concrete declaration on a contemporary social issue. In 1932, in the midst of the ecumenical peace-movement, Dietrich Bonhoeffer declared that:

> The word of the church to the world must ... encounter the world in all its present reality from the deepest knowledge of the world, if it is to be authoritative. The church must be able to say the Word of God, the word of authority, here and now, in the most concrete way possible, from knowledge of the situation.[1]

'From knowledge of the situation': but how do we know when we know enough to speak? In principle it might be said in any situation, and for ever, 'We're still learning. When we know a bit more, we shall issue a statement.' This, however, is to set *knowing* and *learning* over against each other as completely antithetical. In fact one can know enough on a particular issue to be able to speak responsibly, without claiming to know everything. One can still speak while admitting one is still learning. It can almost become a cliché to say that the more one knows about a situation the more one realizes how much is still to be learnt, but it does frequently correspond with the case.

If the church is to speak 'from the deepest knowledge of the world', it must be asked what particular 'knowledge' the church can claim to have, or rather, to be learning. In fact it is vital that the church should recognize that it does have a certain knowledge of how things are in the world, and not let that knowledge be ignored or undervalued. To learn, it has been said since Socrates, requires an admission of ignorance. But if we were *totally* ignorant we would never be able to learn anything. Learning requires an *inquisitive* kind of ignorance, a curiosity born out of what we do know already and yet which puzzles us and draws us on to know more. Moreover, that

[1] D. Bonhoeffer, *No Rusty Swords*, Collins, 1965, pp. 162f.

motivation is likely to be increased once we realize that we do in fact know more than we at first realize. The resources have been there, but hitherto not recognized and interpreted as such.

To be educated requires a certain degree of confidence in what one knows already, as the basis on which more can be built. To be told simply that one has to be 'educated' can be demoralizing and de-skilling. The church must not allow itself to be so demoralized and de-skilled in face of the world that it is made to feel incapable of learning. Educationists (not least when dealing with adults) can at times be forbidding people, so concerned to tell people that they need to 'develop' that they unwittingly send signals to their pupils that they are *unable* to develop. Such a complete demolition job is done on what they thought they knew, confidence is so shattered, that there is no foundation left on which to rebuild. The most effective teaching is that which gives people the feeling that they do already have something to contribute to their own development, that they already have resources which need unlocking, that they already know important things without realizing it. What they have and are can be looked at and valued in a new way. Once that happens, learning really takes off.

I well remember once taking a class of Baptist ordinands in practical theology. The subject was the minister as educator, and we began by tabling the various ways in which they expected to 'teach' their congregations: through preaching, bible studies, house-groups, training courses for church membership, special programmes for training in particular tasks like counselling or evangelism, and so forth. There were no surprises. It was the standard menu on offer among local churches in suburban Britain today. Then I put a rather different kind of question to the group: 'Can you think of experiences in your own lives when you really learned something important for your spiritual development, when you really came to understand something new about yourself, or other people, or the world in general — or God?' It needed only a minute or two's quiet reflection before the answers tumbled out, as varied as the students themselves. About the only thing the answers had in common, was that hardly any of them referred to sermons they had heard, or bible studies they had attended, or anything else organized for their 'education' in the church, or which, evidently, they intended providing for their own congregations in due course. 'It was watching the birth of our first baby.' 'It was when I was in the army and came under sniper fire.' 'It was when with other women in our village I started a support scheme for Vietnamese refugees.' 'It was when I went to work in an inner-city night refuge and really saw poverty for the first time.' Moments such as these were their truly 'educative' experiences. Yet — and here they were only typical of their background — they had not really thought of them as educational, nor of what implications might be drawn from them for their own future 'teaching' work in the church. But of course the implications were immense, and it was from that point that the way was open for the class to explore just what we mean by 'education', how people actually learn, what is the true significance of such activities as preaching and bible studies in relation to that learning process — and in a much more creative way than simply presenting a shopping list of 'goals and methods' would have done. One hopes that they were on the way to becoming better teachers because they were now more aware of themselves as learners, and were now alerted to becoming better learners because they had discovered that they did in fact know more about education than they had realized. What had simply been floating around as an odd collection of memories had been retrieved and identified as crucial, instructive growth-points for their own and others' formation. Confidence and curiosity, one hopes, had both been quickened. After all, that is what evidently happened with Jesus' use of parables, whereby he appealed to what people already knew and experienced, and invited them to see a new significance in it: 'Which of you, having a hundred sheep ...?', 'If you then, evil as you are, know how to give good gifts to your children, how much more ...'.

To advocate that the church's basic role is that of a learning community is not therefore derogatory, a demand for a perpetual inferiority complex in face of the world. To be a learner is not to deny that one already has knowledge of real substance and significance. It is, rather, to value properly that knowledge and awareness as providing the basis for yet further discovery. It is therefore vital that the church should retrieve and properly value the knowledge which it does have, of 'what is going on in the world'. It may not know everything, or even as much as it would sometimes like to claim, but what it does know is of real significance.

The church's knowledge of the world: basic structure

It was a bitterly cold November day in 1978. In the Marienkirche in East Berlin (as it then was) the heating system had broken down, and the large congregation huddled together in the pews to try to reduce the chill. The Cold War was, in every sense, all too evident. The preacher, basing his sermon on the Book of Daniel, posed the question, 'Who are the really powerful people in history?' The truly powerful, he declared, are not those with scientific, technological or military might at their disposal, but those who, like Daniel, can interpret the vision. Exiled, captive among aliens, one of a people who humanly speaking had no future, Daniel nevertheless proved more powerful than the mighty Nebuchadnezzars and Belshazzars because he could read the signs, the writing on the wall of history. To such as him, the future belonged. This was a sermon whose import was clear from start to finish. It needed no concrete 'application'. That was provided by the very context in which it was preached, only a minute or so's walk from the Soviet Embassy, and under the shadow of the mighty television tower dwarfing the Marienkirche, built to symbolize the prowess of the socialist regime. It was a sermon of hope, neither an other-worldly hope nor a triumphalistic secular optimism, but a hope which had taken on board all the facts of present-day life, bleak as they were, and saw God's alternative history in their midst, inviting faith in a different future. At the time, to many no doubt it would have sounded naive. The Soviet empire and the socialist system seemed there to stay. A few days after that service, I found myself on a train between Erfurt and Wittenberg. I got into conversation with the lady sitting opposite me. Soon she had discovered that I was an English Protestant minister, and I had found out that she worked for the Herrnhuter missionary community. Rarely have I learnt so much from anyone in half-an-hour. On the other side of the coach sat a huge Red Army officer, staring straight ahead, hands clasping his briefcase, evidently oblivious of the animated dialogue being whispered just feet away from him — and which concerned him and his future more than he knew.

On my return home, I felt moved to reflect further on that Marienkirche sermon and the other experiences of the visit, and especially on the way in which the East German regime was attempting to re-shape German cultural and religious history, from both the distant and more recent past, to suit its ideological interests. These reflections eventually took shape in a BBC radio talk, 'What Luther Says to Marx'[2] in which I suggested that a major problem for the communist regime was that there was simply *so much* history to be re-interpreted, so many sites of rich cultural and religious significance in East Germany to be 'explained', that eventually in fact it would be Luther, not Marx, who would probably have the last word. The broadcast received severe criticism from certain quarters on account of its 'naivety'. How could the historic buildings of Wittenberg and Eisenach outface the power of Soviet-imposed Marxist-Leninism? How could a church marginal to the power-structures of such a society be viewed as offering any alternative future to the regime?

Now that the Cold War and the Berlin Wall itself are part of history, it is of course tempting to say, 'I told you so'. Luther is indeed once again having more say than Marx. But in retrospect I find it more instructive to ponder the kind of 'knowledge' claimed by those of us who perceived hope for Eastern Europe and its churches, however cautiously, when politically it was still deep in winter. Such 'knowing' comprised at least two elements: what can broadly be called factual information, and the perspective of faith.

The information gleaned by those who were able to travel to the eastern bloc countries, as distinct from those dependent solely on western media and propaganda, was based not only

[2]Published in *The Listener,* June 21, 1979.

on what government representatives were saying officially, but on observations of how people were actually behaving, and on what many people were able to tell us in private. The picture that emerged was not quite that of a totally inhumane, absolutist tyranny of utter darkness, and equally it was different from the rather rosy picture of a successful welfare society producing fulfilment and happiness for all its members, which the government itself and its apologists abroad attempted to promote. The actual picture was of a system which, for many years at least, achieved a significant degree of economic progress and welfare provision, which was undoubtedly repressive, and often cruelly so, but which had far less of a secure hold on controlling the loyalties of its citizens than was often supposed (either by itself or its enemies). The insecurity came out in many ways, from the overly self-justifying tone in which government representatives would talk, to their admission that their people enjoyed tuning into western television stations far more than watching the state television. It came out in the many confessions people were even then making that to survive within the system required not just sacrifices but often moral compromises. 'Deep down,' I recall one government employee and party member saying, 'I feel I'm still a Christian, whatever else I've done.' What was known, was the artificiality of the imposed ideology to which much of national life and thought proved impervious even if, to all appearances, submissive. It used to be said in East Germany that in the universities it was only the theology students who took the compulsory lectures on Marxism seriously. The long-term future of such a society could only be in doubt.

The sermon in the Marienkirche, however, saw hope not just in the inherent shakiness of the structures behind the facade of socialist progress, but in the sovereign purpose of God in history. As stated in earlier chapters, *this* is what the community of faith 'knows' above all. It is a praying community, and central to its prayer is the petition 'Your kingdom come', a prayer of both yearning and confidence. The knowing of this community is primarily an eschatological awareness: to this world, the kingdom is coming. It is a knowledge which answers to the profound question to the future which is posed by

human consciousness in every context, a consciousness
beautifully evoked in Anne Ridler's poem 'St Ishmael's':

> This valley waits. For whom is it waiting?
> This valley is holding its breath. Till when?
>
> Not far off, the gnashing sea,
> Gobbled rock and wind-lashed headland;
>
> Here, a calm viridian valley,
> Sap and silence.
>
> Down in the deep wood stand the fruit-trees
> Laden with apples. Who will pick them?
> Thick woods crowd against the wall,
> Within the wall is woodland crowding
> Outwards: where is the house, the garden?
> Gone. Where is the wonder who
> Should make his entrance? Not yet come.
>
> The valley is waiting. Not for us.
>
> No-one stirs, not a bird; only
> An idiot down in the cove jabbers
> And fights his shadow: cocks a snook,
> With Peep Bo behind the wall.
> His part's designed: the Anti-Masque
> To a solemn drama — mocks the hero
> Still awaited. Rusty rocks
> That dip in a level estuary sea
> Hundreds of millions of years have waited.
>
> Part the bamboo thicket: there
>
> Is the grey chapel you thought to find,
> Eyebrow-deep in rhododendrons,
> Dittany-of-Crete with dangling crimson,
> Flaring pokers, pallid fuchsia.
>
> The valley is waiting.
>
> So our lives wait for the blaze of glory
> Always expected. Each with a secret,

Cluttered with leaves, with flowers and fruit,
Silence caught by the sleeve, to stay
Till the new glory enters the scene.
But when, or how, is out of sight;
Or whether it is for death we wait,
And his the called-for, marvellous entrance.[3]

The blaze of glory, the Christian community can claim, has already been lit. It is celebrated in anticipation on every occasion of eucharistic worship, as the word is proclaimed of the Christ who has come and will come again, and the foretaste of the messianic feast of the kingdom is shared together. But it is important not to lose sight of the two-foldness of this knowledge of the coming kingdom. It is a knowledge of the kingdom which is coming, *and* a knowledge of that to which it comes, namely, the world as it is at present. If these two co-ordinates are separated from each other, or if one is emphasized at the expense of the other, then the critical nature of the knowledge of the kingdom is lost. It degenerates either into endless talking about the world and analysis of secular problems, or into a context-less, disembodied idea of a kingdom which comes to nowhere in particular.

In this light, the 'knowledge' which the church may claim to have of 'what is going on in the world' can be considered at three levels. These are, a factual awareness of what is observable in current history; a reflection upon the significance of what is happening based on a theological understanding of human, creaturely existence; and an understanding of the interaction between the coming kingdom — the alternative history of God — and the present order. In what follows, I shall be describing what will at times seem to be a wilfully Utopian picture of 'what the church knows', perversely at odds with the real state of affairs in the churches, confused or complacent, or both. But I am speaking of a *potential* knowledge, a knowledge which is stored in the very being of the church as a community gathered around its scriptures and liturgies and enmeshed in the world of its time and place, and as such a knowledge which awaits

---

[3]*Faber Book of Modern Verse*, ed. M. Roberts and D. Hall, Faber and Faber, 1965.

wider recognition and articulation throughout the believing community. The case of the church, corporately, is not so different from that of those theological students who did already have more resources than they realized in their personal experience and life-histories, awaiting retrieval and employment.

Factual knowledge of what is happening

Recently, church bodies in Britain were deeply concerned about the situation in Malawi where a referendum was to take place on whether to introduce a multi-party system after many years of one-party, presidential rule. Late in the afternoon of the day of the referendum, the phone rang in the manse of one of the Scottish church leaders who were following the situation closely. It was a Foreign Office official, kindly offering a briefing on what had been happening, based on reports from the embassy staff in Malawi. It was a pleasant if slightly embarrassing task, for the clergywoman to express gratitude yet also to explain that for several hours telephone calls and faxes had been arriving from Africa in the headquarters of her church, and if anything, it should be the church offices which should have been briefing the diplomatic staff. The churches' own network of partner churches in Malawi, mission agencies and aid organizations on the ground, had been in full and effective operation, as in fact they had been for several months. The church is not always so heavenly minded as to be of no earthly use.

This point should of course not be exaggerated. But it is a fact that by its very nature as a human community, spread through all communities and part of them, the listening and looking church can be expected to know a very great deal of what is going on in the day to day world of secular affairs. The point is missed by those politicians and leader-writers who declare *ad nauseam* that when church bodies speak on affairs of the day they are, by definition, making judgments on matters they know nothing about — or judgments which they should not in any case even be trying to make. Recently, the Council of Churches for Britain and Ireland sent to a number of British

Members of Parliament a sample of its briefing material on the conflict in the former Yugoslavia, based on a recent visit to the region by church representatives, with the offer of supplying further such material on international affairs if the recipients thought they would find it useful. One MP replied:

> While I am in no way querying your sincerity I believe very strongly it appears to be contrary to the advice of scripture for the Church to be involved in coming to any collective view on political issues ... It is not the function of the Church community to arrive at political decisions — what they should be concerned about are the motives of which they come individually to judgments on particular issues.

The writer had completely missed the point. No mention had even been made about collective judgments on political issues — merely that the church had something to contribute to the thinking process from its actual awareness and experience in the contemporary world. The respondent's attitude typifies what, as long ago as the turn of the century, the Congregational theologian P. T. Forsyth named 'ethical vulgarism'.[4] Equally it has to be said that the overwhelming majority of the replies were positive and appreciative, confirming that this was a simple but important way in which the church in the world can fulfil its servanthood. The factual knowledge of the world to which the church has access may not be inherently different in nature or content from that gleaned by other agencies but that does not diminish its importance. In some contexts the church may indeed have its unique contacts and sources to exploit. In others it may be able to amplify, confirm or correct impressions conveyed by the media or even specialist researchers. In May 1991 a British church official found that his report on a visit to Lebanon, the first such visit after several years of extreme difficulty and danger for westerners in that land of civil war and hostage-taking, was much appreciated by, among others, the British Foreign Office. It was simply that the churches in

---

[4] P. T. Forsyth, *Christ, the Gospel and Society*, Independent Press, 1962, p. 33. These lectures by Forsyth are of striking contemporary relevance to Christian engagement with public issues.

Lebanon enabled the visitor, in a very short space of time, to have contacts and conversations with an extraordinarily wide cross-section of people from all walks of life and political and religious persuasions, and to travel to parts of the country previously thought to be no-go areas even for many Lebanese themselves.

But we need not be so exotic to underline the point. At home, too, the Christian community, simply by virtue of what it is and does, knows a great deal of what is happening on the ground. In the first place, when we talk about the church we mean the totality of its membership, the *laos*, in their day to day existence where they live out their faith. The church is the bus-drivers and home-helps, the doctors and the farmers, the teachers and the bank clerks, the shopkeepers and the nurses, the production-line workers and the computer programmers, the local councillors and the social workers ... and all who seek to live by faith within the human scene. Here lies the basic data-gathering of the church in the world, by those who experience most fully the pressures thought of more abstractly in political and economic terms. As was stated in Chapter 1,[5] in recent years the recognition of the primacy of the mission of the 'laity' has regrettably diminished. We need to listen again to Hendrik Kraemer, J. H. Oldham, Ralph Morton and Mark Gibbs and to revitalize the work of the lay academies.

Viewed in terms of the totality of its members and its rootedness in local congregations and parishes, the church is the most widely-distributed network of concern and information exchange in the nation. This self-image, potentially so rich and creative, needs to be promoted in face of all the demoralizing talk, within and outside its ranks, about the decline and marginalization of the church in a secular, post-Christian society. The church may be thin on the ground (not in fact as thin as all that), but what matters more is that it is *actually on the ground*, in inner-city areas as well as in lush suburbs, on the council estate as well as in the village. The 1985 Church of

[5]See above, p. 18.

England report on urban poverty *Faith in the City*[6] provoked controversy and drew much criticism from the political right because of its alleged left-wing — indeed according to some even Marxist — bias. It withstood such accusation and not simply because of the inherent strength of its arguments and the considerable expertise on which it drew. What it finally depended upon for its integrity was the irrefutable fact that the church spoke from within the situations it was talking about. The church is *there*, however tenuously in some instances, where unemployment, housing decay, racism and violence are blighting human life. The report voiced the actual street experience of people and clergy living and ministering there, often at real cost. It made visible a world which many of the critics hardly knew. The same is true more generally. It is not a trendy departure from the pastoral, spiritual ministry of the churches, but a direct outcome of simply carrying it out, when concern is voiced over what is happening to schools, hospitals, rural bus services and the environment. It is impossible to be a dutiful priest or pastor, one who visits and listens, praying with eyes and ears, and not to know about such things; let alone to exercise a more specialized sector ministry in industry, the health service or education.

The point emerges still more forcibly if we return to the international scene. The world church, the church of the *oikumene*, the whole inhabited earth, is potentially the most formidable international intelligence-gathering agency in existence. It is on the ground literally almost everywhere, from China to Nicaragua, from South Africa to Indonesia, from Russia to Sri Lanka, from Iraq to Canada, sometimes thinly but also often thickly too. Like the golden lampstand it is a physical sign of the Spirit, the eyes of God ranging over all the earth (Zech. 5.10, Rev. 11.4). The churches of Europe and North America, if they listen to their partners in the south, can never let themselves be accused of ignorance or naivety about the actual state of the world and the experiences of conflict,

[6]*Faith in the City. A call to action by Church and Nation.* Report of the Archbishop of Canterbury's Commission on Urban Priority Areas, Church House Publishing, 1985.

oppression and poverty which are the fate of millions. When during the mid-1980s churches and ecumenical bodies in Britain and the United States began calling for their governments to recognize the African National Congress as the main representative of the aspirations of black South Africans, and to enter into dialogue with its leaders, it was not because they were wilfully espousing an avant garde political radicalism flirting with 'terrorism'. Nor need it be attributed to any remarkable 'prophetic' insight or revelation, though events since early 1990 have amply confirmed their perception. They had simply been listening to the churches of the townships and squatter camps. When a reckoning is made of the totality of the links within world communions and confessional bodies, mission organizations, ecumenical bodies such as the World Council of Churches, and especially the considerable expertise of the church-related aid and development agencies, and of bodies such as the Catholic Institute for International Relations in the UK, the potential knowledge-resources of the churches on the world scene are indeed considerable. Whether the churches themselves at present fully exploit this potential is of course another question. The point is that this knowledge is to hand (and I have presupposed in this section that the church will be aware that this knowledge, like all knowledge, is *socially located*, and that in the light of the gospel some social locations are more significant than others). The Christian community is not ignorant of the world, and what it can know should encourage it to learn still more.

Frameworks of understanding the world

The church can claim not only to know a good deal of what is going on in the world, but also to understand *why* many things happen, or don't happen as they might be expected to. This claim is not based on the application of techniques of penetrating social and political analysis, though the churches must be prepared to learn from these, but is rather the direct outcome of the fundamental perspectives of confessing the faith as a believing and worshipping community. Archbishop William Temple was provocatively on the mark when he used to say that the world will be saved by worship. By the very fact of gathering as a community to praise the one God who has created all, redeems all and sanctifies all, the church is witnessing to an understanding of crucial significance for the nature of the world and human existence within it. It is thereby given to the Christian community to know of certain ineluctable features of the human condition which mark the most public as well as the most personal and inward dimensions of life. Again, what is argued here is not that the contents of this awareness are a monopoly of believers, but that they are direct implications of the confession of the biblical, apostolic faith. Even if not spelled out explicitly in sermons, lectures or books on social ethics, they are already implicitly *known* when God is praised as creator of all that is, when prayer is offered for the forgiveness of sins through the cross of Christ, when the call to faith and commitment is made through proclamation of the gospel, when people are baptized into the new life in Christ, and when the community breaks bread and shares the common cup of thanksgiving as a foretaste of the coming kingdom. Four forms of knowledge at this level may be identified.

First, there is *the coincidence of givenness and freedom* and the tension between them, which is written deep into human existence as created by God. Human consciousness never starts with a blank sheet. We are born into, and have to live in, a particular time and place, set in a particular environment of physical and cultural features. We cannot choose our parents, our genetic make-up, or the peculiar furniture, historical and natural, which we have inherited from the past and with which we have to deal. I might wonder what it would have been like to have been a medieval abbess in rural France, but in fact I am a male living in twentieth-century urban England. That, I have to accept. We are creatures, not the Creator. But equally, as part of our human creatureliness we have a degree of freedom. We are not *simply* products of our physical and historical past, nor our immediate social context. We can make choices, above all moral ones. We are responsible beings, accountable for our decisions, and ultimately accountable to God in whose image we are created. We are shaped by many factors beyond our control, but we ourselves can give a shape to history, our own and that of those still to come. We cannot do anything about the history from which we have arisen, but we can do *something* about the history we pass on to others. Our place is given to us, but what we do with it is our responsibility which we cannot duck at the end of the day. Choices are no less serious, but even more so, precisely because they are limited. We have to accept both our historical givenness and the responsibility which cannot be shuffled off on to nature, the system or the faceless 'them'. This is the truth enshrined in Reinhold Niebuhr's famous prayer for serenity to accept the things that cannot be changed, courage to change what can be changed, and wisdom to tell the difference. Here is a knowledge as relevant to political as to personal life. We are creatures — and ever before the God who is to be freely worshipped, trusted and obeyed.

Second, there is the knowledge of *the endemic misuse of this freedom.* In T. S. Eliot's words:

Why should men love the Church? Why should they love her laws?
She tells them of Life and Death, and of all that they would forget.
She is tender where they would be hard, and hard where they like to be soft.
She tells them of Evil and Sin, and other unpleasant facts.
They constantly try to escape
From the darkness outside and within
By dreaming of systems so perfect that no one will need to be good.[7]

It was another of Reinhold Niebuhr's quips to suggest that 'original sin' is the one empirically verifiable Christian doctrine, given the all too obvious phenomena of cupidity and self-seeking at every level of human life. Prior to Niebuhr, the Apostle Paul may be claimed as the supreme human realist in confessing 'I do not understand my own actions. For I do not do what I want, but I do the very thing I hate' (Rom. 7.15). This awareness of the profundity of sin as the 'heart turned in upon

[7]T. S. Eliot, 'Choruses from "The Rock", 1934', *The Complete Poems and Plays of T. S. Eliot,* Faber and Faber 1969, p. 159.

itself' (*Cor incurvum in se ipsum*, Martin Luther), however, involves more than just a pious way of saying that human beings often behave badly, or even habitually do so. It is a recognition that sin not only touches and taints every human activity in some way, but that it has the capacity to disguise and camouflage itself. Self-seeking at the expense of others has developed the art of drawing the good, the noble and the idealistic, even the holy, into its stratagems. Paul's critique of the role of law in religion does not argue that the law itself is bad; it is in itself 'holy, and just and good' (Rom. 7.12). But sin, like a parasite, seizes on the commandment of God and turns even that into a means of self-assertion, enabling us to say in effect, 'Look at me, how good and religious I am'. Or, for that matter, 'How radically concerned for justice and truth I am' — with its implication that others had better watch out. It is precisely in its battening on to, and camouflaging itself within, moral and idealistic aspirations that the exceeding sinfulness of sin is to be seen. An awareness of this has clear implications for discernment in the social and political sphere. Political and social movements, and often the policies of governments and other corporate institutions, precisely because they need to energize deep human loyalties if they are to be effective levers of change, are prone to presenting themselves in highly moralistic and even religious terms. Civilization, justice and world order are held to be at stake, when a more sober analysis would indicate that it is the self-interest of a certain class, nation or group of nations that is really at issue.[8] It is certainly the case that the moral basis of political life is to be voiced by the church. Paradoxically, that may mean first of all a demoralizing of the political language and rhetoric being bandied about in a given situation, a pricking of sinful presumption. Our vision is always limited and somewhat warped, given our tendency to see what we want to see rather than what is actually there. Our declamations run far ahead of what we are actually committed to achieving, given our propensity for words and impressions rather than actions. In situations of conflict, our tendency to demonize the opposite side grossly

---

[8]See Reinhold Niebuhr, *Moral Man and Immoral Society*, SCM Press, 1963.

overreaches any objective consideration of the facts, being generated by our felt need to idealize and justify ourselves. As well as these forms of pride, *hybris*, there are the contrasting sins of resignation, of believing that nothing can be done and things are best left as they are. These are basic parameters of human behaviour conditioned by the old and tiresome but irreplaceable word *sin* and as such will be known to the church (which of course also has its own forms of all these types of sin to confess). Some years ago a well-known British politician was the guest on the BBC Radio Programme *Desert Island Discs*. His final choice of eight records he would want to have with him in his castaway existence, and the one above all he would choose out of the eight, was Gregorio Allegri's sublime setting of the penitential Psalm 51, the *Miserere*. The reason he gave was that its theme of sin and forgiveness was the message that politicians most needed to hear again and again.

Third, the faith of the church brings with it a deep awareness of *the historicality of human existence, its limits and its significance.* The faith is in an eternally living God whose loving purpose is made known in earthly, creaturely history, yet who also transcends that history. History, the sphere of human decisions from the most intimate to the most public, is the theatre where we meet God, the 'Eternal You' in the midst of all 'yous' and 'its'. That gives history its significance. Its import at every level is underlined in the creed, from the hidden mystery of the conception of Jesus in a woman's body, to his death in the secular, public and political scene 'under Pontius Pilate'. In short, if banally, history matters: God started it, God will end it, and God has put Godself in the midst of it. But we never know the whole of history, which in any case is riven by dark chasms of tragedy. The limits are real enough. We live in time, each at a particular time. We cannot jump out of time, nor live for all time. Our lives are but fragments of the whole. The limitation and fragmentariness of human life are above all signalled by death. We are not immortal, for from dust we were made, to dust we shall return. It is the Creator, not the creatures, who alone is immortal. We are *destined* for eternal life which is not, however, the continuation of this life but its utter transformation through the life-giving Spirit who raised crucified Jesus from the dead. Paradoxically, therefore, we grasp this hope not by denying our finitude and temporality running towards death, but by accepting them; not by indulging in myths that we and what we create shall never die or that death is not real, but by acknowledging the mortality of ourselves and all we set our hands to. Because the resurrection is the ultimate gift to us, we are freed from the burden of trying to make ourselves last for ever and from having to cling to our artefacts as that on which our security is finally built:

> Pride of man and earthly glory,
> Sword and crown betray his trust.
> What with care and toil he buildeth,
> Tower and temple, fall to dust.
> But God's power,
> Hour by hour,
> Is my temple and my tower.[9]

This is a profound implication of the biblical faith (Ps. 90, Is. 40.6f., etc.). It is far removed, however, from resignation and pessimism. History, for all its fragmentariness, is the sphere of human responsibility. It is where we love God and our neighbour. Indeed there is a real sense in which we are responsible for history, seen as human community extending backwards and forwards in time. We take what is bequeathed to us from the past and do something with it for the future. The ultimate question for a responsible person, says Dietrich Bonhoeffer, is not how one is to extricate oneself heroically from the affair, but 'How the coming generation is to live'.[10] The fact that what we receive from the past may not be wholly to our liking, and what we are able to do for the future may seem rudimentary in face of the daunting challenges of our time, is no reason for not deciding and acting. Our vocation is neither to run away nor to pretend that we can manage the whole of history with its irrationalities and perversities. 'I have seen a limit to all perfection, but your commandment is

---

[9]Hymn by J. Neander (1650–80), transl. R. Bridges.
[10]D. Bonhoeffer, *Letters and Papers from Prison*, SCM Press, 1971, p. 7.

exceedingly broad' (Ps. 119.96). 'The grass withers, the flower fades, but the word of our God will stand for ever' (Is. 40.8). We are not to put our final trust in princes who perish like all mortals (Ps. 146.3) but we are to honour governmental responsibility under God (Rom. 13.1, I Tim. 2.1f. etc.). There is always something to be done. There is here a knowledge of political responsibility which runs deeper than the resignation which lets things slide into evil, and the Utopianism which so often becomes tyrannical and evil by playing God over human life. The political task therefore remains of paramount importance, though particular political leaders, movements and ideologies have their day and pass away. In themselves they are not of ultimate importance, despite the hype and rhetoric in which their pretensions may be cloaked. Only by an unusual humility can it be confessed:

> The old order changeth, yielding place to new,
> And God fulfils Himself in many ways,
> Lest one good custom should corrupt the world.[11]

History is the medium in which hope and responsibility are transmitted from generation to generation.

Fourth, the faith of the church cannot be apprehended without knowing *the fundamental sociality and solidarity of human existence.* By its very nature as a worshipping *community* in which we are 'members one of another' (Eph. 4.25) the church witnesses to the fact that human beings are created for existence-in-relation. The seal of that relationship and bonding is the forgiveness of sins through Christ, the one who on the cross outside the city wall took upon himself exclusion from the whole society, and from his Father, in order that all might be included in the new covenant of communion with God and with each other in the Spirit. The community of redemption does not, however, simply gloat over its own experience of togetherness, but points by its very existence to a fundamental fact of all creatureliness, of which it is the fulfilment. Humanity

---

[11]Alfred, Lord Tennyson, 'Morte d'Arthur'.

has been created not as a being-in-isolation, in self-sufficient individuality, but as a being-in-relation; in Karl Barth's phrase, as 'fellow-humanity' or 'co-humanity'.[12] In its most primal form, co-humanity is seen in the way that humanity does not exist authentically and fully as either man or woman in isolation, but as man and woman together and for one another (Gen. 1.27; 2.18–24). In the biblical story, people exist in families, tribes, peoples, whose stories interconnect as an ultimate whole, including a crucial relationship with the whole created order. Adam and Eve are set in a relationship of stewardship to the whole earth and its living creatures (Gen. 1.28f.); or, as in the second creation account, Adam names the animals and tills the garden (Gen. 2.15ff.). Individuality is set within a holistic vision. The earth is the Lord's and everything in it, the world and all who live on it, for he has established it over even the apparently uncontrollable watery floods which represent the extreme of atomized, disconnected existence (Ps. 24.1f.). The psalmist laments that, incomprehensibly, God has caused 'friend and neighbour to shun me' (Ps. 88.18). Job, the loneliest man in literature, is anguished precisely because he is deprived of any real comforter. His final vindication is sealed in the gift of a reborn family and offspring (Job 42.10–17). Nothing and no-one exists, or can be truly understood, in isolation. The ultimate Christian affirmation of this is that in Christ all things in heaven and earth co-exist and hang together (Col. 1.17) and that the final peace of the cosmos has been secured by the blood of his cross (Col. 1.20). To confess Christ as Lord thus carries with it the knowledge of the interconnectedness of all that he is Lord over. John Donne gave this knowledge classic and familiar expression: 'No man is an Island, entire of itself; every man is a piece of the Continent, a part of the main.' The truly Christian community can never be other than attuned to the bell which tolls for the death of each individual and member of the whole. In social terms this means a knowledge that no-one, and no group or community within the whole human family, is to be dismissed as insignificant. Put more positively, it knows that precisely

[12]K. Barth, *Church Dogmatics* Vol. III, Part 2 (*The Doctrine of Creation*), p. 228.

those who *are* being written off are to be affirmed as the most
significant, the 'little ones' to whom the kingdom belongs. It is
those being left out or pushed to the edge who are brought to
the centre (Mk. 5.25–34; 9.36f.; 10.13–16; 10.46–52). This is a
knowledge of what true community is about, from the most
personal and domestic level to that of the whole city and
nation, and to the most inclusive international and global
level. Actions and policies which do not recognize this are
courting disaster, for to damage one piece in the structure will
at some point rebound upon the whole. When European
bankers write off black Africa as economically insignificant
for the 'developed' world and not worth serious attention, the
church, regardless of its expertise or otherwise in economic
affairs, recognizes here a profound and dangerous ignorance
of human reality. There is indeed a point at which the church,
even if only a passenger among the professional navigators, is
entitled to say in effect, 'Sirs, I can see that the voyage will be
with danger and much heavy loss ...' (Acts 27.10).

The believing church, then, does have a significant
knowledge of how things are in this world. Not the only
knowledge, never a perfect knowledge, and often an imperfect
awareness requiring a great deal of further education and
enlightenment, but a knowledge nevertheless, giving it the
status of an informed enquirer amidst the human community.

Knowledge of the coming kingdom

We return to the point from which we began this chapter. The
knowledge which most distinctively marks the community of
disciples is eschatological. Every time it gathers to hear the
word of its Lord and to celebrate the eucharist it is praying for,
expecting and celebrating the arrival of the reign of God. It
cannot be content simply to be an authority, however well
informed and insightful, on the present state of the world. In
its prophetic vocation it opens the rent in the present order.
Here it has no abiding city but seeks the city which is to come
(Heb. 13.14), calling attention to the alternative history of God
at work in the world and striving towards fulfilment in the final
new heaven and earth. It sees the present world as one which

is 'passing away' (I Cor. 7.31). The night is far spent, day is at
hand (Rom. 13.11f.). Advent, the season of candles glowing in
the dark, is not just a liturgical preparation for Christmas but
a frame of expectant mind for the whole Christian year and for
all Christian activity in the world. The most profound Christian
understanding of the world is therefore that it is a world to
which the kingdom is coming, in judgment and grace.

Precisely how in any given moment and context the church
gives concrete expression to this hope in the affairs of the world
is a matter of crucial decision for its witness. Two diametrically
extreme temptations are always to hand. One is to maintain that
the future reign of God is in fact so 'other', so transcendental,
that it can never be directly discerned or embodied in any
present human form, whether in the world or even in the visible
church. The kingdom is completely hidden, the seed growing in
the complete secrecy of inward faith, the leaven working so
mysteriously that it is not outwardly apparent whether the
dough is even rising at all. Some versions of Lutheranism have
encouraged this pessimistic attitude and so handed over the
public and political sphere entirely to the realm of the sword
where only the 'law' operates, in complete antithesis to the
'gospel'. The other temptation, as was mentioned in the
preceding chapter, is to rush into saying of the kingdom 'Lo
here, lo there'. The coming kingdom is immediately identified
with an institution or movement directly to hand, perhaps the
church itself and its growth upon earth. The Roman Catholic
Church in the nineteenth century could scarcely contemplate
the loss of the territorial papal states as anything but incompatible
with Christ's promise to St Peter that his church would be built
on a rock against which the gates of hell could not prevail. At the
same time, western Protestantism was happily acclaiming the
worldwide spread of Christianized European culture (or
Europeanized Christian culture) as the growth of the kingdom
of God. It was then but a short step to identifying western
political and commercial power with the kingdom. Among both
British and German Christians were many who saw a messianic
calling of their peoples being fulfilled in the growth of empire:
a vision which culminated in the bloodbath of Flanders fields.
Today, the temptation is no less apparent to baptize movements

of social and political liberation simplistically into Christianity (though the more discerning political and liberation theologians themselves are well aware of this danger).[13] By the same token, reactionary and conservative movements are frequently regarded as not even being in need of baptism: by being seen to maintain the *status quo* they are regarded as already 'Christian', almost by definition.

A truly eschatological faith knows that in one sense the kingdom always lies 'beyond' the world as it is, and the church as it is. The Swedish ecumenical leader Bishop Nathan Söderblom used to describe the kingdom as always 'just around the corner'. In another sense it is here already. This has often been expressed theologically as the tension between the 'already' and the 'not yet'. Liturgically it is recognized in the great eucharistic affirmation 'Christ has died, Christ is risen, Christ will come again'. The 'already', for its part, cannot be left as a pure abstraction, and we cannot be content with negative statements about the kingdom's utter invisibility — not if Christ has indeed come and if the Spirit is at work. There is Pentecost as well as Advent. We should be prepared at least for *signs* of the kingdom to be discernible: some disturbance of the soil where the seed is germinating, some aeration of the dough where the yeast is fermenting. There must be some concrete manifestations of the coming reign of God.

The danger comes when it is assumed that the hope of the kingdom celebrated by the believing and worshipping community can and should always be translatable directly into a comprehensive programme for the public sphere. Here is where the notion of the 'secret discipline' noted in Chapter 3 as a mark of the early church and revived by Bonhoeffer, becomes significant again. It means a recognition that the exact form of witness in the world cannot be unrolled in advance any more than the course of the world itself can be predicted and controlled. How the ministry of word and sacrament will authentically bear fruit in service and ethical action cannot be set out as a complete programme. It can only

[13]See e.g., G. Gutiérrez, *A Theology of Liberation*, SCM Press, 1974; Jose Miguez Bonino, *Towards a Christian Political Ethic*, SCM Press, 1983.

be discovered from one historical context to another in repeated ventures of faith and discipleship, in the expectation that there will be *some* concrete response possible to the claims of the kingdom. In the perception that the church has of the world as the place where God loved to be in the incarnate Jesus, and therefore as the place to which his reign is coming, the church knows that *some* alternative ways can be found out of the dead-ends of the present order. Just what these ways are, it cannot and need not pretend to know in advance, but through its faith it knows enough to launch the enquiry. It knows enough to reject the apparent inevitabilities which destroy life, community, freedom and dignity. It knows enough to be able to utter a decisive 'No!' to war as means of settling international and inter-communal disputes, and above all to war involving weapons of mass destruction. It knows enough to say a fundamental 'No!' to economic systems which are inherently inhuman and commit vast numbers of children, women and men to unending misery and degradation. It knows enough to say an unconditional 'No!' to all these in the light of its knowledge of the alternative history of God, God's coming reign which speaks of another way.

At times the church may feel that it is not in a position to make such a witness, because as yet it cannot provide advice on just what the alternative way is. It may feel lost and inadequate when it comes to the technical process to be followed. This, however, is illogical and becomes a pretext for the evasion of its proper vocation. The German theologian Helmut Gollwitzer, one of the most radical Christian voices in the post-war Federal Republic, recalls a debate on nuclear weapons in the Synod of the German Evangelical Church in the early 1960s. A prominent bishop declared that the church must not pronounce a definite 'No' unless at the same time it could tell the politicians how they could carry out this policy in political action. 'This showed that he was treating the "No" like a decree of the leaders of the church, which could not of course be issued by them if they could not at the same time show how it was to be implemented.'[14] That, argues Gollwitzer, was to confuse a fundamental call to

---

[14]H. Gollwitzer, *The Demands of Freedom*, SCM Press, 1965, p. 40.

witness with expediency — with disastrous results for the church's integrity. Or, as I would prefer to say, it exemplified a false presumption, masquerading as humility, that the church is indeed called to know everything and that, given time and ideal conditions, it would. That is a basic misconception. It is perfectly consistent for the church, basing itself on its fundamental awareness of what God requires, to call for a radically alternative way to be found, while at the same time confessing that as yet it does not itself know the technicalities of the application. In so witnessing, it is offering an invitation to the world to learn, and is not ashamed to admit that it is itself still a learner, a community of discipleship *in via*.

It is not the case of course that all social and international issues immediately call for a decisive 'No' or 'Yes'. They involve rather a discussion of priorities and a patient search for sensible ways ahead. This especially applies in situations of deep and seemingly intractable conflict between communities as, for example, in Northern Ireland, former Yugoslavia, the Middle East or Sri Lanka. But the same principle applies, of a fundamental knowledge which the Christian community brings to them. That even these apparently hopeless situations belong to the sphere to which God's reign is coming, means that they are not finally hopeless and to be written off. The immediate, or even longer term, answers may not be discernible and the temptation must be resisted to produce ready-made 'solutions'. As stated before, we may have to recognize that we are dealing less with problems to be solved than with sins to be repented of, past histories to be forgiven and long memories to be reconciled. Indeed, we may speak of the church's public witness as primarily that of identifying the points at which repentance needs to be made and forgiveness received, and which can thereby be the birthplace of hope.

Not as a superficial optimism, not by denying the inescapably tragic element in human experience, but out of a profound awareness of the significance of the cross and resurrection, the Christian witness has continually and persistently to speak of hope. That has to be said even when the hope cannot be exactly identified for the present. The direction is known, even if not the precise route. In Bunyan's *Pilgrim's Progress*, it is the discovery of the key called Promise which finally enables Christian and Hopeful to escape from Doubting Castle. Perhaps that can suggest a slightly more modern image for the pilgrim church in service to the wider community, that of a group of explorers seemingly lost in a subterranean system of caverns and passages. The Christian community is that which knows that somehow there is a way out of the labyrinth, in one direction rather than others. It does not claim that it alone will find the way, but keeps alive the hope that the way will be found, amid the threatening despair that all ways are dead ends, and the nightmare that there is no upper world of light and air to be reached at all. Already, the current of the fresh air of the Spirit can be felt on the face.

The church, then, does have significant knowledge of the world, and at more than one level. As a worldwide community on the ground it knows a good deal of what is going on in an observable, factual way. By virtue of its faith in creation and redemption it can claim an understanding of much of the dynamics of human life in community and history, its possibilities and limitations. In the light of its expectancy of the coming kingdom it knows the world as a place to which hope is given, a world already being claimed and disturbed by the coming kingdom. It is tempting to pursue an analysis of the three levels of this knowledge in terms of their orientation in time: the factual, observable level looks to the immediate present, the theological perspective on human nature looks to the past out of which the present situation of human existence has arisen, while the eschatological awareness is obviously directed to the future. In practice, however, the three dimensions closely interrelate to form an almost indivisible whole, an image in which present, past and future ceaselessly shuttle between each other: the world as it is, yet also as created and being redeemed by the God made known in the incarnate Christ.[15] This is a knowledge which entitles the church as a learning community to call for further learning by itself and the world. The question now arises, how are the churches of today utilizing this possibility?

[15]Cf. for example the analysis in Ernst Bloch, *The Principle of Hope* (3 Vols.), Basil Blackwell, 1986.

7

As Those Being Taught: Three Regional Experiences

To be prophetic requires a willingness to be as 'one who is taught' (Is. 50.4). The ear must be opened before the mouth. The community, no less than the individual, who would teach can never be other than a learner, for 'you are all students' (Mt. 23.8). Such has been the theological argument of the preceding chapters. The church that would speak authentically to the world must ever be in the discipleship mode, of seeking to discern the signs of the kingdom amid all that is happening in its midst and in its wider context. It does not speak for the sake of making a noise, of joining in the perpetual chatter of self-advertising voices, but for the sake of its proper identity and calling as the servant community of *God* in the world. It insists on clearing a properly theological space for what it has to say, as it did at Barmen in 1934 and in the *Kairos Document* of 1985, as it must do whenever it would claim to be pointing people to a kingdom which, while certainly in this world, is not from this world in its goals and methods. It uses its actual knowledge drawn from its involvement in the life of this world, from its fundamental understanding of the world and humanity integral to its life as a worshipping community, and from its indefatigable expectancy of the coming kingdom. Starting with what it knows already, it confesses its need to know still more. It is driven, repeatedly, to ask 'Who are you, Lord?' — for our contemporary world. It therefore teaches as one that is continually being taught.

The church's learning, which is a learning in order to speak, has several dimensions. It requires a continual encounter with its own traditions of life and thought, biblical and historical, always asking of any assumed position, 'Is this really what the gospel is about?' It requires an openness to contemporary experience, always asking, 'What is actually happening here?' And it requires a continual interaction between these two kinds of question, for it is the central insights of the tradition which enable the community to identify the significance of what is happening in the world, and it is encounter with the contemporary world which enlivens and opens up the tradition. There is an unending, mutually reciprocal relation here.

All this sounds fine, but where, if anywhere, is such a learning taking place today? If these theological statements mean anything at all, then they should at the very least provide a frame of reference for assessing the actual life and thinking of real Christian communities, rather than just portraying an idealized church. One may of course hope for more than this, and that we might be able to give examples where such learning and re-learning is actually taking place. In this chapter, therefore, we shall flesh out the preceding argument by looking at certain situations where churches are being challenged, especially by rapid social and political change, to learn again what it means to be the church in that context, and to read again the signs of the times. We shall look briefly at three contemporary contexts, South Africa, the Middle East and eastern Europe, and then in the light of this survey consider very briefly some of the more universal implications for the churches.

South Africa: learning to say 'Yes'

The incident in Cape Town in March 1988 supplied one of the most dramatic pictures of public Christian witness this century: church leaders, black and white, of all traditions, kneeling on the pavement in front of St George's Cathedral, face to face with the ranks of police with their batons, water-cannon and dogs. They had set out from the Cathedral to march to the nearby Parliament building to demand from President Botha the lifting of the recent ban on a whole range of groups working for political and civil rights, on trades unions and student organizations. It was a supreme moment of saying 'No' to the totalitarianism of the racist regime. The church still had a voice and was using it on behalf of the voiceless, publicly and decisively.

Two years later, such a scene already seemed a thing of the past. President Botha had gone, President de Klerk had come, Nelson Mandela had been released from prison and the African National Congress had been unbanned. Under pressure from ceaseless and mounting internal opposition, and from ecocomic and political pressure from outside, the apartheid state was cracking and crumbling. Change was in the air, although for two years and more many of the actions of the National Party government remained deeply ambiguous and it was not at all clear that the movement towards a non-racial, democratic South Africa was irreversible. Not until late 1993 did Nelson Mandela feel able to announce to the international community that economic sanctions could be lifted. But change there undoubtedly was despite all the questions, not least about who was instigating much of the violence in the townships.

It was not surprising that some church leaders were among the most euphoric at the early signs of change. In November 1990 there met at Rustenburg the most inclusively ecumenical gathering in South Africa for decades. The change in atmosphere was signalled especially by the presence there of the white Dutch Reformed Church. Testimonies of white repentance and black forgiveness were offered on the platform. An end seemed to have been reached — but what was to be the nature of the new beginning? Archbishop Desmond Tutu, foremost among the prelates who had knelt before the police that day in Cape Town, was not alone in feeling initially that, with undoubted change now under way, the church leadership might be able to retire from the political scene, leave politics to the politicians and concentrate on the urgent pastoral tasks which during the years of opposition to apartheid had not received their full due. This view was not just a case of weariness after the long struggle. It exemplified an entirely healthy attitude towards the proper autonomy of the political sphere.

The previously voiceless now had a voice of their own, they did not need the church as amplifier. The opportunity and responsibility were now there for the political groups to organize themselves and prepare for democratic government. There are too many examples in history of churches unwilling to relinquish the public power and prestige which historical circumstance has bestowed on them, whereas here in South Africa was a church which was ready to let go. Sometimes the church's service does lie in stepping back, just as one of the most demanding tasks of parenthood can be to allow the growing child to walk alone. This in itself was an important instance of the church being prepared to learn a new role.

There were also sternly practical reasons which made the churches face this need for a new role in a changing situation. The pressure was particularly felt in the South African Council of Churches (SACC), which not only brought together in united witness the mainline and independent churches who shared the anti-apartheid platform (although the Roman Catholic Church was not a member), but also provided support and sanctuary for many of the activist opposition groups such as those working for detainees and their families. Indeed the accusation was sometimes levelled at the Council that it was acting as the religious wing of the ANC. But with previously banned groups now able to operate more freely, many activists who had been working under the SACC umbrella now quite rightly felt able and called to work in the overtly secular sphere. Further, funding agencies and partners abroad were reassessing their priorities and, with change now the order of the day in South Africa, were increasingly directing their resources to what they judged were now regions of greater urgency. Such developments alone were effecting a slimming down of the SACC's programmes. To visit Khotso House, headquarters of the SACC, in early 1992 was by comparison with the 1980s like going into a quiet (though efficient) provincial aiport after the teeming hustle of Heathrow.

It also became apparent, however, that any thoughts of the churches completely retiring from the public and political realm were premature. Confusion and uncertainty vied with hope as the 'peace process', far from proving automatic, lurched from one crisis to another and a host of new questions arose on the agenda of moving to a genuinely post-apartheid society. How could the white and black political leaderships be kept in dialogue with each other? How could the mass of the population, for whom 'democracy' had been only a dream for generations, be prepared for the challenges and responsibilities entailed in actually using their vote? On the local level, how could civil society and structures of communal decision-making be developed in the wasteland left by decades of repression? How could returning political exiles and their families be received and integrated into a scene which, in many respects and in all honesty, had had to manage without them for so long? Most urgently of all, what was to be done about the mounting violence in the townships, much of it evidently instigated by elements within the white political establishment and security forces, which was not only wreaking untold grief but threatening to derail the peace process and plunge everything into chaos?

Not to face such issues would have been a sheer abdication of responsibility by the churches, not least because they constituted a vital resource as a wholly nation-wide, non-governmental network of communities with experience of leadership, communication and education. The question had to be asked, 'What does God require of us *now*?' Underlying the recognition of the need for a new orientation was an abiding theological conviction, expressed by Frank Chikane, General Secretary of the SACC: 'The role of the church is to be in active solidarity with all processes that promote justice, exercising that solidarity in a critical prophetic manner. The churches must promote the ethical ideals, the things that approximate the kingdom of God. They must evangelise, helping people change their minds and their old ways and to start a new way.' There was also, however, another temptation than retirement that had to be resisted, namely, that of plunging into a vain attempt to do everything that seemed important. Because resources and capabilities were only too finite, priorities had to be identified and particular goals established. An agenda which was both theologically sound and (albeit by grace) humanly manageable, had to be set. This was itself a challenging exercise in re-learning, for it was to invite and indeed require open and honest debate and controversy.

Early in 1992 this first priority of defining its new role in the changing situation was embraced head-on by the SACC. A four-pronged analysis of priority concerns and lines of possible inititiative was launched, with ecumenical task-forces assigned to the issues of, respectively, Violence, Political Justice, Education for Democracy, and Economic Matters. This exercise, it should be noted, was considerably encouraged by a Joint Consultation held by the SACC and the World Council of Churches in Cape Town in October 1991 — the task of re-definition of goals and roles was no less important for the international ecumenical community which had played such a vital role of solidarity during the years of struggle and resistance. A similar mood of enquiry and reassessment, amid frank admission of uncertainty, was manifest in the Roman Catholic Bishops' Conference. In January 1991 the bishops issued a pastoral letter, 'A Call to Build a New South Africa', addressing the same range of concerns as the SACC task-forces and with suggestions on how local congregations, discussion-groups and individuals might examine their contribution to the building of peace, democracy and economic justice.

Among the priorities that emerged from these enquiries, that of addressing violence became pre-eminent. The result was the Ecumenical Monitoring Programme for South Africa, whereby groups of volunteers from within the country and from abroad, working in close co-operation with local networks, placed themselves in many of the most volatile and dangerous situations — not only to 'observe' and report on what was happening and why, but also in many cases by their very presence to help defuse what would have become even more violent incidents. But such projects had only become possible through the willingness of the churches and ecumenical bodies to undertake a rapid and radical self-examination, to re-learn in a fast-changing situation.

This re-learning, however, has not been solely at the immediate and pragmatic level. The question 'What does God require of us now?' is after all an eminently theological one, and the Christian resistance to apartheid had always both relied upon and generated much profound theological reflection. This theology had never been static, but always in motion. In the 1960s, as embodied in the such organizations as the Christian Institute led by Beyers Naudé, the opposition was considerably influenced by the example of the Confessing Church of Germany — as might be expected of a movement led largely by dissidents from a white Reformed tradition whose interpretation of Calvin had been put at the service of the ideology of racial supremacy. The neo-orthodox emphasis upon the Word of God as sovereign over all human thought-forms, critically encountering all other claimants to human loyalty especially those in 'religious' guise, once again became of decisive significance for those seeking an alternative to civil religion subservient to the state. Moreover, of course, the parallels between the racial issues in both contexts could not be ignored. As a result, Barth and Bonhoeffer found a new home in South Africa. Indeed Eberhard Bethge, Bonhoeffer's friend and biographer, was once asked during a lecture tour of South Africa in the early 1970s, 'When did Bonhoeffer visit South Africa? He knows our situation from the inside!'[1]

During the 1970s the churches' opposition to apartheid became increasingly a *black* responsibility, and as time went on such a consciousness found its chief affinities lying with contemporary theologies of liberation in the Third World rather than with struggles on the white, European scene a generation or more earlier — though the significance of the German Church Struggle has never been forgotten. The newer movements emphasized the necessity of social and political analysis of the contemporay context as the prerequisite of any authentic theology. Such an emphasis found notable embodiment in the Institute for Contextual Theology and its supreme expression was the *Kairos Document* of 1985:[2] the utterly decisive 'No' to the racist state and its religious support apparatus among the churches.

---

[1]See J.W. de Gruchy, *Bonhoeffer in South Africa. Theology in Dialogue*, W. B. Eerdmans, 1984, p. 4.

[2]See Chapter 2, above.

But what are the questions which theology has to address in the confusing time of change. when the issues are not so much about how to stop the oppression of the people, but how to enable them to build their own new society, even while many of the features of that oppression continue? Grey twilight, whether at dawn or evening, is a difficult time in which to get one's bearings as compared with broad daylight — or for that matter pitch darkness when a well-aimed beam at least throws objects into sharp relief. It is a time when myriad tasks facing the country can no longer be avoided: from ensuring a decent level of employment and housing for the masses in the townships and squatter camps, to correcting the massive imbalance in educational provision between whites and blacks; from tackling the need for land redistribution after the decades of expropriation, to ensuring an adequate water-supply for Cape Town by the year 2000; from enabling a participatory, civil society to emerge in the wastelands left by near-totalitarian rule, to providing safety and security for all citizens within the framework of an accepted code of human rights enshrined in constitution and statutes. But none of this can be achieved overnight. How, in what order, should all this be tackled? And which come first, individual rights or the right of the community to economic development, on which so much else depends? It is a time of confusing priorities, goals and means. As one theologian, who had himself known the inside of police cells after demonstrations in the 1980s, said to me in Cape Town in March 1992: 'For years we've been saying "No". Suddenly, now we're beginning to have to learn to say "Yes" — but what to?'

This point was vividly brought home to me during that visit by a conference on 'Church and Development' at the University of Stellenbosch, organized by the Ecumenical Foundation of Southern Africa, an interdisclipinary body which brings together theologians, lawyers, economists, sociologists and others to examine specific social questions. Much was heard of the need for an 'economic theology' as an extension of liberation or political theology in the new South African context: 'Political ideologies do not provide bread for the poor.' But very specific questions also arose. For example, was there now to be a role for bodies such as the Development Bank of Southern Africa (formed by the government to deal with the so-called 'homelands', cornerstone of the apartheid system) and the Independent Development Trust? There was lively discussion between those who considered these creations and instruments of apartheid to have no place in building the post-apartheid economy, and those who thought that despite their origins they were capable of being adapted and redirected for the ends of justice. One might say that underlying this debate was a nice theological question: is anything so depraved as to be utterly unusable?

In such a context, a new kind of ethical discourse is having to be learned. The resistance to and overthrow of apartheid required absolute moral imperatives. Now, it is being realized that while moral imperatives still apply, their application requires proximate steps towards realization. 'Middle axioms', once thought to be typically Anglo-Saxon products of evolutionary rather than revolutionary social policy, are being talked about again in South Africa. Rebuilding always requires more sophistication than does demolition.

One theologian who exemplifies this new approach is Charles Villa-Vicencio of Cape Town, who believes that theology's main challenge is now to address the task of national reconstruction.[3] In the context of nation-building, the insights of liberation theology must be extended and refined in conjunction with legal theory and practice, the understanding of human rights and political economy. Essential to his argument is the need for a continual, fresh re-learning by theology:

> At the centre of this theology is the integration of an ultimate vision which disturbs the *status quo* that emerges at any given time, while promoting concrete proposals which provide the best possible solution to the specific needs of the time. Such a theology can only emerge from a thorough and careful understanding of the nature of the society it is seeking to address. In this sense, it is

[3]C. Villa-Vicencio, *Theology in Reconstruction. Nation-building and human rights*, Cambridge University Press, 1992.

marked by contextual particularity, while drawing on
historical and global insights as a basis for providing a
thoughtful and critical social ethic.[4]

Such an approach, argues Villa-Vicencio, must be inter-
disciplinary, inter-faith, participatory and democratic. In other
words, theology cannot stand in splendid isolation handing
down its directives to the waiting world. The world will not so
wait for it, but pass it by. On the other hand, Villa-Vicencio
insists that the the goal will be definite proposals in the socio-
economic field: some projects should be supported, not others,
and some may be proposed by the church itself. It is significant
however that Villa-Vicencio acknowledges the church's fallibility
here — which is no reason for not making choices. Serious
mistakes may be made, but the church in every age is under
God's judgment. The fear of being wrong must never be
allowed to dominate, for the church is no less vulnerable or
more privileged than other groups. Or, as I would put it, the
church itself is a perpetual learner. It means a preparedness for
theologians to get into issues to the point where they have their
minds confused by the debates and admit they have no clear
answers — for the sake of the answers that may come. In a time
of transition, the church has to surrender something of its own
present identity because it does not know exactly what it will
become.

This of course is by no means a complete story of South
African theology. There have been and are other theological
approaches than those described, even among those who have
rejected apartheid. All that has been told here is a story of
certain Christians who have been remarkably ready to learn,
learn more, and then re-learn what the kingdom of God means
as the context changes. Their ability to remain prophetic
depends crucially on a continual humility, as those who are
taught.

[4]Ibid., p. 275.

The Middle East: learning for more than survival

The Bekaa valley in Lebanon runs north-eastwards between
the Lebanese mountains to the west, and Mount Hermon and
the other hills bordering Syria to the east. Wide and flat, the
valley floor is one of the most fertile areas of the Middle East.
Fields of corn, potatoes and other crops (including here and
there the white opium poppy) stretch for miles into the
distance. For centuries it has also been a highly strategic land-
route, and the confrontations of the past two decades have
likewise brought to it the rumble of tanks and anti-aircraft fire.
The Syrian army is still in occupation of the valley, and when
I visited it in 1991 there seemed to be check-points every mile
or so as we drove north. For the valley is also stronghold of the
radical Islamic movement Hizbollah, especially in the area
around the ancient city of Baalbek with its spectacular Roman
ruins.

As one reaches the foothills at the northern end of the valley,
the landscape turns to semi-arid, the vegetation sparse and
ragged, the dusty road clinging to the steep sides of small,
boulder-strewn valleys. The area has a strangely silent, forgotten-
about appearance. Just occasionally, a white minaret or church
tower jabs the blue sky in the distance.

There are other signs of life, even more unexpected, in this
distant corner which the rest of the world seems to have passed
by. Close by one village, Hermel, stands a set of small, neat,
recently-erected buildings. Children of varying ages cheerfully
greet their visitors at the gate. This is Foyer de la Joie, a day-
school for children with mental and physical handicaps. Apart
from the seeming oddity of its remote situation it looks at first
sight just like many another centre for children with special
needs in almost any part of the world. There are wheelchairs
and other aids for those with walking difficulties; the young
staff are obviously deeply devoted to the work and there is a
smiling confidence between them and their pupils; displayed
on tables are brightly coloured pictures, toys and household
decorations which the children have made themselves. A place
of joy indeed, but beyond that nothing particularly remarkable,
it would appear.

But this is Lebanon, a land which from 1975 until 1990 was synonymous with one of the most bitter and destructive civil conflicts this century has known, in which thousands died and which tore the fabric of the country to shreds. Still today much of Beirut is a concrete skeleton, while out in the countryside what once were villages are strips of whitening rubble. Deeply and tragically entwined in that conflict was religious affiliation: Christian, Muslim and Druze. Until the early 1970s, Lebanon with its near numerical parity of Christian and Muslim populations, the political rights of each community recognized in a carefully balanced democratic constitution, had in many eyes symbolized the hope that a genuinely pluralistic society was possible, even among the passionately maintained identities of the Middle East. That equipoise finally capsized as trust between the political leaders of the communities broke down, the strain increased to breaking-point by the large Palestinian refugee presence and liberation movements, and by Israeli collusion with the ambitions of the Christian political leadership. The rest, one might as well say, is history at its bloodiest.

Seen against that background, Foyer de la Joie is more than just another centre for handicapped children. For the children include both Muslims and Christians and so does the staff. The land and buildings are managed by a committee comprising members of both communities. The venture and others like it — for there are similar schools elsewhere in the Bekaa — arose out of a deliberate and carefully thought-out policy under the auspices of the Middle East Council of Churches and its diakonic programmes of relief and reconstruction in the country. Just as in South Africa, when it became clear that the apartheid system was crumbling irreversibly, the South African Council of Churches started to re-examine its role and priorities, so too as the end of the war seemed to draw nearer the ecumenical community in Lebanon asked: 'What kinds of ministry will now most clearly witness to the gospel and the kingdom of God?' Of course, in the aftermath of such human catastrophe there was no shortage of tasks of healing and reconstruction that could have been undertaken. Any one of them, any clinic or school or welfare centre, anywhere, could have been described as a 'practical expression of the love of

God'. But the question being asked was more precise, more searching: it was about what would *most* clearly indicate the values of the kingdom at this particular point in the history of Lebanon. The question therefore became still more concrete. Which communities in Lebanon are tending to be most forgotten? Beirut, after all, was already having a lot of attention paid to it, not least by the church agencies themselves, and likewise the Palestinian refugee camps. Answer: people in the remote villages such as in the upper Bekaa. And who, in such places, are the most vulnerable and under-resourced people? Answer: children with mental and physical handicap. And how, given the tragedy of the recent past, might such service witness to hope? Answer: by being open to, serving, staffed by, managed by, people from both Christian and Muslim communities. To serve the weakest, in the furthest and most hidden places, and to do so in a way which transcended the walls of enmity, was considered to be the most adequate kind of response to the challenge and promise of the gospel of hope and reconciliation.

The choice of this kind of ministry in Lebanon represents a determination of Christians to re-learn their role in a society where confessional affiliation has for generations been locked into a struggle for domination. No matter that many of the 'Christians' and 'Muslims' who rained shells and rockets at each other, reducing much of Beirut to rubble, may have been nominal rather than committed adherents of their respective religious belief-systems (just as 'Protestant' and 'Catholic' in Northern Ireland have come to signify political rather than purely theological differences). The fact that religious identity may be misused for political purposes does not let religious leaders off the hook, but rather increases their responsibility to retrieve and demonstrate a more authentic understanding of their traditions in the service of justice and peace for all, rather than the partisan rhetoric driven solely by the fears for one's own survival as a distinct community. The kind of venture exemplified by Foyer de la Joie signifies a recognition of the need to turn away from saying that this land or city or village belongs to *us*, and learning instead to say that *we* all belong to *it*. In terms of conscious commitment this line may at present be embraced by only a minority, but the quality and creativity of prophecy and discipleship have never been a function purely of numerical strength. The point is that a new Christian and ecumenical humility *is* being learnt in Lebanon, seen for instance in the fact that even the Maronite Church, traditionally almost as dismissive of the Orthodox and other Christian confessions as of the Muslims, and from which the most partisan political Christian figures in the country have habitually come, has now joined the Middle East Council of Churches. The alternative history of God, the striving for justice, reconciliation and peace, as against the triumph of one sector by force at any cost, is being discerned and embraced. The vision is frail but alive, like the roses I found blooming blood-red in the rubble of a burnt-out house on the mountain above east Beirut.

This particular example of prophetic re-learning, however, needs also to be set within the longer and wider history of Christianity in the Middle East. Lebanon is unique in the relative numerical strength of its churches. Over most of the region, for nigh on thirteen centuries since the Islamic conquests, Christians have had to exist as minority communities. Accorded *dhimmi* minority status under Islamic law they have been tolerated and indeed have often worked out an agreeable *modus vivendi* within Islamic societies. But, often effectively second-class citizens in a culture which insists that the Koran lays down the basis for society and politics no less than religion, for generations it has been their very survival as distinct communities which has been the horizon of their aspirations. Kenneth Cragg summarizes the situation: 'The Islamic conquest effectively orphaned the churches within its range and by the *dhimmi* system both perpetuated their divisions ... and consigned them to a limbo of irrelevance — as far as Islam was officially concerned.'[5] One might say that for Arab Christianity ever since the seventh century, history has been one long experience of learning simply to survive. That, inevitably, does not lend itself to a very dynamic or creative image in the eyes

---

[5]Kenneth Cragg, *The Arab Christian. A History in the Middle East,* Mowbray, 1992.

of the world, especially for those in the west who have tended to view Arab Christians (if they have been conscious of them at all) as suspiciously inculturated to and quiescent amidst Islam. The crusaders who sacked Jerusalem in 1099 slaughtered Muslim and Christian alike, and today many western Christian pilgrims to the Holy Land pay scant regard to the historic churches there which are dismissed as quaint irrelevances amid the archaeological sites beloved of piety. No less than with Islam, it is with the imperialist or patronizing attitudes of western Christendom that the churches of the Middle East have had to learn to cope over the centuries, with varying degrees of success.

The questions facing Christianity's role in the Middle East have been given a fresh twist with the rise of Arab nationalism. There has been both opportunity and danger for Arab Christians on the nationalist agenda. What identifies an Arab nation? Is it not, as many Muslim political leaders have argued or assumed, the religion of Islam? But people were Arabs long before there was Islam, and many Christians among them. Can there not be a sense of Arab nationhood, then, which embraces both Muslim and Christian? Here is the real dilemma for the churches of the Middle East, since many of them (especially the uniate churches which, regardless of the language and form of their liturgy, acknowledge the jurisdiction of Rome) lie under an inherent suspicion of being western-orientated or western-dependent and therefore intrinsically non-Arab in ethos. Is there any way of being decidedly Christian yet non-western, of being non-Muslim but Arab?

These are the questions which have set the agenda of learning for the most creative minds in Middle Eastern Christianity in recent years. Nowhere are they more urgent than among the Palestinian Arab Christians. The establishment of the State of Israel and the displacement of large numbers of Palestinians from their homes, the wars of 1956, 1967 and 1973, the continued Israeli occupation of the Gaza Strip and the West Bank, and the *Intifada* uprising have all formed the context of asking 'What does it mean to be Palestinian and Christian?' Certain factors have conspired against facing that question. The 'Arabness' of some churches has been compromised by relying on external personnel rather than truly local, Arab leadership, as for instance (at least until very recently) in the Greek Orthodox Church. Then, too, it is a paradox that it is precisely the 'success', in human terms, of some forms of Christian mission in the Middle East, especially in schooling and higher education, medical care and social service, which has unwittingly loosened the hold of Christianity in the region. These forms of ministry, often under the auspices of western Protestant missions, have played an outstanding part in the development of many areas of society in the region. But one untoward effect of them has been to create a relatively privileged, highly educated and trained population of Christians who can hardly be otherwise than tempted to seek greater employment opportunities, and more security, in Europe and North America in face of an increasingly uncertain future in the region of their birth and nurture. This has been one factor in the serious and much publicized 'exodus' of Christians from the Middle East in recent decades.

Those who do remain in the region therefore have to pursue their questions in an increasingly isolated and vulnerable context, where at least the issues become inescapable. There is always the alternative, of course, of retreating into an introverted preoccupation with maintenance of liturgy and parochial pastoral duty. In a setting where the only meaning of the environment is threatening, meaning can be looked for in the inner apparatus of the church and its continued functioning. But there are also those who dare to ask, not merely what promise the contemporary scene has for the church, but what new meaning for the wider community might be brought out of the tradition of the Christian family. This means learning to look beyond survival, indeed to suspend sheer concern about survival and to let that rest upon the only thing that *is* ultimately worth surviving for, namely God's *shalom* for all people and all creation.

The town of Beit Sahour lies close to Bethlehem in the occupied West Bank territory, and indeed it boasts the traditional site of the Shepherds' Fields where the angels heralded the birth of Jesus. The Bethelehem-Beit Sahour region is also one of the few Palestinian areas where Christians are still, just, in a majority. The town has a lively Orthodox community, and only recently the Arab Orthodox Club — the biggest cultural and sports club in the town — celebrated its twenty-fifth anniversary. Christians and Muslims here live in relative harmony, not least because Christians have been to the fore in resisting the injustices of the Israeli occupation, notably the taxation system imposed by the Israelis. A tax boycott was organized, and that in itself required a theological learning process on the part of the Christian community, especially in face of the derisive accusations by the Israeli authorities that Christians had no business to refuse taxation in view of what the New Testament, including Jesus himself, had to say about the matter. Members of the Greek Orthodox community went and asked their priest for guidance on the matter. He could not help them. He was not equipped either by training or experience to handle such a concrete contemporary dilemma. So, said the committed laity, we had to work out an answer for ourselves. Basing their arguments on the biblical insights of justice, they refused to acknowledge that a regime in illegal and oppressive occupation had a moral right to tax them.

The group most active on these issues in Beit Sahour is called Rapprochement. It might at first be thought that the Christian-Muslim harmony there is possible only because of a common enemy, Israel. But one of Rapprochement's chief aims is to facilitate contact, dialogue and understanding between all parties to conflict in Israel-Palestine, and not least between Palestinians (of whatever faith) and Israelis. As well as small, discreet meetings and family exchanges there have taken place large public gatherings — some of them in the Shepherds' Fields on Christmas Eve. Here therefore is a community prepared to learn how to practise justice and peace for all — and to see their own survival as having meaning only within that process. It is a costly learning, calling for a readiness to tread ways previously uncharted by the tradition in that context. It is discipleship and prophecy in one.

This learning of how to face critical day-to-day questions of living under occupation and deprivation, is being accompanied by some far-reaching theological reassessment, exemplified in the work of the Anglican priest and teacher Naim Ateek.[6] It is a reassessment which goes to the very heart of the interpretation of the sources of Christian faith within the bible. *Hermeneutics,* the science of how we understand and interpret writings from the past or another context, has become a central concern of theology this century, and not least in contemporary theologies of liberation. From what perspective and out of what concern do we read the bible, the creeds or the confessions and traditional writings of our particular churches? Theologies of liberation challenge churches, first, to become aware that they *do* already bring a perspective to bear on the text from their own social context, and secondly, to recognize that if the gospel is first of all good news to the poor and powerless then to be authentically understood it must be read from the perspective of the poor themselves. Such has been the creative thrust of theologies of liberation from Latin America and other parts of the Third World. A theologian such as Ateek has learnt much from them, and indeed the relevance of such theology is clear for the Palestinians who see their own situation of poverty, oppression and deprivation as akin to those in which so many communities elsewhere in the world are practising liberation theology. Ateek, however, knows also that there is one almost universal feature of liberation theology as known hitherto, which will *not* do for the particular Palestinian scene of today: the *exodus* motif of liberation. The biblical story of the triumph of Israel over Pharoah and above all of the conquest of the land of the Caananites has become virtually unreadable to Palestinian Christians, for it has become used as the justification for their deprivation and ejection by the present State of Israel. This was memorably brought home to me personally at a tea-party of Palestinian members of the Anglican congregation in Beirut, all of whom had had to leave their homes in 1947-48. The charming politeness of the occasion (it would have graced an English vicarage) abruptly changed to agonized outbursts of disbelief that any interpretation of the

---

[6]Naim Stefan Ateek, *Justice and Only Justice. A Palestinian Theology of Liberation,* Orbis, 1989.

Old Testament promises of possession of the land could possibly apply to the contemporary state of Israel.

Ateek argues that any theology of liberation for Palestinians must take as its controlling motif, not one particular story or theme from the Old Testament, but the character of God as made known in Jesus: the compassionate energy for an *inclusive* peace which embraces justice for all. This is a costly peace based on the cross, and to be made in a cross-bearing way. 'Christians become involved in the work of peacemaking without illusions. They embark on it with trepidation, fear and trembling.'[7] This must be undergirded by a threefold theological imperative. First, there is attention to the biblical concept of God and God's inclusive love. Second, there must be the exposition and speaking of truth, making the facts of the situation known, including the pervasiveness of sin and injustice — not claiming that the church has 'specific answers to complicated political problems' but a sense of justice and a continual readiness to cry out against injustice. Third, there must be kept alive a concept of peace, informed by a *vision* of peace, that it is possible to attain if people are willing to accept a change in their war mentality.[8]

All this means, argues Ateek, coming to *a new knowledge of God*, a need which must be acknowledged even — and indeed especially by — the church hierarchies, and be embodied in new ecumenical and inter-faith relationships and ministries of service and reconciliation, amid all the pressures of minority status and opposition from the ruling powers:

> The Church lives in the power of the cross. Its strength comes from its crucified and living Lord. It is enlivened by the Holy Spirit. This power enables the Church to overcome its physical and psychological weakness as a minority, and transcend any bitterness or hostility resulting from the political conflict, in order to assume the role of the servant and, for Christ's sake, to become the agent of both peace and reconciliation.[9]

[7]Ibid., p. 149.
[8]Ibid., p. 154.
[9]Ibid., p. 161.

Ateek is one who can speak with great personal integrity of this need for re-learning, devoid of all self-righteousness, because as he makes clear in his deeply moving autobiogaphical testimony, this is a journey of discovery he has been making throughout his life in his own Palestinian soul — 'a journey of faith' — struggling against hate, anger and humiliation.[10]

In the work of Ateek and other peacemaking figures such as Father Elias Chacour[11] we see prophecy and discipleship emerging — and most certainly stemming from that readiness to learn anew, to be taught and re-taught in the Spirit for the contemporary situation. Theirs is a re-learning involving not a rejection of the tradition in which they have been nurtured, but a new penetration into what that heritage of faith means for the present and future. We see enfleshed in them an apprehension of those truths which the church 'does know', as we examined in the preceding chapter, yet needs to retrieve properly and know afresh: from the facts of everyday life right down to the knowledge of God, from an awareness of the world as it all too cruelly is to the knowledge of the coming kingdom and what the world might be in that light.

The need for re-penetration and new exposition of religious tradition is particularly crucial and urgent in the Middle East. As Kenneth Cragg puts it:

> The vital test of any faith ... is its ability to identify and resist the evils that are collective in their origin and their momentum and to do so most of all when the faith itself is their source and sanction. An honest review of the Middle East story may conclude that all such hope is vain. When they most need to be self-critical and in doubt of themselves, where the passion of creed and greed, of tribe and trade, is rampant, they most readily aid and abet.[12]

As Cragg argues, if Christianity has a creative future in the region it will be through a new discovery and articulation of 'God in Christ', incarnate and crucified, the gospel of 'the God

[10]Ibid., p. 164.
[11]See Elias Chacour and David Hazard, *Blood Brothers*, Old Tappan, 1984.
[12]Cragg, op. cit., p. 292.

whose sovereignty fulfils itself in the love that comes, suffers, and reconciles, in the measures we can identify in Jesus and the cross'.[13] Only a hold on such central convictions, to which the ancient creeds pointed in their abstractions that became badges of disunity, triumphalism and strife, will be adequate both to the tradition itself and to the daunting realities of attempting to live as neighbours with Muslim and Jew.

Eastern Europe and former Soviet Union: learning after survival

If the chief concern of the Christian churches in the Middle East has for so many years been *how* to survive, the main challenge facing the churches in the countries recently released from communist rule is that of coming to terms with the fact that they *have* survived, and now need to learn what to do with that survival.

January 27 is the feast day of St Sava, Serbia's patron saint, first archbishop of the Serbs in the thirteenth century, effective founder of both the church and nation of Serbia. The church of St Sava in Belgrade is packed to and beyond the doors for the three-hour Mount Sinai liturgy, presided over by the diminutive figure of Patriarch Pavle, the present head of the ehurch. As so often with Orthodox liturgy, description vainly struggles against superlatives. The intoning and chanting by the celebrants is answered with the rich, sonorous harmonies from the choir in the gallery, the sound breaking over and resounding round the church like some great tidal wave of devotion. As the gospel is read, two elderly women struggle forward through the solid mass of worshippers standing before the screen to kneel and clutch hold of the azure and silver vestments of the priest. Incense wafts across the dais. A young woman, madonna-like as she holds her baby to her shoulder, stands as if transported, tears running down her cheeks.

This is devotion that has survived and revived. Tito's Yugoslav communism was, in the opinion of most observers, a relatively mild version compared with that imposed on the Warsaw Pact

[13]Ibid., p. 292.

countries, a bloc from which Tito remained resolutely independent. It was nevertheless a system barely tolerant of religion, and the large Serbian Orthodox and Roman Catholic Churches, together with the smaller Protestant communities, found themselves severely marginalised from official social policy. Virtually no new church building was permitted in Belgrade. In part Tito's policy on religion was part of his determination to override the distinctive nationalities of the Yugoslav republics with their majority religious identities — Slovenian and Croatian Catholicism, Serbian Orthodoxy, Bosnian Islam and so forth. By the same token, under the unifying socialist ideology the churches, and none more so than the Serbian Orthodox Church, found a powerful and sustaining sense of purpose as bearers of historic national and cultural identity. That mission, clearly, has been fulfilled in the outliving of the communist Yugoslav state, and the St Sava's day liturgy is a celebration of that triumph.

Here of course is where the questions begin for the Serbian Orthodox Church. The very same national aspirations which it helped to preserve under Tito have now been ruthlessly exploited by the opportunistic politicians bent on creating a 'Greater Serbia'. Patriarch Pavle and many of his bishops have distanced themselves from the regime of President Milosevic and have courageously denounced the brutality of the war with Bosnia and Croatia, yet seem powerless to effect any leverage over the war-lords wreaking havoc there. Furthermore, their own idealizing of the unity of the Serb people would seem to render ambiguous any stated commitment to peace in the Balkans as a whole. In such a situation, can a national church be other than nationalistic? The same question, it should be said, applies equally to the Roman Catholic Church in Croatia.

'Eastern Europe' is too large and complex a concept to allow easy generalization, especially where its churches are concerned, not to mention the countries of the former Soviet Union itself, but the same fundamental question finds parallels in so many particular contexts: what have the churches survived *for*? It ill behoves westerners who never experienced the oppressive years at first hand to denounce from a distance the 'triumphalism' of church leaders in the east. The symbol of the cross *has* outlived the hammer and sickle. For our purposes here, the issue is whether and how Christianity in the countries concerned is capable of recognizing in the very moment of liberation the need and opportunity for re-learning, the apprehension of a role which will contribute to their societies' new struggles for an order based on peace, justice and human rights. Times of rapid social transition can be exciting to watch from the outside, but bewildering to experience from within. The kind of experience was symbolized for me in an almost amusing way when being shown around the Baptist theological seminary in Budapest in the great year of change, 1989. A fine new building was being erected on the present site of the seminary. A few months earlier, the Baptists had run into trouble with the government planning authorities, who refused them permission to include a baptistery in the new seminary chapel. Such a device, said the officials, would not be required if the chapel was indeed for use by the seminarians (the authorities obviously did not wish the chapel to become, by design or default, another centre for a local congregation). But these were the months of change and by the time of my visit the authorities could not care less what went into a Baptist seminary chapel (if western money was coming in so much the better). This however was not the end of problems. Carrying out the original plan for the seminary extension would have required the removal of several large trees at the rear of the site — and now the local 'Greens' were objecting to this and so further modifications were required. From communist bureacracy to pluralist democracy in a space of months!

Such a transition does demand a readiness for new learning by the churches, and especially those which by virtue of their size and historic role in the life of their nations may assume that all that is now required is a return to their rights and privileges denied them under state socialism. And to speak of a 'spiritual vacuum' after the collapse of Soviet communism is not untrue. Watching, on a bleak February morning, the long queues of wreath-carrying pilgrims winding their way through the snow flurries across Red Square to pay their respects at the tomb of Lenin, it was hard not to feel that here was an ersatz religion performing its liturgy. Inside the Kremlin, on the walls of the sublimely beautiful Cathedrals of the Assumption and the Annunciation, left intact as museums, the large-eyed ikons of the saints were waiting with timeless patience for the return of the faithful to Christian worship, and they have not waited and prayed in vain. But what do the churches have with which to fill that vacuum? Or are they themselves, dread thought, part of that vacuum, one group among others simply competing for sectional power?

'The rivalry of communism and Christianity has had a decisive impact on our age. This period is now coming to an end. On this giant battlefield, as far as the eye can see, there are no more heroes, only the starving still wandering around. We are all surrounded by a feeling of emptiness. One looks back nostalgically to the time when there were motivations other than emptiness.'[14]. So writes a Polish Catholic, Josef Tischner, from a national context where for a time it seemed as though Christianity in its Catholic form was offering a simple, solid, triumphal alternative to communism. and which has provided a Pope announcing a project for the 're-Christianization' of Europe. As Tischner states, in Catholic Poland the church stepped in as mainstay of freedom and brought liberals, disillusioned with marxism, into the Catholic camp. 'But now doubts are spreading in the church's camp as well. Before our eyes there is a turning away from the church — both Christianity and religion in general have to accept a sharp drop in numbers. Might it be that liberalism will prove to be the only idea that is victorious?'[15]. Another observer of the Polish and Central European scene, Patrick Michel, identifies the problem facing the church as one of reorientation to a pluralist scene, of becoming a creative force in the political sphere without itself simply filling the vacuum left by communist totalitarianism with an authoritarianism of its own.[16] The fact that the Polish Catholic authorities still speak of the nation needing to preserve

---

[14]J. Tischner, 'Christianity in the Post-Communist Vacuum', *Religion, State and Society*, Vol. 20, 3 & 4, 1992, p. 332.

[15]Ibid., p. 331.

[16]P. Michel, 'Religious Renewal and Political Deficiency: Religion and Democracy in Central Europe', *Religion, State and Society*, Vol. 20, 3 & 4, 1992, pp. 339-344.

its Catholic identity, Michel argues, indicates that the church
has yet to reflect on the very nature of democracy:

> The church has applied itelf to helping Polish society to
> give birth to political modernity. Today the church must
> find its place within this modernity. Yet all the indications
> are that this is difficult to achieve. The church will have to
> abandon all claims to the central position that it occupied
> by force of circumstance during the years of resistance.
> 'To live in pluralism,' said Adam Michnik, 'is to know how
> to limit oneself, to know that we live with others and to
> make that cohabitation viable.' 'Limiting oneself',
> however, has to entail leaving the realm of totality and
> entering the realm of the relative. Yet the Polish church
> seems to have some difficulty in resolving to do so; its
> victorious confrontation with a Soviet-type regime has in
> fact done little to prepare it for its meeting with
> modernity.[17]

A stern re-learning exercise indeed, and similar tests face the
churches in all ex-communist societies, albeit in varying degrees.
Even in the former East Germany where the Protestant churches
made a notable venture of living in 'critical solidarity' with
socialism, and where the rapid and bloodless change of 1989
was justifiably heralded as the 'pastors' revolution' by virtue of
the churches' initiation of public debates, adjustment has not
been without pain. Learning, as many did, how to live with a
certain critical detachment from political authorities, has not
by itself made it easy for Christians now to adopt a citizenship
which readily *carries* political responsibility. On his recent
return from a year in Berlin, one close observer of the German
scene in both east and west commented to me that in this
respect he felt that Catholic laity in the east, who during the
communist era had been encouraged by their leadership to
adopt a lower, non-political profile, were perhaps proving
more capable of adjustment to liberalization and reunification.
(Perhaps also significant here is the story of the Baptist
community in a village in the east, who with the sudden onset

[17]Ibid., p. 342.

of local democracy were descended upon by their neighbours to supply a mayor and other leaders in the new local authority on the grounds that they at least, because of their self-governing congregational polity, were presumed to know already what this democratic business was all about.)

It is in Russia itself, however, that the most critical scenario is emerging. Lurid tales are reaching the west of an Orthodoxy seeking sheer restoration of the pre-revolutionary scene, blessing resurgent Russian chauvinism, anti-semitism and even fascism, while still contaminated by KGB-infiltrated clergy who know how to pull political strings to suit their own power interests. The picture is, as usual, more complicated and at least two levels of 'Orthodox' activity need to be distinguished. At one level there are the political movements in which priests and believing laity are involved, which seek to imbue the social scene with an Orthodox ethos of one kind or another. At another level, there is the official church position as represented by its hierarchy. And yet another factor is how these two levels relate to each other. All this takes place within the whirlwind of social change already occurring, let alone being talked about, and the release of one stage of fragmentation after another. As one commentator observes:

> The phenomenon of post-communism is marked by distinct and often contradictory tendencies. The aspiration to democracy is accompanied by an ambivalence to rationality and a search for new meta-truths to replace the shattered bearings of the old society. In this context, religious life is an act of both psychic and social reintegration. Society is uniquely open to revealed truth, and at the same [time] prey to charlatanism and unscrupulous operators. The phenomenon of the 'practising non-believer' emerges, in contrast to the prevalance of the 'non-practising believer' in the West.[18]

On the level of political groupings and parties, much interest has centred on the Russian Christian Democratic Movement

[18]R. Sakwa, 'Christian Democracy in Russia', *Religion, State and Society*, Vol. 20, 2, 1992, p. 158.

which emerged in 1990, and with which a number of priests have been associated including the well-known dissident Father Gleb Yakunin. This has indeed, as with the Catholic-inspired Christian Democratic parties in western Europe, genuinely sought to promote democratic values in society within a strongly communal ethos, and to rescue the church from 'Sergianism', that subservience to the state which allegedly as was held to marked its behaviour in the totalitarian communist era. In its liberalism it stops well short of endorsing western 'individualism' and its social philosophy owes much to the communal, personalist thinking of well-known Orthodox figures of an earlier generation such as Nicolas Berdyaev. Nor does it seek to romanticize any particular era of the past as a mythical example of society to be restored. It seeks a 'free church in a free state' and an 'enlightened patriotism'.[19]

A critical question is clearly the relationship between such a movement and the official church leadership. On the one hand the movement sees itself as a friend of the church and as promoting Christian values in the shaping of the new society. On the other hand, the church hierarchy have sought to distance themselves from this as from all political parties (while under suspicion in some quarters that they are still playing their own political game through direct and close links with figures in government). The question then has to be asked as to how the Orthodox Church views its own calling and role in the reconstruction of the new society. Is it enough simply to offer itself, as it is, as the vacuum-filler? How is its great tradition of liturgy and spirituality to be transposed into values and goals for citizens to embody in secular social life? There can be no democracy without autonomy for people and their social institutions. Does the church recognize this necessity and how it will affect its own style of leadership? Or is it assuming that the only valid method of spiritual leadership in society is that of direct, authoritarian control?

Is the church itself prepared to *learn*, to come to terms with some new thing, at this critical point in its and Russia's history? This is an especially significant question for the Orthodox

[19]Ibid., p. 155.

Church, since the very strength and solidity of its venerable tradition of doctrine, liturgy and spirituality seems to foreclose any role to it except that of teacher. The danger with having a tradition is to assume that it can be maintained merely by repetition, without seeing that it can *live* only through being put to new use under new conditions and thus developing in the process, although without losing its real identity. The social significance for today of the teaching of the fathers and saints will not emerge simply from reciting them. They require reflection and questioning from within the context of the pressures and issues of today's world, if they are to speak to that world. It is this awareness for which one Russian priest, Nikolai Balashov, has recently argued.[20] In a trenchant attack on the assumptions behind the current revival of interest in ascetic spirituality he dismisses the belief that the saving and healing word of God will reach the spiritually impoverished Russian people 'through the mere recitation of instructive stories from the lives of the desert Fathers'.[21] These stories have a certain enchantment, and were used to educate Orthodox Russia over nine centuries. 'Yet this did not prevent the revolution, the establishment of a totalitarian regime with its death toll of millions of lives, or the post-revolutionary tragedy of the Russian Church.'[22] Nor, states Balashov, will it now suffice for the creation of a Christian form of statehood, economy, community and culture:

> As if nothing has happened, a vast majority of our pastors continue to preach a one-sided view of Christianity and the Church as predominantly an ascetic school, with individual spiritual education under the guidance of a starets or elder. Elders are not easy to find nowadays: genuine elders are in short supply. But never mind: any amount of clerics readily offer themselves to play the part, even those who were ordained as recently as yesterday. It is no problem: the less one knows, the fewer doubts one

---

[20]N. Balashov, '"Holy Russia" and related problems', *Sobornost*, Vol. 15, 2, 1993, pp. 39-43.

[21]Ibid., p. 39.

[22]Ibid.

harbours; answers to any questions are available at the drop of a hat.

Since the church Fathers already said everything of importance long ago, every creative effort becomes suspect in the eyes of the custodians of tradition. All outward activity is perceived as vain, distracting one from what is crucial: the interior life, the life of the spirit. In any case, they would insist, it is useless taking any part in social life. As long as a person is enslaved by sin, can he or she have any positive influence on others?[23]

This dominance of the unexamined ascetic ideal, Balashov insists, far from being creative in the life of the contemporary church, is resulting in an arid sterility, preventing any engagement of faith with the everyday world outside the church or beyond the immediate gaze of the ikons. But, crucially, he identifies the fault not with the Fathers themselves, but with the contemporary Christians who blindly repeat their words without noticing how time changes their meaning. The Fathers spoke, in a uniquely personal way, out of a burning love of God and a mysterious freedom. Today there is a servile imitation of them instead of an enkindling by their spirit. 'The result is our inability to deal creatively with the challenge of modern times and our consequent and cowardly retreat from reality into a parallel phantom world of pseudo-spiritual dreams.'[24]

Such a critique exposes a vital lesson which applies more widely than Balashov's immediate Russian context. One can go through all the poses and forms of being taught without really learning anything. There can evidently be a great deal of teaching but little learning, little real prophecy and discipleship. What learning there is can amount to little more than a conditioning to subservience, not the liberating curiosity to know more through venture and engagement in one's own experience, not the truth which will make us free. But so long

[23]Ibid., p. 4.
[24]Ibid., p. 43.

as voices like those of Balashov are making themselves heard, there is prophecy. It is a voice challenging the church, the church manifestly at its strongest, the church of the unbroken tradition of creed and liturgy, and now the triumphantly surviving post-communist church, to become a learning child all over again, for its own sake and the sake of those whom it would serve and lead.

Learning to learn: a paradigm for everywhere

We could of course have looked at many other contexts in which churches today are learning that ... they have to learn. The exciting implications of the 'base Christian communities' in Latin America and certain experiments in Christian living and learning in Asia would more than merit comment if space permitted. But even just the three national or regional cases we have examined have illustrated that prophetic speech and action can only spring from communities that are undergoing re-education, often costly and painful, through their present historical experience and through fresh apprehension of their traditions. These are churches where some, at least, realize that prior to speaking to society they have to learn what is to be said. They have to be hearers and doers of the Word of God before presuming to speak it. That means they have to admit that they themselves are in need of teaching, that they are ignorant, that they do not yet have answers. And that is hard to bear.

Churches in western Europe and North America may well look on these contexts as particularly 'critical' ones, in the sense that they are in rapid or near-explosive social change. But this whole book presupposes that the situation in the 'west' is also critical (as well as, on the socio-political and economic levels, helping to generate crisis after crisis for the rest of the world). All contexts for the Christian community are 'critical' in that over every situation, those of apparent ease and security no less than those of breakdown and conflict, there stands the ultimate 'crisis', the judgment, revealed in the cross of Christ. Within every context the alternative history of God has to be discerned. The crisis in the west has many symptoms, not least the fact that the churches are steadily becoming minorities, and even those which call themselves 'national churches' can, in secularized societies, no longer pretend they carry the same sort of influence in public life which they once had. There is a learning to be undertaken on being a creative minority (as distinct from being an introverted or aggressive one) in society. That creativity means a re-learning of the missionary role of the church within society. Such a mission in its multi-dimensional and many-faceted nature has continually to be renewed and reconceived, in the west no less than elsewhere. T. S. Eliot is once again apposite:

> In order to arrive there,
> To arrive where you are, to get from where you are not,
>   You must go by a way wherein there is no ecstasy.
> In order to arrive at what you do not know
>   You must go by a way which is the way of ignorance.
> In order to possess what you do not possess
>   You must go by the way of dispossession.
> In order to arrive at what you are not
>   You must go through the way in which you are not.[25]

The late David Bosch, one of the outstanding missiologists of our time, has argued that mission demands a new paradigm today, a paradigm not of expansion, domination or conquest, but of identification with the liberating mission of the incarnate, self-emptying Jesus under the cross — 'the only place where it is ever safe'.[26] Mission faithful to the biblical vision knows that there are seemingly irresolvable tensions; for instance, as was recognized at the 1989 Meeting of the Conference on World Mission and Evangelization at San Antonio, Texas, between the belief that there is no salvation other than in Christ while at the same time limits cannot be set to the saving power of God. Bosch comments:

> Such language boils down to an admission that we do not
> have all the answers and are prepared to live within the

[25]T.S. Eliot, 'East Coker' from 'Four Quartets', *The Complete Poems and Plays of T.S. Eliot*, Faber and Faber 1969, p. 181.

[26]David J. Bosch, *Transforming Mission. Paradigm Shifts in Theology of Mission*, Orbis, 1991, p. 519.

framework of penultimate knowledge, that we regard our involvement in dialogue and mission as an adventure, are prepared to take risks, and are anticipating surprises as the Spirit guides us into fuller understanding. This is not opting for agnosticism, but for humility. It is, however, a bold humility — or a humble boldness. We know only in part, but we do know. And we believe that the faith we profess is both true and just, and should be proclaimed. We do this, however, not as judges or lawyers, but as witnesses; not as soldiers, but as envoys of peace; not as high-pressure salespersons, but as ambassadors of the servant Lord.[27]

Or, if one dare add to that list of 'not as ... but': not as 'experts' but as researchers whose every new discovery makes them both want to share it with others and to learn still more for themselves.

[27]Ibid., p. 489.

8

Forms of Speech

Sometimes it is possible to speak in a way which not only comments upon, illuminates or even influences a situation, but actually creates a quite new state of affairs. As far as the Christian church is concerned, one of the most dramatic recent instances of this is from Malawi. Independence came to Malawi in 1964, in the flood tide of anti-colonial movements sweeping through Africa. Hopes of genuine liberation however were short-lived, as the government of President Hastings Banda imposed one-party, autocratic rule. For nearly thirty years the people of Malawi were subjected to an increasingly totalitarian regime, with all political opposition and dissidence silenced by the heavy apparatus of a police state. With the 1990s, as democratization once again began to awaken in Africa — even South Africa — no less than in eastern Europe, internal discontent made itself felt together with economic pressure from aid-donating northern countries and financial institutions. President Banda eventually agreed to a referendum, held in June 1993, in which a clear majority of the people said 'Yes' to multiparty democracy.

What by common consent proved to be the decisive catalyst for change came from a somewhat unexpected quarter. On 8 March 1992, in all Roman Catholic churches in Malawi there was read out a pastoral letter from the bishops of the church protesting about the current state of affairs in the country and calling for a society of participation, equality and human rights whereby justice and true national unity could be achieved.[1] Such

---

[1] *The truth will set you free. A statement by the bishops of Malawi*, Church in the World 28, CAFOD et al, 1992.

205

a statement was costly and risked suffering. The government labelled the document seditious, possession of it a crime. The bishops for a time were subjected to house arrest and there were real threats against their lives. However their action was also fruitful. It precipitated, for the first time, a truly open dialogue between government and opposition. Soon the other Christian leaders, especially from the Anglican and Presbyterian Churches, along with Muslim leaders, lawyers and a variety of political opposition groups, were involved in forming an insistent platform of pro-democracy voices which could no longer be ignored by the government, leading to the referendum of June 1993.

It is no exaggeration to say that a new Malawi was born on 8 March 1992. The 'culture of silence' had been broken[2] by the very fact of speaking out. One of the Catholic bishops confessed that he himself had experienced a real liberation through speaking. This is not to deny, of course, that the statement was to inaugurate difficulties of a new order, as always happens when breakthroughs generate further responsibilities and complexities. The Exodus is but the beginning of trials for Moses. But it is clear that the pastoral letter *was* a breakthrough and fully merits attention, not least by churches outside the Third World, as a classic case of courageous speech by a church confessing the faith in a context of political oppression. It confronted human rights abuses with stark clarity:

> Nobody should ever have to suffer reprisals for honestly expressing and living up to their convictions: intellectual, religious or political.

> We can only regret that this is not always the case in our country ... Academic freedom is seriously restricted; exposing injustices can be considered a betrayal; revealing some evils of our society is seen as slandering the country; monopoly of mass media and censorship prevent the expression of dissenting views; some people have paid dearly for their political opinions ...

[2] *The Referendum in Malawi: Free Expression Denied,* Article 19 (Issue 22), April 1993, p. 3.

This is most regrettable. It creates an atmosphere of resentment among the citizens. It breeds an atmosphere of mistrust and fear. This fear of harassment and mutual suspicion generates a society in which the talents of many lie unused and in which there is little room for initiative.[3]

This was certainly speaking the truth. The church was speaking of what it knew of day to day life and political reality. But the very title of the pastoral letter indicates that it was also speaking truth at another level: *The truth will set you free* (cf. Jn. 8.32). What marks the bishops' statement is its firm *theological* grounding. It begins with a crisp affirmation of the dignity and unity of humankind, created in God's image, as the basis on which human rights and equality are to be proclaimed. Quoting from Pope Paul VI it proceeds to an outline of the church's role as including concern for human temporal welfare as well as 'religious' matters. Only then does it launch its analysis and comment on the state of affairs in the country. The final sections of the letter return to Jesus' words on the liberating power of the truth, and his affirmation of his ministry in the Spirit to liberate the captives (Lk. 4.18f.), as expressing 'a deep human reality'. Significantly, the tone is not one of over-righteous denunciation, but one which presents issues 'for our reflection' which 'God invites us to consider seriously'. 'We hope that our message will deepen in all of us the experience of conversion and *the desire for the truth and the light of Christ*' (emphasis mine). Here is the learning church calling others and itself to a new humility of learning before God.

It is appropriate that we have begun the final chapter in this exploration of what it means for the church to speak authentically to the world, with this statement. It exemplifies so much of what has been argued for in earlier sections: the theological clearing of space and establishing of the ground of specifically Christian witness; the citation of clearly known facts of life and suffering, 'from the deepest knowledge of the world' (cf. Bonhoeffer, Chapter 6 above); not a claim to an achieved ecclesiastical righteousness but the confession of the

[3] *The truth will set you free*, p. 5.

need to learn; a teaching which is not a display of one-way didacticism but an invitation to join the enquiry. As such we can hold it before us as an inspiring and encouraging example of how the church can in every sense speak truthfully. That it is an instance from the Third World is even more matter for reflection and should prepare those of us in the north to be further educated by the south, where the main life and energy of Christianity in today's world is increasingly to be found.

It may however be felt that such an instance, precisely because it comes from a singularly fraught and dramatic situation, has — like Barmen and the *Kairos Document* — a charismatic quality which does not relate easily to the more mundane and muddled contexts in which most churches and Christians live for most of the time. Only comparatively rarely do we find ourselves *in extremis*. Not every moment is necessarily a 'kairos'. It is splendid when the church speaks out for political freedom, democracy and human rights when these are utterly denied. Once some measure of these values is established, however, the questions begin. Democracy brings with it argument about goals and how to achieve them, about social priorities and the use of resources. How does the church enter such debates? Should, could, there be a clear 'Christian voice' on them? It is one thing for the church to be a partisan *for* democracy, but quite another for it to be partisan *within* democracy; one thing for it to be the voice when all other voices are silenced, another for it to be a voice once the public address system is reconnected. That, as has been noted, has already been found to be the case in Malawi, as in South Africa too.

We need, then, to return to the question of what manner of speaking may be appropriate for the church in a variety of contexts and circumstances. We have emphasized throughout that to be genuinely 'prophetic' requires a certain discipline. It also requires imagination. The 'church speaking' should not become fixed on certain staid stereotypes of statements by church leaders and official bodies. For one thing, local churches, parishes and ecumenical groups should be encouraged to make their own ventures into 'prophecy' much more than at present, and not be continually looking for 'leadership' at national level to speak. As was seen in Chapter 2, the German

Church Struggle was primarily resourced and inspired in its early stages by *local* proclamations and liturgies of confession, and likewise the Kairos movement in South Africa was a network of locally contextual theologies. For another, as part of the learning process far more imaginative use needs to be made of statements once they are made. If the speaking of the church is not to be cheapened into a series of ephemeral noises, then statements need evaluating with the passage of time. In some cases they should be tested as providing guidelines for continuing action by the church — and therefore as criteria against which the fulfilment of the church's mission can be measured. Churches can hardly expect the world to take what they say seriously, if they themselves regard their statements as mere pieces of paper for filing.

Among the most important disciplinary elements in seeking authentic and effective utterance on public issues is an awareness of the kind of thinking and speaking that is already taking place on the matters concerned, especially among the political decision-makers themselves. In fact, for all the talk about 'taking the world seriously on its own terms' which has been popular among socially-minded clergy for three or more decades now, paying attention to how the politicians themselves are actually approaching the issues confronting them, and the conditions under which they are operating, is usually just about the last concern of the church anxious to speak. This of course matters not one jot if the point of speaking is simply to get something off the ecclesiastical chest and into the religious press. If, however, the intention of speaking is actually that of making some difference, of influencing in however small a way the political decision-making process, thought needs to be given to how that process is working and to the appropriate angle at which intervention should be attempted.

At an ecumenical gathering of church representatives in Britain recently, a group was assigned the task of constructing a letter to be sent to the British Prime Minister at the forthcoming European Community summit meeting, at which he would be acting as President. One of the group, a former Treasury official, was asked how such a letter should be written. 'So it will be noticed by a civil servant at two in the morning,' he replied. The remark can be taken as more than of immediate and practical relevance. 'Two in the morning' is a convenient figure of speech for the whole peculiar perspective from within which politicians and those who advise them operate. More than once in his autobiography *The Time of My Life* (Penguin, 1990) Denis Healey quotes Dean Acheson's comment that while academics reach conclusions, politicians have to reach decisions. And while academics may give themselves plenty of time to reach their conclusions, politicians never have enough time before the decisions are made for them. That is not to say, however, that policy decisions in principle and in detail are purely pragmatic with no intellectual direction. It is mistaken either to exaggerate or ignore the conceptual element in political affairs. What is important is that those who would bring a conscious moral perspective to bear on the process should be alert to the actual frame of reference within which the politicians are operating. This can vary — and should not be assumed to correlate purely with ideological position. I wish to illustrate this with particular reference to international affairs.

International affairs: the three-fold approach

Too often, churches and other morally-conscious bodies approach international issues with an assumption that whereas they stand for the values broadly described as 'internationalist', governments of their own and other countries are inevitably 'nationalist', 'ethnocentric' or in some other sense inherently committed to the narrow self-interest of the nation-state and its people at the expense of the wider community. This may at times, perhaps often, be true, but it also ignores the way in which governmental thinking on international issues is far from monochrome in its approach.

Martin Wight was an outstanding British scholar and teacher on international relations, who died at a sadly early age in 1972. Only quite recently has the full fruit of his teaching become available in published form.[4] Wight's main thesis is that in the

[4]Martin Wight, *International Theory. The Three Traditions*, (ed. G. Wight and B. Porter), Leicester University Press for Royal Institute of International Affairs, 1991.

modern world both the theory and political practice of international relations manifests three main approaches: the 'realist', the 'rationalist' and the 'revolutionist'. With each of these approaches Wight associates an archetypal thinker — not necessarily the founder of the respective approach but certainly a seminal philosopher whose thought has great affinities with its main line, who may often have expressed it and who can symbolize its main principles.

Thus, first, the *realist* approach is that which sees the world as essentially a realm of competing states and political authorities, each engaged in maintaining and if possible increasing its power over the others. Its philosophical patron is Machiavelli whose work *The Prince* has become the archetypal study of statecraft based on the premise that what the ruler needs to know is how to safeguard and, if desirable, extend his power. Today its approach is summarized in the term *Realpolitik* and its definitive example is provided by a figure such as Bismarck who in starkly unsentimental fashion recognized no interests to be real beyond those of the nation-state: 'I have always found the word Europe on the lips of those politicians who wanted something from other Powers which they dared not demand in their own name.' The key-word for realism is power. Its ethos is that of the threatened in this world, the fortress mentality.

Second, the *rationalist* approach views the world as essentially a single, comprehensive system of interests to be held in balance, whether of states or other entities such as trading groups, industries etc. Crucial to balance and harmony is the concept of a commonly recognized code. Its definitive early expression was found in Hugo Grotius and his application of natural law principles to the life of nations. The key-word for rationalism is authority. It does not pretend that the present world order is ideal, and indeed the rationalist has a marked aversion to investing any political institution with absolute, final value. Content with the best available in the circumstances, rationalism does not expect too much from the political sphere. It is enough to know that here lies one's duty, though not one's final destiny as a human being. In England, Edmund Burke still stands as its most eloquent advocate: 'We must do the best we can in our situation. The situation of man is the preceptor of his duty.' Many would argue that, from Gladstone onwards, rationalism has been the main feature of British foreign policy. Its ethos is that of the secure and fairly comfortable in this world, concerned for equipoise and the minimum of disturbance.

Third, the *revolutionist* approach brings to the world a moral imperative of universal import. History is to be subjected to a moral claim from beyond itself. In this respect it is Kant who is the philosophical patron here. The existing order is to be measured against the plumb-line of a given ideal or ideology and, if found wanting, to be destroyed and reconstructed. Whereas the rationalist denies the ultimacy of politics and the finality of human institutions, the revolutionist condemns the existing system of power in order to replace it with another — though still political — system. There is thus a tendency almost to 'divinize' the political category as prescribing human goals and providing the sphere of moral judgment and duty. 'Revolutionist' can of course cover a diverse range of particular political goals and ideologies, from right-wing to left-wing, from pacifism to the armed struggle. The free-market capitalism for which Margaret Thatcher and Ronald Reagan crusaded in the 1980s was every bit as 'revolutionist' as the marxist-leninist ideology to which they were so bitterly opposed. (In fact it can be argued that Marxism is far from being purely 'revolutionist' in this sense, being something of a blend with rationalism and its notion of an immanent historical process.) Its ethos can equally be that of the hurt and aggrieved, whether in their own name or that of others.

Two points need to be noted in Wight's thesis. First, these approaches are not just those of political theoreticians. They are manifest in the actual practice of statecraft by real politicians in office and by others active in the public sphere. Second, these approaches are not necessarily mutually exclusive in any one government or politician at any one time. They can find expression in varying degrees of combination.

Bearing these points in mind, Wight offers us a useful framework for interpreting political thinking on international affairs in any particular context, and one to which morally-minded communities such as the churches would do well to pay great heed. The question can then be asked, What main approach is being followed by decision-makers in relation to this particular issue of the moment? The kind of knowledge or wisdom which the church should bring to the situation, and the manner in which it should speak, will then be greatly affected by whether it is the realist, the rationalist or the revolutionist mode (or a peculiar compound of them) which is operating. The assumption often made by Christian thinkers is that because they themselves represent a deep moral commitment, theirs is by rights always the 'revolutionist' approach. The moral imperative is that which they have to impress on politicians who are hidebound either in *Realpolitik* or in that cautious form of rationalism which believes in studying the situation intensely and doing nothing. But for one thing, as was shown in Chapter 6, the church knows things other than purely moral dictates. There is a Christian knowledge of information about the immediate world, and of the realities of human nature in society. For another, it is not unknown for governments to adopt a moralizing tone themselves in dealing with international issues. The recent moves by western governments and financial institutions to link aid to African countries with progress on human rights and democratization is a case in point.

The three approaches can be taken as indications of the different kinds of discourse which may be holding sway at any one time among those dealing with international politics. It is important that those who wish to engage with them from a particular moral perspective should recognize which kind of discourse is being pursued by the decision-makers, and should decide just how the moral perspective in its turn is going to join in the conversation. If for instance a sternly 'realist' line is being taken by the powers that be on, say, the promotion of arms exports, then it needs to be decided whether the 'realist' approach is going to be challenged in the name of moral considerations ('profits and jobs at home and political clout abroad, are not the only things that matter — so do lives and human rights'), or whether the 'realism' is going to be challenged on its own terms as not being realistic enough: 'our national interest is *not* served by swamping countries with arms which could well be turned against us and our friends in due course ...' If the approach to an issue is largely rationalist, for example that of third world debt, again, it has to be decided whether the church will argue against rationalism in the name of 'higher considerations', or become as a rationalist to the rationalists, perhaps by insisting that the 'facts of the case' must include those of brutality and human misery which are too often conveniently folded away out of sight of the comfortable, rationalist world-view. If the discourse is the revolutionist rhetoric, the need may well be felt irresistible to oppose the ideology being proclaimed as a 'false gospel', or it may be felt that the ideology is quite consistent with and indeed expressive of the gospel and its claims — but can even the most humane ideology by itself cope with human failure? Ideologies and idealisms, even and perhaps most especially those with the loftiest conceptions of humanity and aspirations for human betterment, cannot forgive — least of all those who fail in their cause. Yet at the end of the day it is forgiveness that people need most, for and from each other, and without it there is no hope for community.

This is to bring us back to central theological questions. The church's address to the world obviously needs to be geared to the particular features of the secular context, but equally must also stem from the heart of its own belief. Its manner of speaking is a question of theology at least as much as that of 'how to communicate in contemporary society'. That being so, is one form of speech specially appropriate? With what kind of grammar should faith address the world on worldly issues? In contemporary Britain and elsewhere a number of answers to this question are being given.

A manner of speaking: the indicative

John Habgood, Archbishop of York, is deeply committed to Christian engagement with social and international issues yet cautions against any expectation that Christians can supply distinctive prescriptions for public ills.[5] The prime Christian

---

[5] J. Habgood, *Church and Nation in a Secular Age*, Darton, Longman and Todd, 1983.

contribution to social ethics, he argues, lies in the indicative rather than the imperative. That is, it speaks in terms of the principles by which people should live and by which societies should order themselves. Christians cannot offer much that could not be said by all reasonable people of good will. What Christian belief does offer, is an insight into what kind of place the world is, the locus of human sinfulness and divine grace, and so provides 'the context within which the intractable realities of social and political life can be tackled with wisdom and integrity'.[6] We might describe Habgood's approach as that of reason informed by faith, or faith tempered by reason, and as such characteristically Anglican. It is very much in the William Temple tradition. So too is the approach of David Jenkins, until recently Bishop of Durham, who, despite his media-fed notoriety as a troublesome political priest, does not wish to claim too much, too soon, for the social illumination provided by Christian faith. He is worth quoting at length on this:

> Faith, as such, clearly cannot give us details, but surely it can, and must, give us direction. For instance, it seems to me that Christian faith underwrites and develops the conviction that men and women are meant to be free, that all human beings are of worth, and are meant to share and to belong and to count; meant to have their own part to play in whatever relationships and livelihoods are available. Now that faith, that insight and hope does not tell us directly about details and patterns of behaviour or about the workings of things like markets, banks and industries, distributive networks and the rest of it. But surely our faith does and must warn us if we see any absolutizing of economic theories and explanations which lead people to declare, in answer to questions about effects and the cautions about prospects, that there is and can be no other way. Faith here surely joins up with prudence ... That joins up with common sense ...[7]

[6]Ibid., p. 168.
[7]David E. Jenkins, *God, Politics and the Future*, SCM Press, 1988, p. 79.

Critics of Bishop Jenkins' 'radicalism' will surely have to admit that all this boils down to a very Anglican position alongside Temple and Habgood. Faith and reason are allies in helping us understand the world we live in. The Anglican *via media* approach supplies immense strength for social teaching as well as ballast for ecclesiology and, as Henry Clark has argued in his survey of social pronouncements by the Church of England in recent years, the material produced by the Church of England Board for Social Responsibility is consistently of high quality.[8] It is a stance highly appropriate to reasoned debate in a parliamentary democracy. We should note, however, that Jenkins sees a decidedly critical potential in faith-cum-reason's view of the absolutizing tendencies of political dogma. Further, immediately following the passage quoted above, he posits the need to question 'a certain narrow exclusivism in the presentation of the appeal to facts', to be found for instance in claims that the economy is doing well when literally thousands of our fellow-citizens are in fact doing badly in terms of deprivation, unemployment and alienation.[9] This is very much in line with the identification we made in Chapter 8 of the church's capacity to speak out of a real knowledge of what is actually going on in the world, as well as out of its claim, based on certain perspectives belonging to the givenness of its belief, to have insights into abiding realities of human existence.

It has to be asked, however, whether an emphasis upon the indicative alone is adequate to a church which is not only part of society but has a specific *mission* within and to that society. Habgood is right in stating that when it comes to specific issues what Christians have to say may be no more than what any person of sound sense and goodwill has to offer. The question is whether that sense and goodwill are actually offered when vested interests are grabbing at the microphone. The world, unfortunately, is not populated entirely with people as sagacious and fair-minded as the bench of bishops. Reason alone cannot always advance or even defend reason, even a reason informed

[8]Henry Clark, *The Church under Thatcher*, SPCK, 1993.
[9]Jenkins, op. cit., p. 79.

by faith. The cause of reason in the world needs an inspiration, a passion even, from beyond itself if it is to survive. Brutality is abroad as well as commonsense. Part of its wickedness lies in delighting to cloak itself in apparent reasonableness, especially in the economic sphere. Else why would we be accepting with such equanimity the cruel marginalization of so many in our own 'advanced' societies and the degradation of millions of our neighbours in the poorer world? Shakespeare's characters walk in our midst, as Bonhoeffer observed in Nazi Germany — and not only there.[10] We should not therefore be too worried if the church can 'only' say what is reasonable. What should concern us is whether the church is actually saying it and saying why it matters. If the church is the only community left to say it, or if it has to ally itself with others who are saying it, then that is truly part of its calling. The church *is* to be on the side of the classical virtues of goodness, truth and beauty. The point is that these values cannot stand by themselves without a word from beyond them. The indicative is not the only possible and necessary form of speech.

A manner of speaking: the imperative

For another emphasis we journey to Scotland, land of the Calvinist rather than the Lutheran-Puritan-Catholic reformation of Anglicanism. In the courtyard outside the Assembly Hall of the Church of Scotland and the Theology Faculty of New College stands the authoritative figure of John Knox. The Reformed tradition (which has also heavily influenced the Free Churches of England) speaks much more markedly of the word of God having a direct claim on human citizenship. God calls us immediately into an *obedient* faith, justifying and sanctifying in one movement of grace.

Duncan Forrester, Professor of Christian Ethics and Practical Theology at New College, is a contemporary exponent of this tradition in relation to social and political affairs. He is, on the one hand, sharply critical of what he sees as a self-delusion on the part of all the mainline churches in the west as regards their actual standing in society:

[10]D. Bonhoeffer, *Ethics*, SCM Press, 1955, p. 46.

Post-Christendom churches represent minorities which no longer have a recognized right to influence power. They are more likely to reflect rather than shape values and policies. They tend to use the remaining fragments of their former influence to defend the institutional interests of the Church. Beyond that, they may issue broad hortatory generalizations on the issues of the day, which are not expected even by those who produce them to affect significantly subsequent events. The Church understands itself as standing above the political process and viewing it from on high.

Political theology generated in such a context tends to be 'from above' — Church leaders and professional theologians speaking on behalf of the institutional church to the powerful and the decision-makers. In this dialogue of élites, the shared assumption is that the Church is still a significant part of the power structure of society, and that theology has the capacity to resolve, or assist in solving, the problems of 'the world'.[11]

On the other hand, freed from the trappings of power, their very marginalization can be a stimulus for the churches to become a creative minority in a new way: a rediscovery of a pre-Constantinian role in the post-Constantinian world. He is critical of Habgood and others for their emphasis upon the inability, rightly or wrongly, of the church to utter anything more than generalities about society.[12] This is to fail to see, remarks Forrester, that Christianity 'is inherently a bad civil religion, and that to force it into this mould is corrosive of its Christian identity'.[13] Furthermore, while the church does indeed have things to say in the indicative about the human condition, there is more to be said. There are *imperatives* as well as abstract statements. But even to speak with a tone of command is not enough:

[11]D. Forrester, *Theology and Politics*, Blackwell, 1988, p. 142f.
[12]Ibid., pp. 53f.
[13]Ibid., p. 54.

Church statements are surely intended to effect something
— to change attitudes, to influence the way people vote,
to affect decisions. But do they in fact make any difference?
Only when church statements are clearly and cogently
argued, make a distinct contribution to the discussion,
and are followed through are they likely to have much
influence, to be heard, and to affect the way things go.[14]

The church should not feel it necessary to speak about every
single item on the public agenda, nor should it be assumed that
it is a *Christian* contribution simply because it is the church
which is speaking. Forrester has subjected to rigorous critique
the track record of the Church and Nation Committee of the
Church of Scotland.[15] Too often, he finds, both the Committee
and the General Assembly to which it reports have been
content to reflect immediate church, or even just Scottish,
opinion on a variety of matters 'without offering any particular
vision or distinctive slant, assuming that theology has little if
anything to say in relation to worldly affairs'.[16] Exceptions
include reports on Central Africa during the 1960s, and on the
exploitation of North Sea oil in the 1970s.

The classic Church of Scotland contribution to public affairs,
according to Forrester, was however the Commission for the
Interpretation of God's Will in the Present Crisis, which worked
under John Baillie during the Second World War and made its
report in 1944.[17] This combined rigorous theological thinking
with a realistic appreciation of the technical problems involved
in any social issue. The *way* in which a just distribution of
wealth is to be achieved in society is a technical matter on which
religion as such has no more expertise to offer than any other
approach. Nevertheless, the Commission affirmed, in every
problem there is a spiritual and ethical dimension. There
should be controlling principles, not detailed prescriptions,

---

[14]D. Forrester, *Belief, Values and Policies*, OUP, 1989, p. 63.

[15]D. Forrester, unpublished MS, 'When Churches Speak on Public Policy: The
Church of Scotland'.

[16]Ibid., p. 18.

[17]See *God's Will for Church and Nation*, SCM Press, 1946.

[18]Ibid., p. 62.

but more than abstract principles about the human condition, or what might be described as 'middle axioms'. Thus, 'economic power must be made objectively responsible to the community as a whole. The possessors of economic power must be answerable for the use of that power, not only to their own consciences, but to appropriate social organs'.[18] 'Extreme inequalities of wealth must be controlled, and a living wage provided for every adult citizen.'[19] 'The common interest demands a far greater measure of public control of capital resources and means of production than our tradition has in the past envisaged.'[20]

Forrester views much of the subsequent work in the Church of Scotland as falling far short of this combination of theological grounding — the concomitant, I would add, of a willingness to learn afresh what that theology is all about — with broad but directional imperatives for social policy. One may reflect that the consequences for failing to provide a continual theological undergirding and existential Christian commitment to such social values are now becoming very evident. The historian John Kent[21] argues that while William Temple may have had much to do with promoting the ideal of the welfare state during the Second World War, the churches as a whole have not been able to supply a continued religious motivation to its values which since the late 1970s have fallen prey to the new right-wing ideology of privatized existence within the free-market economy. There *is* therefore a place for the imperative mode, provided it arises out of a genuinely theological perception and not just a wish to shout one's prejudices or to get one's irritation with the government off one's chest, and provided it faces the realities and possibilities of the actual society which it addresses.

Above all, of course, the imperative is a thoroughly biblical manner of speaking: 'Cease to do evil, learn to do good; seek justice, rescue the oppressed, defend the orphan, plead for the widow' (Is. 1.16c–17). To be true to the biblical dynamic of

---

[19]Ibid., p. 63.
[20]Ibid., p. 157.
[21]J. Kent, *William Temple*, Cambridge University Press, 1993.

witness, and to the calling of the church as a missionary body rather than just a 'religious institution' within society, the church must strive towards concreteness in its utterances. If there are principles, then the risk must be taken of saying what these principles mean for *this* situation. If there are indicatives, the venture must be made of saying 'what is really going on' *here and now*, not simply in history as a whole, to which a response must be made.[22] If it is prepared to learn, the church can and will have something to say in this mode as occasion requires. And having spoken, it will learn still more as it seeks to follow through its statements by faithful actions.

Status confessionis?

The imperative might indicate a moral course to be taken, either in broad terms or in specific detail. It could however indicate something still more fundamental. In Chapter 2 we examined the nature of the 1934 Barmen Theological Declaration as a *confession* of the faith of the church in a specific historical situation of crisis. In terms of Reformation theology, the Synod of Barmen had identified the scene as one of a *status confessionis*; that is, one where the issue concerns nothing less than the gospel itself and the church's loyalty to it, and its rejection of a false gospel. The attempt to introduce a racial requirement into the qualifications for ministry in the church, together with models of ministry and leadership drawn not from the bible but from the National Socialist ideology, were not just 'practical' matters of indifference to the truth of the gospel, mere *adiaphora*. To accept them would mean denying the gospel, and embracing a church very different from the church of Jesus Christ.

A measure of the fruitfulness of Barmen is the way in which, since the Second World War, more and more situations facing the church in various parts of the world have been viewed as potential or actual examples of *status confessionis*. As we have seen, the most widely recognized parallel to the German case

---

[22]Cf B. Thorogood, *Judging Caesar*, United Reformed Church, 1990, esp. Chapter 11, 'In the Imperative Mood'.

was that in South Africa, where a number of churches eventually came to brand apartheid not simply as morally wrong, but quite specifically as a *heresy*.[23] Churches which not only acquiesced in apartheid in society, but moreover actually allowed it to operate within their own fellowships and structures, were not simply failing to witness to the gospel (all churches are failures to some degree) but actually *denying* it and expressing a very different 'gospel'. On the strength of this conviction the white Dutch Reformed Church has for a number of years been suspended from membership of the World Alliance of Reformed Churches. A further test case was, in the opinion of a number of Christians in western Europe, provided by the manufacture, possession and threatened use of nuclear weapons of mass destruction. Karl Barth in 1958 called for a church confession in view of the 'godless' nature of nuclear weaponry which effectively denies the Christian creed's affirmation of God as Creator, Redeemer and Sanctifier. In 1981 the Reformieter Bund Churches of the German Federal Republic declared that a *status confessionis* had been provoked by the marshalling of nuclear weapons amounting to 'a blasphemy destroying all life', and a heated controversy with other German churches ensued. Still more recently, the injustice of the world economic order (or disorder), in which the churches of the north no less than their societies have deep complicity, has been strongly argued as presenting a *status confessionis* by the German theologian Ulrich Duchrow.[24]

When does a serious moral issue become a *status confessionis*? Or is this just a term used to heighten the rhetoric and over-dramatize a situation? Deep within us, after all, lies the desire to 'see history made', if not actually to make it ourselves. The temptation to absolutize every issue into one of ultimate importance must be acknowledged as a way of compensating for the mundane character of most of the lives of most of us. It is hard to live with the fact that not every stream is a Jordan to be crossed, not every skirmish an Armageddon. But the term

---

[23]J. W. de Gruchy and C. Villa-Vicencio, *Apartheid is a Heresy*, Eerdmans, 1983.
[24]Ulrich Duchrow, *Global Economy. A Confessional Issue for the Churches?*, WCC, 1987.

does remain with an integrity to be respected, and its occasional misuse does not demand its total disuse. In broad terms, a *status confessionis* is reached when it is clear that not only is a policy or practice 'wrong' but that the church's complaisance in it would make impossible the proclamation of the gospel. Or, to put it another way, when complicity in the wrong actually imposes the preaching of a different message, a different faith, a different God, to that of Jesus Christ. In this respect, a *status confessionis* will normally have some clear directive and prescriptive import for the life of the church itself. A clear practical imperative emerges as an either/or between the gospel and heresy: Do not withdraw from table-fellowship with gentiles! (Gal. 2.11–14). Stand by the non-Aryan pastors! No colour-bar in the church! With certain issues, however, the fact of the church's complicity, and therewith the clarity of the imperative, may not be quite so obvious. The church itself does not possess nuclear weapons — but may tacitly approve them (and even sanction prayers and blessings for their use as in the commissioning of British nuclear submarines). The churches do not themselves run the world economic order, though they may well benefit from it and allow it to continue by default. Moreover, as Duchrow argues, the world economic order is indeed an intra-church as well as socio-political affair, since rich Christians in the north are in fact part of the system whereby they are in practice oppressing their sisters and brothers in the south.

The point has been made by such as Ronald Preston[25] that to make a rejection of the world economic system into such a confessional issue is of limited value, since it gives no guidance on the actual choices faced by people in the economic system. Having said 'No', to what are we to say 'Yes'? The point is well made, but does not in fact invalidate the case for a *status confessionis*. In some circumstances for the present it may be enough to say 'No', and to begin the search for a new 'Yes' without knowing what that 'Yes' will actually prescribe. Abraham goes out 'not knowing where he is to go' except in faithfulness to his God. In that case, the confession consists of a definite

[25]Cf. Forrester, *Beliefs, Values and Policies*, p. 93.

commitment to a search for a new beginning, a wholly other direction. Forrester, for his part, affirms the place for occasional emphatic, confessional statements. 'Theology must speak from the heart of Christian belief, or hold its tongue.'[26] A confessional statement, we might say, is a macro-order of utterance. As at Barmen, it speaks of what the ultimate theological basis of all social and ethical teaching of the church is to be. It clears a space for that basis against the pressures of the time. It insists on the claim of the church to be the church, to speak and act as such in the name of Jesus Christ and no other name. The confession may, or may not, itself get down to concrete particulars. It will certainly open the way to such definite utterances. But its own imperative is 'Let us hear the Word of God, amid all the other words around us'. For this kind of utterance, the church must always be ready.

There is, however, implicit in such an imperative another form of speech. As was seen in Chapter 2 in dealing with Barmen and *Kairos*, the effect of the most decidedly confessional utterances is to *question* the church on its actual standing in relation to the gospel, and to question the world on its fulfilment of the divine claim upon it. But do we in fact have to wait until this point is reached before adopting the interrogative mode?

A manner of speaking: the interrogative

One of the signs of growing maturity is the acquisition of a wider and richer range of forms of speech. The infant seems at first to speak in sheer exclamations. Presently the indicative comes along (usually in the present tense, with or without actual verbs), closely followed by the imperative, often imperiously so. The sign that someone is increasingly at home in the language and would like to be more at home in the world, however, comes with the asking of questions. As every parent knows, they can be endless. In fact the question is a highly sophisticated manner of speaking. It is a statement designed to provoke another statement. It is a statement about a perceived oddity or incompleteness of the world as one

[26]Ibid.

experiences it, as against what one imagines it could be or ought to be. On the basis of what one knows already, one would like to know something more or something else, a quest born out of trying to imagine what it would be like to know. It expresses the curiosity which, knowing something, would like to know more. The question is born out of the alternative imagination.

The question — even and perhaps especially the child's question — can be both disturbing and liberating. 'Why isn't the emperor wearing any clothes?' The question raises the possibility that there is quite another way of looking at the world, or maybe even that there is another world to look at altogether. Even words like 'inevitable', 'essential' or 'necessary' have to come to the bar of judgment and answer the simplest yet most searching question, 'Why?', or 'Why not?'.

How strange then, that the interrogative mode should have been used so little in church speech on public issues. There are situations in which the question can be the most effective form of speech, if the aim is to draw the powerful and decision-makers into the open to give an account of themselves and to explain their policies, or to uncover underlying issues and attitudes. Of course, like every other manner of speaking the interrogative can be abused when it becomes sheer aggressive rhetoric as in the old chestnut 'Have you stopped beating your wife?' But, as the most rudimentary wisdom in counselling knows, the most effective questions are not those which are aimed at straight 'yes' or 'no', but rather the more open-ended 'why?' and 'what?' and 'what next?' questions. Those are the enquiries which invite and commit the client to talk and talk ... in ways that are often unexpectedly revelatory to him- or herself no less than to the questioner. There is of course a vast difference between an individual who is consciously seeking help, and a government or other corporate institution with powerful interests to defend which does not welcome in the least any attention or 'concern' from those whose real business is imagined to lie elsewhere. The point is that the question requires a response which is hard to evade — and even an evasion will itself become doubly significant. The purely indicative or imperative statements may or may not receive a comment in return, of greater or less relevance to the points raised. They can be water off the duck's back. The question, however, cannot be so easily disregarded. It *has* to be answered — and a naive or banal reply can only invite still further questioning. Put another way, whereas the indicative and imperative moods may be forms of 'declaring' the truth, it is the question which, in many situations, is the most appropriate means of *exposing* the truth, of calling it out of the shadows.

In this respect especially, the interrogative mood has a deeply biblical pedigree. 'Adam, where are you?' (Gen. 3.9) is the word with which begins the whole divine redemptive approach to humankind. The human pair can no longer hide. Other questions quickly follow: 'Who told you that you were naked? Have you eaten ...?', 'What is this that you have done?' (vv. 11, 13), 'Why are you angry, and why has your countenance fallen?' (4.6), 'Where is your brother Abel?' (v. 9). The indicative states how things are, the imperative says what ought to be done, but it is the question which challenges the responsible persons themselves to acknowledge how things are and what has to be done. Hence the interrogative is such a central feature of the prophetic style: 'When you come to appear before me, who asked this from your hand?' (Is. 1.12); 'Are you a king because you compete in cedar? Did not your father eat and drink and do justice and righteousness? ... Is not this to know me?' (Jer. 22.15f.); 'What does the Lord require of you, but to do justice, and to love kindness, and to walk humbly with your God?' (Mic. 6.8). Jesus' speech is vibrant with questions: 'Which one of you, having a hundred sheep ...?' (Lk. 15.4); 'What do you want me to do for you?' (Mk. 10.51); 'What were you arguing about on the way?' (Mk. 9.33).

To realize that one is free to ask questions is itself liberating. We are not bound to silence because we have not yet complete knowledge of the situation and competence in the area concerned. Indeed it is precisely because we do not know everything, that questions are put which are not purely rhetorical. The questions and the responses they invoke may be more revelatory of the truth of a situation than any attempt to declaim upon the truth in olympian, omniscient style. And the question can be as concrete as imaginable. The way is always open, therefore, for even an uncertain, confused and hesitant church to speak concretely, if not the truth then for the sake of the truth, by using the interrogative mood. It is the style appropriate to the church's role of *scrutiny*, to use Bernard Thorogood's term,[27] of policies and the values underlying them. At the same time, in asking the question we are not thereby necessarily putting ourselves in the position of judges, but risking exposure to judgment ourselves, inviting the counter-question, 'And what have you yourselves done about this?' As Bernard Thorogood puts it:

> We are Caesar. We are involved, part of the body politic, sharers in the whole process, casting our vote and paying our taxes, influencing one another. We are the newspaper reporters and the radio announcers, the bankers and the stockbrokers, the dramatists and the artists, the schoolteachers and judges. In judging Caesar we judge ourselves. All too often it is our priorities which have appeared in parliament and we do not like what we see. Our xenophobia appears in the wretched guise of the immigration laws. Our delighted consumption of the good things of life ends up as resistance to full environmental planning. So our prayer for Caesar and for ourselves as citizens is all of a piece. It is that we may do justice and love mercy and walk humbly before God.[28]

It is the interrogative mood which is most consistent with the role of the one who is being taught, who knows enough to want to know more. It is in the interrogative that teacher and learner, prophet and disciple, coalesce as one. It is at this point, too, that new images and models of the church can spring into view. We have frequently in these pages spoken critically about the 'didacticism' which besets a church which wishes to put the world to rights. The image we have attacked is that of the self-important, finger-wagging occupant of the podium who knows what is best for the audience and the world they live in. But of course there are other images of teacher. The most creative of

[27]Thorogood, op. cit.
[28]Ibid., p. 127.

all is that of the teacher who is also a researcher and who, far from setting off teaching and research against each other (significantly, that is increasingly one of the greatest problems in higher education these days) sees each as necessary to the other. It is the scientist leading a team of colleagues and assistants and research students, and letting the keener undergraduates also know what is going on. For such, teaching becomes an invitation to others to share in the quest in which the teacher, ultimately, is still a pupil and sets the example of what it means to be a student. The church should ponder the potential of such a model, seeing itself as the leading enquirer into what it means to be human in the light of the gospel, repeatedly experimenting with the interaction between the apostolic faith and the contemporary (and about-to-be contemporary) realities of life, experience and responsibility.

This is to recognize that as well as a time for the statement, considered and reflective or urgently imperative, there is a time for the enquiry. The colloquy deserves to be reinstated in church life as a major means of decision on theological and ethical issues. Literally, *colloquium* simply meant 'speaking together' or 'conversation' but it also acquired the technical meaning in some church circles, especially in Protestantism, of a judicial and legislative court. The most famous colloquy of the Reformation was of course that held at Marburg in 1529, in an attempt to resolve the sacramental dispute between Luther and Zwingli. Whatever precise purpose it may have served in history, the essence of the colloquy lies in its being a corporate enquiry into a matter of contemporary and public moment for the church, in which a judgment is sought through open discussion and rigorous questioning of all views which are presented. Central to its method is the *hearing*. Those with particular expertise or perspectives who are invited to contribute must expect to spend most of their time answering questions rather than delivering set-piece discourses. Indeed, the whole exercise is shaped by the questions of those mandated to seek a judgment. Too many conferences and 'consultations' take place in church and ecumenical circles which are largely opportunities for theologians and other experts to deliver prepared papers assured of publication afterwards. 'Discussion' is all too often a superficial, desultory and incoherent accompaniment to them, and often as badly recorded as it is conducted. There is a proper art to enquiry through dialogue which must be learnt, or perhaps re-learnt when we recall the medieval conduct of disputations. For a start, the quality and usefulness of such events would be enhanced if no assurance about publication were given to 'main contributors' beforehand, but far more attention were to be given to the facilitating of properly open, thorough and progressive discussion. The publication should properly be of the *proceedings*, rather than simply the main presentations (which in any case can often be relatively brief), and what should appear in the report should be that which, according to the decision of the gathering as a whole, most fully merits wider circulation in order to illuminate the decision-making process and the salient points of argument. The colloquy, quite apart from its conclusions, by its very nature is implying something crucial: that there is more to the issues than the unexamined prejudices and superficialities, the slick slogans and sound-bites, which the public debate has hitherto afforded them. That in itself is to make a statement of fundamental importance.[29]

Indicative, imperative, interrogative: there can be no rigid rule as to which mood is appropriate for which context. Mission is a matter of living response, in the Spirit, to situations and challenges for which there can be no fully adequate preparation in advance (Mk. 13.11). If, however, we lay these three moods alongside the threefold analysis of political approach provided by Martin Wight in the international sphere, something like a rule of thumb emerges. When the political game is *realist* then is the time to address it in *indicative* terms, for then is the moment to remind the power-brokers of the broader and deeper 'realities' of the world in which they are living and with which they themselves must come to terms. When political thought and speech is at its most *rationalist*, then may well be the occasion for the sharpest *imperative*

[29]Among the experiences which have helped to shape these reflections, particularly significant was that of organizing an ecumenical colloquy during the Gulf Crisis in late 1990.

address from the church with its prophetic adrenaline running hot, in order to disturb the bland equanimity which is excusing and camouflaging injustice and oppression in the name of 'balance'. Finally, it is when the *revolutionists* are in their most decidedly imperative mood, that the *interrogative* note most needs to be struck, querying whether the wrath of humankind is serving the justice of God, let alone his mercy. But to repeat, this can only be a rule of thumb.

Indicative, imperative, interrogative — the church that is learning to speak will be aware of the possibilities and appropriateness of all forms of speech. It will be sufficiently imaginative and aware so as never to become hooked solely on one mood. It will also, of course, know that on occasion silence too can be eloquent — not of evasion but of the need for something *so serious* to be said that it must be awaited in patience and in reverence for the truth, as against deference to the demands for chatter. And having opened its mouth, let there be a reticence about saying anything more until what has been said has been followed up and fulfilled in the life of the church, after the example of the new pastor who refused to preach to his congregation after his first Sunday until he saw signs that his flock were indeed beginning to love one another as the sermon had enjoined.

Instead of a conclusion: a checklist

The whole argument of this book has been to qualify the need for the church to 'speak out' on public issues. Let us summarize these qualifications in the form of a checklist of questions which should be applied whenever it is asked, 'Will you be issuing a statement?'.

1. What is the church's primary responsibility in this situation, and does it necessarily involve speaking at all? Might there not be more important things to *do*?

2. What are the drives and promptings urging us to 'speak out'? How great is our desire to be heard and seen, as distinct from actually making some real difference to the situation? To what extent is this an exercise in self-justification? Who is really to benefit from this speaking?

3. Given that we genuinely do feel the need to say something, what is to be specifically Christian about what we say? How does it arise directly out of the centrality of our beliefs in the gospel? How is that gospel basis to be made clear in the utterance? Or are we simply proffering another 'solution' to a 'problem'?

4. What is the church stating about itself in this utterance? That it is the community which claims to have all the answers? What does the church need to confess of its own ignorance, failures and need to learn?

5. When whatever has to be said has been said, what steps will be taken by the Christian community to follow up the statement? Will it simply be recorded as a statement, or will it be used as a criterion for monitoring the actions of churches and Christians in relation to the issue concerned? Precisely who is being committed to do something — and to do precisely what?

The church speaks because it has been, and still is, being taught — and it speaks in the anticipation of learning more. It issues a word, not as the final word but as an offering to the Lord who alone is the final word, and who is Lord of the church's future. The church speaks and asks 'What will the Lord do with this word? Where will it lead us? What new things will emerge from it?' In the end, Christians have to be as wise as serpents and innocent as doves (Mt. 10.16). There will be many times when 'knowledge' itself seems inadequate. Ultimately, and not as a sanction for intellectual or moral indolence, it is the promise of the Spirit which becomes operative pricely at the point of danger and vulnerability (Mt. 10.19f.). The church is true church not by never making mistakes, but by being the most willing learner from its own mistakes. The gospel is not a guarantee of success, but the promise that even failures can be fruitful, sometimes even more fruitful than what the world calls successes.

Select Bibliography

Ateek, N. S., *Justice and Only Justice. A Palestinian Theology of Liberation*, Orbis, 1989.

Barth, K., *Church Dogmatics Vol. I. The Doctrine of the Word of God,*, T&T Clark, 1956.
How My Mind Has Changed, St Andrew Press, 1969.

Bethge, E., *Dietrich Bonhoeffer. Theologian, Christian, Contemporary*, Collins, 1970.

Bonhoeffer, D., *No Rusty Swords. Lectures, Letters and Notes 1928-36*, Collins, 1965.
The Cost of Discipleship, SCM Press, 1959.
Ethics, SCM Press, 1955.
Letters and Papers from Prison, SCM Press, 1971.

Bosch, D., *Transforming Mission. Paradigm Shifts in Theology of Mission*, Orbis, 1991.

Brueggemann, W., *The Prophetic Imagination*, Fortress Press, 1978.

Calvin, J., *Institutes of the Christian Religion, Book IV*, Transl. H. Beveridge (Vol. II), James Clarke, 1957.

Clements, K.W., *What Freedom? The Persistent Challenge of Dietrich Bonhoeffer*, Bristol Baptist College, 1990.

Cragg, K., *The Arab Christian. A History in the Middle East*, Mowbray, 1992.

de Gruchy, J. and *Apartheid is a Heresy*, W.B. Eerdmans, 1983.
Villa-Vicencio, C.

de Gruchy, J.,   *Theology and Ministry in Context and Crisis. A South African Perspective*, Collins, 1987.

Dodd, C.H.,   *The Apostolic Preaching and Its Developments*, Hodder and Stoughton, 1936.

Duchrow, U.,   *Global Economy. A Confessional Issue for the Churches?*, WCC, 1987.

Dulles, A.,   *Models of the Church*, Gill and Macmillan, 1988.

Ellingsen, M.,   *The Cutting Edge. How Churches Speak on Social Issues*, WCC and W.B. Eerdmans, 1993.

Flannery, A. (ed.),   *Vatican Council II. The Conciliar and Post-Conciliar Documents Vol. I*, Fowler Wright, 1980.

Forrester, D.,   *Theology and Politics*, Blackwell, 1988.
                      Beliefs, Values and Policies, Oxford University Press, 1989.

Forsyth, P.T.,   *Christ, The Gospel and Society*, Independent Press, 1962.

Gollwitzer, H.,   *The Demands of Freedom*, SCM Press, 1965.

Habgood, J.,   *Church and Nation in a Secular Age*, Darton, Longman and Todd, 1983.

Jenkins, D.E.,   *God, Politics and the Future*, SCM Press, 1988.

Kinnamon, M. (ed.),   *Signs of the Spirit. Report of the Seventh Assembly*, WCC, 1991.

Küng, H.,   *Infallible?*, Collins, 1971.

McIntyre, A.,   *After Virtue. A Study in Moral Theory*, University of Notre Dame, 1981.

McLuhan, M.,   *Understanding Media. The Extensions of Man*, McGraw-Hill, 1964.

Marcuse, H., *One Dimensional Man. Studies in the Ideology of Advanced Industrialised Society*, Routledge and Kegan Paul, 1964.

Oldham, J.H., *Real Life is Meeting*, (Christian News-Letter Books No 14) Sheldon Press, 1942.

Raiser, K., *Ecumenism in Transition*, WCC, 1991.

Ramsey, P., *Who Speaks for the Church? A Critique of the 1966 Lausanne Conference on Church and Society*, Abingdon Press, 1967.

Schillebeeckx, E., *The Church. The Human Story of God*, SCM Press, 1990.

Scholder, K., *The Churches in the Third Reich*, Vol. I, SCM Press, 1987 and Vol. II, SCM Press, 1988. *Requiem for Hitler*, SCM Press, 1987.

Temple, W., *Christianity and Social Order*, Penguin, 1942.

Thorogood, B., *Judging Caesar*, United Reformed Church, 1990.

Vidler, A.R., *Christ's Strange Work*, SCM Press, 1963.

Villa-Vicencio, C., 'A Life of Resistance and Hope', in *Resistance and Hope: South African Essays in Honour of Beyers Naudé*, eds. C. Villa-Vicencio and J.W. de Gruchy, David Philip and Eerdmans, 1985. *A Theology of Reconstruction. Nation-building and human rights*, Cambridge University Press, 1992.

Weber, D.C., *Discerning Images. The Media and Theological Education*, University of Edinburgh, 1991.

Wight, M., *International Theory. The Three Traditions*, Leicester University Press for Royal Institute of International Affairs, 1991.

Wilson, R.R., *Prophecy and Society in Ancient Israel*, Fortress Press, 1980.

Documents:

The Kairos Document. Challenge to the Church. A Theological Comment on the Political Crisis in South Africa. UK edition, 1985, published by Catholic Institute for International Relations and British Council of Churches.

Evangelical Witness in South Africa. A Critique of Evangelical Theology and Practice by South African Evangelicals Themselves. Evangelical Alliance, 1986.

Faith in the City. A call to action by Church and Nation. Report of the Archbishop of Canterbury's Commission on Urban Priority Areas, Church House Publishing, 1985.

The Truth Will Set You Free. A statement by the bishops of Malawi. Church in the World 28, 1992.

Index

I. PERSONS

236

II. SUBJECTS